TABLE OF CONTENTS

Secret Key #1 – Time is Your Greatest Enemy

Success Strategy #1

Pace Yourself

Wear a watch to the SPHR Test. At the beginning of the test, check the time (or start a chronometer on your watch to count the minutes), and check the time after each passage or every few questions to make sure you are "on schedule." For the computerized test an onscreen clock display will keep track of your remaining time, but it may be easier for you to monitor your pace based on how many minutes have been used, rather than how many minutes remain.

If you are forced to speed up, do it efficiently. Usually one or more answer choices can be eliminated without too much difficulty. Above all, don't panic. Don't speed up and just begin guessing at random choices. By pacing yourself, and continually monitoring your progress against the clock or your watch, you will always know exactly how far ahead or behind you are with your available time. If you find that you are one minute behind on the test, don't skip one question without spending any time on it, just to catch back up. Spend perhaps 45 seconds on the question and after four questions, you will have caught back up more gradually. Once you catch back up, you can continue working each problem at your normal pace.

Furthermore, don't dwell on the problems that you were rushed on. If a problem was taking up too much time and you made a hurried guess, it must be difficult. The difficult questions are the ones you are most likely to miss anyway, so it isn't a big loss. It is better to end with more time than you need than to run out of time. You can always go back and work the problems that you skipped. If you have time left over, as you review the skipped questions, start at the earliest skipped question, spend at most another minute, and then move on to the next skipped question.

Lastly, sometimes it is beneficial to slow down if you are constantly getting ahead of time. You are always more likely to catch a careless mistake by working more slowly than quickly, and among very high-scoring test takers (those who are likely to have lots of time left over), careless errors affect the score more than mastery of material.

Secret Key #2 – Guessing is not Guesswork

You probably know that guessing is a good idea on the SPHR test- unlike other standardized tests, there is no penalty for getting a wrong answer. Even if you have no idea about a question, you still have a 20-25% chance of getting it right.

Most test takers do not understand the impact that proper guessing can have on their score. Unless you score extremely high, guessing will significantly contribute to your final score.

Monkeys Take the SPHR

What most test takers don't realize is that to insure that 20-25% chance, you have to guess randomly. If you put 20 monkeys in a room to take this test, assuming they answered once per question and behaved themselves, on average they would get 20-25% of the questions correct. Put 20 test takers in the room, and the average will be much lower among guessed questions. Why?

1. This test intentionally writes deceptive answer choices that "look" right. A test taker has no idea about a question, so picks the "best looking" answer, which is often wrong. The monkey has no idea what looks good and what doesn't, so will consistently be lucky about 20-25% of the time.
2. Test takers will eliminate answer choices from the guessing pool based on a hunch or intuition. Simple but correct answers often get excluded, leaving a 0% chance of being correct. The monkey has no clue, and often gets lucky with the best choice.

This is why the process of elimination endorsed by most test courses is flawed and detrimental to your performance- test takers don't guess, they make an ignorant stab in the dark that is usually worse than random.

Success Strategy #2

Let me introduce one of the most valuable ideas of this course- the $5 challenge:

You only mark your "best guess" if you are willing to bet $5 on it.
You only eliminate choices from guessing if you are willing to bet $5 on it.

Why $5? Five dollars is an amount of money that is small yet not insignificant, and can really add up fast (20 questions could cost you $100). Likewise, each answer choice on one question of the SPHR will have a small impact on your overall score, but it can really add up to a lot of points in the end.

The process of elimination IS valuable. The following shows your chance of guessing it right:

If you eliminate this many choices:	0	1	2	3	4
Chance of getting it correct	20%	25%	33%	50%	100%

However, if you accidentally eliminate the right answer or go on a hunch for an incorrect answer, your chances drop dramatically: to 0%. By guessing among all the answer choices, you are GUARANTEED to have a shot at the right answer.

That's why the $5 test is so valuable- if you give up the advantage and safety of a pure guess, it had better be worth the risk.

What we still haven't covered is how to be sure that whatever guess you make is truly random. Here's the easiest way:

Always pick the first answer choice among those remaining.

Such a technique means that you have decided, **before you see a single test question**, exactly how you are going to guess- and since the order of choices tells you nothing about which one is correct, this guessing technique is perfectly random.

Secret Key #3 – Practice Smarter, Not Harder

Many test takers delay the test preparation process because they dread the awful amounts of practice time they think necessary to succeed on the test. We have refined an effective method that will take you only a fraction of the time.

There are a number of "obstacles" in your way on the SPHR test. Among these are answering questions, finishing in time, and mastering test-taking strategies. All must be executed on the day of the test at peak performance, or your score will suffer. The SPHR is a mental marathon that has a large impact on your future.

Just like a marathon runner, it is important to work your way up to the full challenge. So first you just worry about questions, and then time, and finally strategy:

Success Strategy #3

1. Find a good source for SPHR practice tests.
2. If you are willing to make a larger time investment, consider using more than one study guide- often the different approaches of multiple authors will help you "get" difficult concepts.
3. Take a practice test with no time constraints, with all study helps "open book." Take your time with questions and focus on applying the strategies.
4. Take a final practice test with no open material and time limits.

If you have time to take more practice tests, just repeat step 4. By gradually exposing yourself to the full rigors of the test environment, you will condition your mind to the stress of test day and maximize your success.

Secret Key #4 – Prepare, Don't Procrastinate

Let me state an obvious fact: if you take the SPHR exam three times, you will get three different scores. This is due to the way you feel on test day, the level of preparedness you have, and, despite SPHR exam's claims to the contrary, some tests WILL be easier for you than others.

Since your future depends so much on your score, you should maximize your chances of success. In order to maximize the likelihood of success, you've got to prepare in advance. This means taking practice tests and spending time learning the information and test taking strategies you will need to succeed.

Since you have to pay a registration fee each time you take the SPHR exam, don't take it as a "practice" test. Feel free to take sample tests on your own, but when you go to take the SPHR exam, be prepared, be focused, and do your best the first time!

Secret Key #5 – Test Yourself

Everyone knows that time is money. There is no need to spend too much of your time or too little of your time preparing for the SPHR exam. You should only spend as much of your precious time preparing as is necessary for you to pass it.

Success Strategy #5

Once you have taken a practice test under real conditions of time constraints, then you will know if you are ready for the test or not.

If you have scored extremely high the first time that you take the practice test, then there is not much point in spending countless hours studying. You are already there.

Benchmark your abilities by retaking practice tests and seeing how much you have improved. Once you score high enough to guarantee success, then you are ready.

If you have scored well below where you need, then knuckle down and begin studying in earnest. Check your improvement regularly through the use of practice tests under real conditions. Above all, don't worry, panic, or give up. The key is perseverance!

Then, when you go to take the SPHR exam, remain confident and remember how well you did on the practice tests. If you can score high enough on a practice test, then you can do the same on the real thing.

Top 20 Test Taking Tips

1. Carefully follow all the test registration procedures
2. Know the test directions, duration, topics, question types, how many questions
3. Setup a flexible study schedule at least 3-4 weeks before test day
4. Study during the time of day you are most alert, relaxed, and stress free
5. Maximize your learning style; visual learner use visual study aids, auditory learner use auditory study aids
6. Focus on your weakest knowledge base
7. Find a study partner to review with and help clarify questions
8. Practice, practice, practice
9. Get a good night's sleep; don't try to cram the night before the test
10. Eat a well balanced meal
11. Know the exact physical location of the testing site; drive the route to the site prior to test day
12. Bring a set of ear plugs; the testing center could be noisy
13. Wear comfortable, loose fitting, layered clothing to the testing center; prepare for it to be either cold or hot during the test
14. Bring at least 2 current forms of ID to the testing center
15. Arrive to the test early; be prepared to wait and be patient
16. Eliminate the obviously wrong answer choices, then guess the first remaining choice
17. Pace yourself; don't rush, but keep working and move on if you get stuck
18. Maintain a positive attitude even if the test is going poorly
19. Keep your first answer unless you are positive it is wrong
20. Check your work, don't make a careless mistake

General Strategies

The most important thing you can do is to ignore your fears and jump into the test immediately- do not be overwhelmed by any strange-sounding terms. You have to jump into the test like jumping into a pool- all at once is the easiest way.

Make Predictions

As you read and understand the question, try to guess what the answer will be. Remember that several of the answer choices are wrong, and once you begin reading them, your mind will immediately become cluttered with answer choices designed to throw you off. Your mind is typically the most focused immediately after you have read the question and digested its contents. If you can, try to predict what the correct answer will be. You may be surprised at what you can predict.

Quickly scan the choices and see if your prediction is in the listed answer choices. If it is, then you can be quite confident that you have the right answer. It still won't hurt to check the other answer choices, but most of the time, you've got it!

Answer the Question

It may seem obvious to only pick answer choices that answer the question, but the test writers can create some excellent answer choices that are wrong. Don't pick an answer just because it sounds right, or you believe it to be true. It MUST answer the question. Once you've made your selection, always go back and check it against the question and make sure that you didn't misread the question, and the answer choice does answer the question posed.

Benchmark

After you read the first answer choice, decide if you think it sounds correct or not. If it doesn't, move on to the next answer choice. If it does, mentally mark that answer choice. This doesn't mean that you've definitely selected it as your answer choice, it just means that it's the best you've seen thus far. Go ahead and read the next choice. If the next choice is worse than the one you've already selected, keep going to the next answer choice. If the next choice is better than the choice you've already selected, mentally mark the new answer choice as your best guess.

The first answer choice that you select becomes your standard. Every other answer choice must be benchmarked against that standard. That choice is correct until proven otherwise by another answer choice beating it out. Once you've decided that no other answer choice seems as good, do one final check to ensure that your answer choice answers the question posed.

Valid Information

Don't discount any of the information provided in the question. Every piece of information may be necessary to determine the correct answer. None of the information in the question is there to throw you off (while the answer choices will certainly have information to throw you off). If two seemingly unrelated topics are discussed, don't ignore either. You can be confident there is a relationship, or it wouldn't be included in the question, and you are probably going to have to determine what is that relationship to find the answer.

Avoid "Fact Traps"

Don't get distracted by a choice that is factually true. Your search is for the answer that answers the question. Stay focused and don't fall for an answer that is true but incorrect. Always go back to the question and make sure you're choosing an answer that actually answers the question and is not just a true statement. An answer can be factually correct, but it MUST answer the question asked. Additionally, two answers can both be seemingly correct, so be sure to read all of the answer choices, and make sure that you get the one that BEST answers the question.

Milk the Question

Some of the questions may throw you completely off. They might deal with a subject you have not been exposed to, or one that you haven't reviewed in years. While your lack of knowledge about the subject will be a hindrance, the question itself can give you many clues that will help you find the correct answer. Read the question carefully and look for clues. Watch particularly for adjectives and nouns describing difficult terms or words that you don't recognize. Regardless of if you completely understand a word or not, replacing it with a synonym either provided or one you more familiar with may help you to understand what the questions are asking. Rather than wracking your mind about specific detailed information concerning a difficult term or word, try to use mental substitutes that are easier to understand.

The Trap of Familiarity

Don't just choose a word because you recognize it. On difficult questions, you may not recognize a number of words in the answer choices. The test writers don't put "make-believe" words on the test; so don't think that just because you only recognize all the words in one answer choice means that answer choice must be correct. If you only recognize words in one answer choice, then focus on that one. Is it correct? Try your best to determine if it is correct. If it is, that is great, but if it doesn't, eliminate it. Each word and answer choice you eliminate increases your chances of getting the question correct, even if you then have to guess among the unfamiliar choices.

Eliminate Answers

Eliminate choices as soon as you realize they are wrong. But be careful! Make sure you consider all of the possible answer choices. Just because one appears right, doesn't mean that the next one won't be even better! The test writers will usually put more than one good answer choice for every question, so read all of them. Don't worry if you are stuck between two that seem right. By getting down to just two remaining possible choices, your odds are now 50/50. Rather than wasting too much time, play the odds. You are guessing, but guessing wisely, because you've been able to knock out some of the answer choices that you know are wrong. If you are eliminating choices and realize that the last answer choice you are left with is also obviously wrong, don't panic. Start over and consider each choice again. There may easily be something that you missed the first time and will realize on the second pass.

Tough Questions

If you are stumped on a problem or it appears too hard or too difficult, don't waste time. Move on! Remember though, if you can quickly check for obviously incorrect answer choices, your chances of guessing correctly are greatly improved. Before you completely give up, at least try to knock out a couple of possible answers. Eliminate what you can and then guess at the remaining answer choices before moving on.

Brainstorm

If you get stuck on a difficult question, spend a few seconds quickly brainstorming. Run through the complete list of possible answer choices. Look at each choice and ask yourself, "Could this answer the question satisfactorily?" Go through each answer choice and consider it independently of the other. By systematically going through all possibilities, you may find something that you would otherwise overlook. Remember that when you get stuck, it's important to try to keep moving.

Read Carefully

Understand the problem. Read the question and answer choices carefully. Don't miss the question because you misread the terms. You have plenty of time to read each question thoroughly and make sure you understand what is being asked. Yet a happy medium must be attained, so don't waste too much time. You must read carefully, but efficiently.

Face Value

When in doubt, use common sense. Always accept the situation in the problem at face value. Don't read too much into it. These problems will not require you to make huge leaps of logic. The test writers aren't trying to throw you off with a cheap trick. If you have to go beyond creativity and make a leap of logic in order to have an answer choice answer the question, then you should look at the other answer choices. Don't overcomplicate the problem by creating theoretical relationships or explanations that will warp time or space. These are normal problems rooted in reality. It's just that the applicable relationship or explanation may not be readily apparent and you have to figure things out. Use your common sense to interpret anything that isn't clear.

Prefixes

If you're having trouble with a word in the question or answer choices, try dissecting it. Take advantage of every clue that the word might include. Prefixes and suffixes can be a huge help. Usually they allow you to determine a basic meaning. Pre- means before, post- means after, pro - is positive, de- is negative. From these prefixes and suffixes, you can get an idea of the general meaning of the word and try to put it into context. Beware though of any traps. Just because con is the opposite of pro, doesn't necessarily mean congress is the opposite of progress!

Hedge Phrases

Watch out for critical "hedge" phrases, such as likely, may, can, will often, sometimes, often, almost, mostly, usually, generally, rarely, sometimes. Question writers insert these hedge phrases to cover every possibility. Often an answer choice will be wrong simply because it leaves no room for exception. Avoid answer choices that have definitive words like "exactly," and "always".

Switchback Words

Stay alert for "switchbacks". These are the words and phrases frequently used to alert you to shifts in thought. The most common switchback word is "but". Others include although, however, nevertheless, on the other hand, even though, while, in spite of, despite, regardless of.

New Information

Correct answer choices will rarely have completely new information included. Answer choices typically are straightforward reflections of the material asked about and will directly relate to the question. If a new piece of information is included in an answer choice that doesn't even seem to relate to the topic being asked about, then that answer choice is likely incorrect. All of the information needed to answer the question is usually provided for you, and so you should not have to make guesses that are unsupported or choose answer choices that require unknown information that cannot be reasoned on its own.

Time Management

On technical questions, don't get lost on the technical terms. Don't spend too much time on any one question. If you don't know what a term means, then since you don't have a dictionary, odds are you aren't going to get much further. You should immediately recognize terms as whether or not you know them. If you don't, work with the other clues that you have, the other answer choices and terms provided, but don't waste too much time trying to figure out a difficult term.

Contextual Clues

Look for contextual clues. An answer can be right but not correct. The contextual clues will help you find the answer that is most right and is correct. Understand the context in which a phrase or statement is made. This will help you make important distinctions.

Don't Panic

Panicking will not answer any questions for you. Therefore, it isn't helpful. When you first see the question, if your mind goes blank, take a deep breath. Force yourself to mechanically go through the steps of solving the problem and using the strategies you've learned.

Pace Yourself

Don't get clock fever. It's easy to be overwhelmed when you're looking at a page full of questions, your mind is full of random thoughts and feeling confused, and the clock is ticking down faster than you would like. Calm down and maintain the pace that you have set for yourself. As long as you are on track by monitoring your pace, you are guaranteed to have enough time for yourself. When you get to the last few minutes of the test, it may seem like you won't have enough time left, but if you only have as many questions as you should have left at that point, then you're right on track!

Answer Selection

The best way to pick an answer choice is to eliminate all of those that are wrong, until only one is left and confirm that is the correct answer. Sometimes though, an answer choice may immediately look right. Be careful! Take a second to make sure that the other choices are not equally obvious. Don't make a hasty mistake. There are only two times that you should stop before checking other answers. First is when you are positive that the answer choice you have selected is correct. Second is when time is almost out and you have to make a quick guess!

Check Your Work

Since you will probably not know every term listed and the answer to every question, it is important that you get credit for the ones that you do know. Don't miss any questions through careless mistakes. If at all possible, try to take a second to look back over your answer selection and make sure you've selected the correct answer choice and haven't made a costly careless mistake (such as marking an answer choice that you didn't mean to mark). This quick double check should more than pay for itself in caught mistakes for the time it costs.

Beware of Directly Quoted Answers

Sometimes an answer choice will repeat word for word a portion of the question or reference section. However, beware of such exact duplication – it may be a trap! More than likely, the correct choice will paraphrase or summarize a point, rather than being exactly the same wording.

Slang

Scientific sounding answers are better than slang ones. An answer choice that begins "To compare the outcomes..." is much more likely to be correct than one that begins "Because some people insisted..."

Extreme Statements

Avoid wild answers that throw out highly controversial ideas that are proclaimed as established fact. An answer choice that states the "process should used in certain situations, if..." is much more likely to be correct than one that states the "process should be discontinued completely." The first is a calm rational statement and doesn't even make a definitive, uncompromising stance, using a hedge word "if" to provide wiggle room, whereas the second choice is a radical idea and far more extreme.

Answer Choice Families

When you have two or more answer choices that are direct opposites or parallels, one of them is usually the correct answer. For instance, if one answer choice states "x increases" and another answer choice states "x decreases" or "y increases," then those two or three answer choices are very similar in construction and fall into the same family of answer choices. A family of answer choices is when two or three answer choices are very similar in construction, and yet often have a directly opposite meaning. Usually the correct answer choice will be in that family of answer choices. The "odd man out" or answer choice that doesn't seem to fit the parallel construction of the other answer choices is more likely to be incorrect.

Why Certify?

PHR: **Professional in Human Resources**
SPHR: **Senior Professional in Human Resources**

- Raise the standards in your field and distinguish your experience.
- Use your credentials to further your career.
- Improve your skills and abilities to manage workers

Candidate Handbook
http://www.hrci.org/AboutUs/HB/

Score

The passing score for each exam (based on a scaled score) is 500. The minimum possible score is 100. The maximum possible score is 700.

Question Types

The SPHR exams are multiple choice and consist of 200 scored questions plus 25 pretest questions randomly distributed throughout the exam (a total of 225 questions). Each question lists four possible answers, only one of which is the correct or "best possible answer." The answer to each question can be derived independently of the answer to any other question. Four hours are allotted to complete the exam.

Strategic Business Management

HR professional

In the past, HR professionals typically played a small role in each individual organization, as they were expected to enforce the organization's policies, but were not actively involved in the organization's policy-making and planning. However, the role of HR professionals is quickly changing and for many organizations HR professionals are becoming a larger part of the organization's strategic planning and operations. In fact, most HR professionals today are not only functioning as an essential tool designed to address the organization's administrative needs, but also as an essential tool for the strategic planning and operational needs of the organization by acting as an analyst, consultant and manager. As a result, the role of an HR professional within an organization has changed from that of a simple administrator to a professional that helps promote the success of the organization by helping to establish the organization's strategic plan, to analyze risks associated with organization operations, to help establish and enforce the policies and practices that help the organization function and by performing many other similar functions throughout the organization.

Mission vs. vision statement

Mission statements and vision statements are similar in some ways as they are both intended to help clarify the objectives of the organization. However, there is a key difference between a mission statement and a vision statement that an individual should keep in mind. Basically, the difference between the two types of statements is that a mission statement is intended to identify the reason that the company exists now while a vision statement is intended to identify the goals that the company hopes to achieve later. In other words, a mission statement is only intended to define the broad mission that an organization is attempting to carry out every day. A vision statement, on the other hand, is intended to define the specific goals that an organization hopes to achieve in the future through their actions. This means that a mission statement defines the organization as it stands now while the vision statement defines what the organization hopes to achieve at a later point.

<u>Mission statement</u>
In order for an individual to contribute to an organization's strategic plan, it is essential for that individual to understand the organization's mission statement. A mission statement is a declaration of the reason that an organization exists, which can be extremely important if an individual needs to determine the standards, values, strategies and other organizational aspects that are required to achieve the organization's goals. This is because an individual that understands the reason the organization exists can use the organization's mission as a guideline for establishing the processes that the organization will have to use in order to achieve its goals. For example, the mission statement of a retail chain might be "to provide the best shopping experience possible for our customers" and, as a result, the chain's executives may decide that they need to implement standards and practices that promote high levels of customer service in order to carry out the organization's mission.

<u>Vision statement</u>
In order for an individual to contribute to an organization's strategic plan, it is essential for that individual to understand the organization's vision statement. A vision statement is a declaration of the goals that the organization wishes to achieve at some future point, which is extremely

important if an individual needs to design and implement the strategies necessary to move the organization towards completing their long-term goals. This is because an individual needs to understand the goals that the organization is attempting to achieve in order to establish the business practices, standards, and values necessary to achieve those goals. For example, the vision statement of a retail chain might be "to become the largest retail chain in the United States" and, as a result, the chain's executives may decide that they need to implement strategies that allow them to expand quickly. These strategies may include strategies that help the chain find new locations, purchase new locations, find and train new personnel quickly, and many other similar strategies.

Organization goals

There are a variety of different ways in which an organization can make sure that each specific goal set is well-defined, valid, and ultimately useful. However, one of the most effective ways for an organization to make sure that a particular goal is valid and ultimately useful for measuring the organization's success is to use the acronym SMART. SMART, in the context of goal-setting, stands for specific, measurable, achievable, relevant, and time-related, which are the five attributes that a valid, well-defined goal should have. This simply means that a valid goal should be specific and well-defined, should be measurable in an accurate fashion, should actually be possible considering the organization's resources and the environment, and relevant to the overall objectives of the organization. A valid goal should also have a specific deadline so the goal is completed as efficiently as possible and so that the goal can be compared accurately with other goals.

Measuring performance

There is a wide range of different business metrics that an organization might use in order to measure its performance. However, three of the most common accounting and financial business metrics are cash flow, return on investment (ROI), and return on equity (ROE). An organization's cash flow refers to the amount of money that the organization takes in, compared to the amount of money that the organization spends during a given period such as a week, month, or year. An organization's return on investment refers to the amount of money that the organization earns from a particular investment compared to how much money the company spent to make that investment. In other words, an organization's return on investment is the ratio between the profit or loss on a particular investment and the money that was originally invested. An organization's return on equity is the amount of money that the organization makes, compared to the average investment of each shareholder.

Business development metrics

There is a wide range of different business metrics that an organization might use in order to measure its performance. However, three of the most common operations and business development metrics are the number of activities, the opportunity success rate, and the innovation rate. The number of activities is an exact or estimated count of how many tasks the organization undertakes during a specific time period. In other words, the number of activities is simply how many things the company is attempting to do at one time. The opportunity success rate is the number of opportunities that the organization has successfully taken advantage of, divided by the total number of opportunities that were available. Finally, the innovation rate is the organization's gross revenue from new ideas, products, and services divided by the total gross revenue.

Marketing and sales metrics

There is a wide range of different business metrics that an organization might use in order to measure its performance. However, three of the most common sales and marketing business metrics are the number of customers/orders for the period, the average amount received for each order, and the gross profit margin. The number of customers/orders is simply an exact or estimated count of how many people have purchased products from the company or the number of orders the company has received during a specific period of time such as the number of customers/orders per day, per week, per month, or per year. The average amount received for each order is simply the total amount in dollars that the company has received for a particular period divided by the number of orders. Finally, the gross profit margin is the total revenue for a certain period of time minus the cost of sales for that particular period divided by the total revenue for that period.

Information technology metrics

There is a wide range of different business metrics that an organization might use in order to measure its performance. However, three of the most common information technology metrics that an organization might use are the number of online orders, the availability of information resources, and the number of views per page/listing. The number of online orders is simply a count of how many orders have been placed by customers using the company's website. The availability of information resources is the percentage of time that the company's servers, websites, e-mail, and other technological resources are accessible at the time that an individual needs to use those resources. The number of views per page/listing is a count of how many times customers have looked at a particular web page or online product.

Metrics related to the general business environment

There is a wide range of different business metrics that an organization might use in order to measure its performance. However, three of the most common metrics related to the general business and economic environments that an organization might use are the current number of competitors and the average number of new competitors entering the market per year, the organization's current market share, and the average income of customers in the target market. The current number of competitors is simply the number of other businesses within the same market as the organization and the average number of new competitors is simply the average number of businesses that enter the same market as the organization during a year. The current market share is the percentage of the local or overall market that the business controls, or in other words, the percentage of the market with which the organization usually does business. The average income of customers in the target market is simply the amount that an average customer for the organization would normally make in a given year.

Financial statements

A balance sheet is usually used to determine how well off an organization is financially at a specific point in time. In other words, if an organization has a relatively large amount of equity and a relatively small number of expenses; then the organization is probably doing well financially. On the other hand, if an organization has a relatively large amount of liability and only a small amount of equity; then the organization is probably not doing well financially.

An income statement is usually used to determine whether an organization has made a profit during a particular period or not. If an organization has not made a significant profit, an income statement may also identify expenses that may need to be addressed in order to improve the organization's overall performance.

A statement of cash flows is usually used to identify how much money is required for operating costs, how much money is currently on hand, and how much money the organization will need to borrow in order to make sure that the organization can cover its operating costs.

Developing strategic plan

Average amount received

There are a variety of different ways that an organization can use the average amount received per order to help develop its strategic plan. However, the average amount received per order is usually used to identify how effective the company's marketing and sales strategies have been for maintaining and increasing their profits from their current customer base. In other words, the average amount received per order helps the organization identify how much each customer is contributing to the organization's cash flow. This can help the organization determine if it should focus on expanding its customer base or if it should focus on encouraging its current customer base to spend more through marketing initiatives such as special sales, discounts, reward programs for frequent shoppers, and other similar strategies.

Customers/orders received

There are a variety of different ways that an organization can use the number of customers/orders received over a specific period in order to develop a strategic plan. However, the number of customers/orders received is usually used to help identify if there is a problem with the marketing and sales strategies that the company is currently employing. If the number of customers or orders for a specific period is significantly lower than other previous periods or the number of customers or orders is significantly lower than the numbers estimated from the company's competitors, it might be a sign that there is something wrong with the way that the company is attempting to sell their product. For example, the owner's of a fast food restaurant may decide to change their menu by adding healthier options and focusing their marketing on these new healthier options in order to expand their customer base. If there is a sudden drop in the number of customers instead of an increase, the owner will immediately know that his or her strategy is not working.

Cash flow metric

There are a variety of different ways that an organization can apply a cash flow metric to its strategic planning. However, there are certain basic advantages to using a cash flow metric. An organization's cash flow offers the organization the opportunity to analyze exactly how much money is coming in, how much money is going out and, most importantly, makes it easy to determine if the organization is making money or losing money over a given period. Understanding the organization's cash flow can be extremely important especially if the organization is losing money, as the organization needs to take its expenses and its earnings into consideration in the organization's strategic plan. Any organization that wants to achieve a certain level of profit by the end of the fiscal year must take into consideration how much money the organization spends on a weekly or monthly basis and plan around those expenses by either finding ways to reduce them, eliminate them, or earn enough to offset each expense.

Return on investment

There are a variety of different ways that an organization can apply a metric such as the return or estimated return on an investment to the organization's strategic planning. However, the return or estimated return on a particular investment is usually used if an organization is attempting to decide between two different investments. Each organization only has a limited amount of financial resources to devote to its expenses and investments and, as a result, the organization needs to make sure that it is only spending money on the endeavors with the greatest return. If the organization can estimate, or even better accurately identify, the return that each particular investment will offer, it is very easy for the organization to create a strategic plan that invests the organization's funds in the endeavors that will earn the most money.

Return on equity

There are a variety of different ways that an organization might consider its return on equity if the organization is attempting to develop a strategic plan. However, it is important to realize that the organization's return on equity is usually at the very foundation of the organization's strategic plan regardless of the specific type of organization. This is because the primary goal of any business, regardless of the specific mission or vision statement that the business has established, is to offer its shareholders the largest return on their investment possible. As a result, a for-profit organization's return on equity is an indication of the organization's overall performance. An organization can usually apply its return on equity to its strategic planning by comparing its return on equity to other organizations in the same industry or field. If the organization is offering a competitive return, the organization should not drastically change its strategic plans. On the other hand, if the organization's return on investment is much lower than its competitors, the organization needs to find a new strategy.

Gross profit margin

There are a variety of different ways that an organization can use its gross profit margin to help develop its strategic plan, but the gross profit margin is usually used to help an organization determine whether or not a particular marketing or sales strategy currently in effect is actually profitable. For example, the executives of a fast food restaurant chain may have instituted a new "less than a dollar" menu and a marketing campaign focusing on this menu about a year ago. These executives certainly want to make sure that their new campaign is actually increasing their sales and the organization is not just wasting money on a pointless, or even worse, detrimental, marketing campaign. As a result, the executives may compare the organization's gross profit margin for the current year to the previous year in order to determine if the organization is making a larger profit off of these lower-priced items. This allows the organization to decide if they should continue to use the current strategy or try something new.

Activities undertaken

There are a variety of different ways that an organization can apply the number of activities undertaken during a given period to its strategic plan, but the number of activities is usually used to determine whether or not the company is taking on a larger workload than what the company can normally handle. Multi-tasking is an important part of virtually any enterprise, but it is important for an organization to identify how much work is too much. For example, if an old-fashioned toy manufacturer that prides itself on the fact that each toy built by the company is handcrafted wants to start building a large array of modern toys, the manufacturer may quickly find that it is not possible to expand the company's toy line without drastically increasing the company's costs or eliminating other activities. This is because each old-fashioned toy takes a significant amount of time to construct and the company may not be able to expand its modern toy building activities without eliminating some of the old-fashioned toys from its product line.

Opportunity success rate

An organization's opportunity success rate can be extremely useful for developing a strategic plan, as it allows the organization the chance to determine whether or not it is using the opportunities that are available effectively. If the organization's opportunity success rate is low; then the organization most likely needs to focus on strategies that boost sales in order to boost the company's ability to utilize the opportunities that are available. If the organization's opportunity success rate is high; then the organization may want to focus on marketing strategies that try to expand the company's customer base, so that there are more opportunities available. However, it is important to keep in mind that an opportunity success rate, even though it is an indication of how the company itself is developing, is closely linked to the company's sales and marketing. As a result, it may not be wise for companies that have short pre-sale periods to use opportunity success rates as these rates can change greatly before new strategies are even implemented.

Innovation rate

An organization's innovation rate can be extremely useful for developing a strategic plan as it allows the organization the opportunity to determine whether or not its new ideas, products and services are actually profitable. If the organization's innovation rate is equal to or higher than its competitors, the organization should probably stay with its current innovation strategy and try to focus on designing products and services that are similar to the new products the company has recently placed on the market. On the other hand, if the organization's innovation rate is significantly lower than its competitors, the organization may want to try a new innovation strategy and try to focus on developing products and services that are not similar to the products the company has recently placed on the market. It is important to realize that the innovation rate is not a measurement of how innovative a company is, but rather a measurement of how profitable each group of new innovations has actually been for the company.

Online orders

The number of online orders that have been placed using an organization's website can be extremely useful for developing a strategic plan, as it allows the organization the opportunity to measure the effectiveness of their website. If the number of orders made online through their website or by e-mail is approximately equal to or greater than the number of orders placed through more traditional means such as in a store or by phone, the company should probably focus on maintaining or expanding their online services. On the other hand, if the number of orders placed online through their website or by e-mail is significantly less than the number of orders placed through more traditional means, the company should consider implementing strategies to improve their online services. The company may also want to compare the number of online orders made through their website to the number of online orders made through websites belonging to the company's competitors as this will allow the organization to determine the effectiveness of the company's website in relation to the rest of the industry.

Information resources

The availability of the organization's information resources can be an essential factor to consider for any organization's strategic plan, as the technology that the organization is using at any given time is only useful if it is working. This means that if the computer systems, websites, e-mail services, or other pieces of technology that the organization's employees or that the organization's customers normally use are inaccessible at a time when someone would normally need to access these resources, then the organization will not be able to function normally. As a result, considering the availability of the organization's information resources is an effective way for the organization to identify problems with the company's IT systems and IT personnel, so that the organization can determine methods of minimizing the effects of these problems in the future.

The number of views per page or views per listing for an organization's websites, ads or other information resources can be an important factor for an organization to consider during the strategic planning process. This is because the number of views per page or views per listing can help the organization measure the effectiveness of its websites and ads. If a particular page or listing receives a large number of views and a large number of customers place orders related to the items or services that are described on that particular page or in that particular listing; then it is an indication that these websites and ads are performing well. However, if a particular page or listing is not receiving a large number of views or if the page is receiving a large number of views but only a small percentage of the customers viewing the page are buying the product; then the organization should probably rethink their website marketing and design.

Competitors

The current number of competitors in the market and the average number of new competitors entering the market per year can actually be a useful set of statistics for organizations that are attempting to develop a strategic plan. The current number of competitors in the market is an effective way for an organization to measure how much competition is currently present in a particular market and the average number of new competitors entering the market per year is a good way for the organization to measure how that competition will change. In other words, these two statistics help the organization determine how much competition is in the market now and how much competition will be in the market in the near future. These two statistics allow the organization to develop their strategic plan with the amount of competition that the organization will face in mind. These two statistics may also act as a warning sign for potential problems in the market if the number of competitors does not rise as much as expected or the number actually decreases unexpectedly.

Current market share

The organization's current market share can be an important factor to consider during the strategic planning process, as it acts as a way for the organization to measure its success and growth in a particular market and compare that success and growth with the organization's competitors. As a result, the organization's current market share is ultimately an indication of how the organization as a whole is performing in the current business environment for each specific market in which the organization is doing business. If an organization's market share in a particular market is continuing to grow or if the organization is maintaining a large, stable market share, then it is usually an indication that the organization's current strategies are working. However, if an organization's market share in a particular market is beginning to decline or if the organization's market share is stable, but low when compared to the organization's competitors; then it may be an indication that the organization needs to try something new.

Average income of customers

The average income of customers in the target market can be an important piece of information to consider during the strategic planning process as it acts as a way for the organization to analyze the current economic environment. The amount of money that individuals within the target market earn can fluctuate greatly from year to year and it is essential for the organization to make sure that the customers in the target market can afford to purchase the product. For example, if a car dealer is attempting to sell a line of new cars that each normally cost $25,000; it may be difficult to convince someone that just had their pay cut from $50,000 to $25,000 a year to purchase the car since the price of the car is equal to the customer's earnings for an entire year. As a result, it is important for the organization to take the amount of money that the average customer would earn in a given period of time into consideration to make sure that the organization can plan around the current economic market.

Common industry practices

There are a variety of sources that an organization might use to find information about common industry practices, industry developments, and technological developments, but the three most common sources are newspapers, magazines, and websites. Large newspapers, especially newspapers that focus primarily on business, will often publish articles that detail major changes occurring in each particular industry as well as articles detailing new technologies that are coming out in the near future. Certain business magazines, specifically those published by the particular industry that the organization is a part of, can be extremely useful as they often detail current trends in the industry as well as how those trends have changed and why they have changed. Certain websites can also be extremely useful as most industries have industry websites that will detail changing trends and major developments that are currently taking place in the industry. The organization may also want to check the shareholder websites for their competitors, as these sites will often identify the practices and acquisitions on which the organization's competitors are focusing.

Current labor pool

There are a variety of sources that an organization might use to find information about the current labor pool including newspapers, magazines, industry websites and other similar print and online publications. Most major publications will print articles about major changes in the work force as soon as they occur so all of these sources can be useful tools for an organization that is attempting to analyze the current labor pool. One of the most useful publications for an organization that is attempting to determine the status of the current labor pool for a particular industry, however, is actually the Occupational Outlook Handbook. The Occupational Outlook Handbook (OOH), which is published by the United States Bureau of Labor Statistics, is primarily designed for individuals seeking employment. However, the OOH also provides detailed descriptions of each occupation, information about the current labor pool, and projections for the next five to ten years of how the labor pool for each occupation is expected to change, which can be extremely useful information for any organization.

Upcoming legislation

There are a variety of sources that an organization might use to find information about upcoming legislation and new regulations that might affect the particular industry that the organization is a part of, but the three most common sources are newspapers, magazines, and websites. Virtually every newspaper covers information related to upcoming legislation to some degree and large national newspapers can often be a good way for an organization to find out about changes to federal and state laws while smaller city newspapers can be a good way for an organization to find out about changes to laws and ordinances passed by the local government that may impact the organization. Industry magazines and publications are also another very useful tool for finding information about upcoming legislation, as these publications will almost always cover legislation that is specifically of concern to members of the industry. Industry websites, government websites and certain professional websites can all be extremely useful as well; as these websites will usually detail the progress of legislation that may be of interest throughout the legislative process.

There is a wide range of methods that an individual, such as an HR professional, might use to influence upcoming legislation, but the three most common methods are by mail, by scheduling meetings with elected officials, or by lobbying. In order for an individual to influence legislation by mail, that individual simply needs to write a formal letter and send that letter to an elected official such as a state senator, a congressman or congresswoman, a local mayor or any other similar official. In order for an individual to influence legislation through meetings, that individual needs to schedule a meeting with an elected official or a member of his or her staff in order to discuss the issue with which the organization is concerned. In order for an individual to influence legislation by lobbying, that individual should find members of other similar organizations, possibly even members of the organization's competitors within the same industry, and have the entire group express their opinions to an appropriate elected official by mail or in person.

Federal bill process

The process of forming a new law begins with the bill being introduced by either the Senate or the House of Representatives. The bill is then referred to a committee that determines if the bill should be considered further by a subcommittee, considered further by the entire floor of the House or Senate, or if the bill should be ignored. If the bill reaches the floor of the House or Senate, the bill is debated and a vote is taken to pass or defeat the bill. If the bill is passed in the Senate, then the bill is passed on to the House to be considered in the same way and vice versa. After both the House and Senate have approved a particular bill, the bill is sent on to the president so the bill may be signed into law, may be vetoed, may be returned to congress, may become law automatically if it is ignored for 10 days while Congress is in session or die automatically if it is ignored until after Congress is out of session.

Functions of management

The five basic functions that are normally associated with management are planning, organizing, coordinating, directing, and controlling. Planning refers to the process of actually determining what the organization is attempting to achieve and how the organization is going to achieve that goal. Organizing refers to the process of obtaining and allocating human resources, financial resources, and other similar resources in order to carry out the plan that the organization has established. Coordinating refers to the process of making sure that all of the resources that have been allocated are functioning together as planned in order to achieve the organization's goal. Directing, also sometimes referred to as leading, is the process of making sure that the work associated with completing the goal is actually carried out in an effective manner. Finally, controlling is the process of evaluating the organization's progress towards the goal. In other words, controlling is the process where the manager actually has to determine whether the plan is working as expected or not.

Project management

Project management is the process of determining and implementing a plan that will lead to the completion of a particular task within certain defined constraints. In other words, project management refers to the process of planning how to complete a particular project and actually making sure that the project is completed so it meets the quality standards expected, accomplishes the task that the organization set out to achieve, is completed within the time allowed and is completed within the financial limits of the project. Project management is important because almost every organization has to carry out a large number of different tasks at the same time and most organizations will often find that there are not enough financial and time resources available to complete every task. As a result, it is essential for an organization to find ways of completing projects cheaply and efficiently so the organization's resources are used as effectively as possible.

<u>Main factors</u>
The three main factors that project managers traditionally have been expected to control while completing a project include the cost of the project, the time spent on the project, and the scope of the project. The cost of the project refers to the total amount of resources spent on the project including financial resources, raw material resources and other similar resources. The time spent on the project refers to the total amount of time spent by the employees of the organization on that particular task, so that the task could be completed. The scope of the project refers to the requirements that need to be met in order to complete the task in the appropriate fashion. This simply means that in order for a project manager to complete a task appropriately, he or she must make sure that the project is completed within the time and cost constraints set by the organization and that the end result meets the requirements of the organization.

Other than the three main factors that project managers have traditionally been expected to control, an important factor that a project manager might be expected to control on a regular basis is the risk associated with a project. Most projects carry some risk of failure and virtually every project carries the risk that the project will not be completed as cheaply as expected or completed before the deadline. As a result, it is essential for a project manager to find ways of minimizing the risk of unexpected delays, costs, or other problems with a particular project. This is because a large project that fails to produce the desired result or a project that ends up costing significantly more or taking significantly more time than the organization had originally anticipated may actually have a significant negative impact on the organization as a whole.

<u>Quality control</u>
In order for a project manager to make sure that the end result achieved from a particular project meets the expectations of the organization, it is essential for that project manager to monitor and control the quality of the work being performed. In fact, the quality of the work being performed for a particular project is usually one of the main factors involved with controlling the scope of the project. This is because most tasks have specific requirements or guidelines that need to be met in order for the task to be completed correctly. If the product, service or other result produced by the project does not meet the quality requirements set by the organization; then the project manager has failed to meet the scope of the project. Therefore, it is extremely important for a project manager to continually monitor the quality of the results produced from a project in order to make sure that the project produces the desired end result.

Gantt chart

A Gantt chart is actually a type of bar chart that is often used to identify the various tasks involved in a particular project and to establish a schedule for completing those tasks. Gantt charts, in general, are actually closely related to Work Breakdown Structures, as the chart is designed to break the larger project down into the specific activities, tasks and other parts that make up the larger project. A Gantt chart lists each main task, referred to as a summary element, and then lists the subtasks that need to be completed to complete the main task, referred to as terminal elements, under the main task. Each task included on the chart then has a bar next to it that indicates how much of the task has been completed and a different colored bar that indicates how much of the task is still remaining. Gantt charts also usually indicate the date or week that each particular task started in and the date or week in which the project needs to be completed.

PERT

The Project Evaluation and Review Technique (PERT) is a method of determining how much time is required to complete a specific project. Basically, the PERT process consists of breaking the larger project down into a series of separate tasks that are necessary to complete the larger project and then organizing each of these smaller tasks into a chart. Each task in the PERT chart is represented by a line or arrow that is drawn from a circle that represents an event or goal, such as the project beginning or the organization completing a task and moving onto the next task, to a circle that represents the next event or goal. Usually each event or goal circle is assigned a number and the circles are arranged based on the order in which they are to be completed or based on the order of importance. The organization can then estimate the amount of time each task will take and note that estimate above the corresponding task line or arrow in the chart.

WBS

A Work Breakdown Structure (WBS) is a method for breaking a larger project down into a series of separate smaller tasks that are necessary in order to complete the larger project. The process of constructing a WBS is based largely off a principle known as the 100% Rule; which simply states that the subtasks included in a Work Breakdown Structure must describe 100% of the work necessary to complete the larger task. In other words, the most important factor to consider in a WBS is does the WBS include every subtask that needs to be completed in order to complete the larger task? Work Breakdown Structures are usually depicted in chart form as tree structures that start off with the larger task and then branch out to the subtasks that make up the larger task. Each subtask is usually then broken down further into smaller subtasks and each subtask is then assigned a percentage based on how much of the project is related specifically to that subtask.

Outsourcing

Outsourcing refers to the practice of hiring third-party companies or contractors to perform tasks that have been traditionally performed by the organization itself. In other words, outsourcing is the process of finding people or organizations outside the organization to perform tasks that were originally done "in-house" by employees or other resources of the organization. There are a variety of situations in which it may be better for an organization to outsource certain tasks rather than perform those tasks in-house, but some of the most important factors that an organization should consider are; the cost of performing the task in-house, the cost of a third-party performing the task, the level of difficulty associated with the task, the level of quality control necessary for the task, the level of quality control available from outside sources, the impact on the organization if the task is not completed when expected or as expected and ultimately how much control does the organization need to maintain over a particular task.

There are a variety of factors that an organization should consider before choosing a third-party vendor regardless of the specific task that the organization is attempting to outsource. However, four of the most important factors to consider are the costs associated with doing business with the vendor, the quality of the vendor's product or service, the ability of the vendor to meet the organization's needs for the specific task and the vendor's experience as it relates to the specific task. The cost associated with a particular vendor simply refers to all of the costs that the organization might incur if the organization chooses to use that particular vendor. The quality of the vendor's product or service refers to the vendor's ability to perform the service or manufacture the product up to the standards set by the organization. Finally, the ability of the vendor to meet the organization's needs and the vendor's experience as it relates to the task are both ways of determining if the vendor will be able to consistently perform the task as expected or not.

Off-shoring

Off-shoring is actually a process similar to outsourcing, as it refers to the practice in which an organization hires an individual or company that is located in another country in order to perform a particular task that the organization would normally perform domestically. In other words, off-shoring is the practice of hiring individuals or companies that are offshore, overseas or simply in a different country from the organization itself so that these individuals or companies can provide a specific product or service for the organization. Most organizations use off-shoring in order to obtain goods or services for less than the organization would typically have to pay if the organization attempted to obtain those goods or services from domestic sources. Off-shoring is very similar to outsourcing, but it is not exactly the same as it is possible for an organization to have an offshore division that provides products and services to the organization but may still actually be a part of the organization.

In-sourcing

In-sourcing is actually the opposite of outsourcing, as it refers to the practice in which an organization performs a task "in-house" by hiring individuals as direct employees of the organization or by acquiring an outside company in order to perform a particular task that had been previously performed by outside vendors. In other words, in-sourcing is the process of finding people within the organization or finding or establishing companies or divisions directly linked to the organization to perform tasks inside the organization instead of having those tasks performed outside the organization. There are a variety of different situations in which an organization may decide to in-source a particular task, but most organizations in-source in order to gain more control over tasks that are extremely complex or extremely important or to eliminate some of the costs associated with outsourcing a particular task.

HRIS

A Human Resource Information System (HRIS) is actually a computer system that is designed to help human resource professionals carry out the day-to-day HR functions that are necessary for an organization to continue functioning normally. Most Human Resource Information Systems are designed to collect and store data related to employee benefits, hiring of employees, placement of employees, payroll, employee evaluations and information about the training of employees. Basically, this means that an HRIS is designed to help an HR professional carry out all of the primary functions associated with the organization's HR needs, which include benefits administration, payroll, time and labor management and HR management; specifically in regards to hiring, placement, training, and other similar needs. However, it is important to note that an HRIS is not only designed to aid the organization's HR department, but also to help make sure that the entire organization continues to function as effectively as possible.

Strategic planning process

There are a variety of ways that an organization can create a strategic plan, but most organizations begin the strategic planning process by establishing the goals that the organization hopes to accomplish in the future. These goals usually include primary goals that are established in the organization's mission and vision statements and secondary goals that need to be accomplished in order to achieve the primary goals of the organization. These goals are actually essential to the strategic planning process because they act as the framework for the structure of the strategic plan, as the organization needs to make sure that the plan will accomplish the goals that the organization has set. However, it is also important to note that these goals not only help the organization structure the plan, but also help the organization measure their progress as a whole and the overall effectiveness of a particular strategic plan.

Once the organization has set these goals, the second step that most organizations take is to analyze the organization itself and the elements in the environment surrounding the organization. This analysis is primarily designed to find the strengths and weaknesses of the organization and to identify the outside influences that may make it difficult or even impossible for the organization to achieve its goals. There are a variety of different ways that an organization can assess its own strengths and weaknesses and assess the outside factors that may hinder or even help the organization including methods such as a SWOT analysis, a PEST analysis, a Porter's Five Forces analysis, and a variety of other similar methods. However, regardless of the specific method that an organization uses, it is important to realize that a good strategic plan must take the organization's merits, flaws and outside influences into consideration.

Once an organization has established a set of goals, identified the strengths and weaknesses of the organization and identified the outside factors that may prevent the organization from, or aid the organization in achieving its goals most organizations then move on to actually constructing the strategic plan. In order to construct the plan, most organizations use the goals that they established at the beginning of the process to establish the objectives that the strategic plan is designed to accomplish. Once the objectives for the plan have been established the organization then develops the strategies that will be required in order to achieve those objectives. The strategies included in the first draft of the strategic plan will usually be very simple, but will become more and more complex as the organization tries to use its strengths effectively, improve areas of the organization that have been identified as weak and try to compensate for outside factors that may interfere with the organization carrying out the plan as expected.

Once an organization has constructed a strategic plan from its goals, taking its strengths, weaknesses and outside environment into consideration, the organization then needs to actually put that strategic plan into action. This step of the process may actually sound simple; but it is often more complicated to put a strategic plan into action than it would appear. This is because an organization's strategic plan is only effective if the members of the organization follow the plan as it is written. As a result, in order for an organization to implement a strategic plan, the organization not only needs to inform each of its members of the plan that they need to follow, but must also make sure that each member actually carries out that plan. If a few members of the organization, or even worse, an entire department, attempt to take shortcuts or fail to follow the plan as expected, the entire plan may fail; so it is essential for the organization to make sure that each member carries out the plan in the appropriate fashion.

Once an organization has actually constructed a strategic plan and put that plan into action the organization must continually go back and evaluate the plan in order to make sure that the plan is still moving the organization towards achieving its goals. This is actually extremely important for any organization, as even the best laid strategic plan may be derailed by changes in the outside environment. The goals that the organization set at the beginning of the process allow the organization to measure the overall effectiveness of the organization's strategic plan and if that plan is not as effective as expected, the organization can make changes to the plan. This is important because it is impossible for an organization to consider every internal and external factor that may play a role in the success or failure of a strategic plan. It is essential for an organization to identify unexpected flaws in the plan as they arise and correct those flaws.

Types of analysis

PEST analysis
A PEST analysis considers four different groups of factors that may affect a particular organization and each letter of the word PEST actually stands for one of these four factor groups. The "P" in PEST stands for political, which primarily refers to the laws, regulations, taxes, and other factors related to the local or federal government that may affect the organization. The "E" in PEST stands for economic, which primarily refers to the current state of the economy as measured through statistics such as economic growth and the inflation rate. The "S" in PEST stands for social, which primarily refers to the culture and demographics of the area in which the organization plans to operate; such as the population size and growth, cultural beliefs, religious beliefs, age distribution and a variety of other similar factors. The T" in PEST stands for technological, which refers primarily to the invention and implementation of new technology, new regulations related to technology, new technology in use by competitors and many other similar factors.

SWOT analysis
A SWOT analysis considers four different groups of factors that may affect a particular organization and each letter of the acronym SWOT actually stands for one of these four factor groups. The "S" in SWOT stands for strengths; which refers to anything that the organization has or does that will ultimately help the organization achieve its objectives. The "W" in SWOT stands for weaknesses; which refers to anything that the organization has or does that may prevent the organization from achieving its objectives. The "O" in SWOT stands for opportunities; which refers to anything outside the organization that may help the organization to achieve its objectives. Finally, the "T" in SWOT stands for threats; which refers to anything outside the organization that may prevent the organization from achieving its objectives. In other words, SWOT refers to the internal strengths, internal weaknesses, the external opportunities and the external threats that may help or hinder a particular organization.

Porter's Five Force analysis
A Porter's Five Force analysis considers five different groups of factors that may affect a particular organization; which includes the threat of substitute products, the threat of new competitors, existing competitive rivalry, the bargaining power of customers, and the bargaining power of suppliers. The threat of substitute products refers to new technology or new products or services that consumers may choose over the organization's current products or services. The threat of new competitors refers to how easy it is for new organizations to enter the market. The threat of

existing competitive rivalry refers to other companies currently in the market that are competing with the organization and how those companies are attempting to stay competitive. The bargaining power of customers refers to the ability of customers to affect the organization's actions by refusing to buy the product or service if it is too expensive, does not live up to the customer's expectations, etc. The bargaining power of suppliers refers to the ability of suppliers to affect the organization's actions by controlling their access to raw materials, supplies, etc.

<u>Cost/benefit analysis strategy</u>
A cost/benefit analysis is a decision-making strategy that examines the total estimated cost of each option that is available, the total estimated benefit of each option that is available and then compares the costs of the option with the benefits of the option to determine if the benefits the organization may receive outweigh the costs. In most cases, the cost and benefit for a particular option refer to the financial cost and the financial benefit related to that particular option; but the cost/analysis strategy can be used for any decision that involves the use and acquisition of resources. The cost/benefit analysis strategy can be extremely useful for an organization that is attempting to determine which option will offer the greatest benefit. However, it is important to note that this strategy is heavily based off estimates made by the organization so there may be instances in which a cost/benefit analysis will not display an accurate representation of the benefits associated with a particular set of options.

Organizational life cycle

The organizational life cycle consists of four primary stages, which includes birth, growth, maturity, and decline. The birth stage refers to the stage in which the organization is forming or has just formed. This is the stage in which the organization conducts all of the activities associated with establishing the framework for the organization; such as acquiring capital, establishing values and establishing an initial business plan. The growth stage refers to the period of time in which the organization expands itself by increasing its market share, its number of employees, its number of locations, the organization's profits and other similar attributes. The maturity stage refers to the period in which the organization's expansion begins to level off and the organization is maintaining its current attributes rather than expanding them. Finally, the decline stage refers to the period in which the organization begins to lose its ability to maintain its current attributes and the organization's market share, number of employees, number of locations, profits and other similar attributes begin to decline.

Response strategies

There are four different response strategies that an organization can use to respond to a risk; which include reducing the effects of the risk, sharing the risk, avoiding the risk or accepting the risk. Reducing the risk includes any action that the organization takes to make the risk less likely to occur or less likely to cause significant harm to the organization. Sharing the risk includes any action that transfers some of the risk to another business entity such as by transferring the risk to an insurance company by purchasing an insurance policy. Avoiding the risk refers specifically to a strategy in which the organization simply discontinues any activities associated with the risk in order to eliminate the risk entirely. Finally, accepting the risk refers specifically to a strategy in which the organization continues to monitor the risk, but does not respond to the risk because the potential benefits of the opportunity outweigh the potential cost.

Creating a budget

The three main ways that an organization can create a budget are: from the bottom-up, the top-down or by using a parallel budgeting system. A bottom-up budget is constructed using estimates provided by each operating manager within the organization. These estimates describe the resources that each manager believes his or her department will require to continue functioning up to expectations. The organization uses these estimates to construct the budget. A top-down budget, on the other hand, is constructed by the organization's upper management and is based solely on resource estimates provided by senior managers. These estimates describe the resources that the senior managers believe each department will require. A budget that is created using a parallel budgeting system is constructed using estimates provided by each operating manager within the organization, but each estimate must meet certain requirements established by the organization's senior management.

Methods
There are a variety of different methods that an organization might use to create a budget. However, the two most common methods that an organization might use are incremental budgeting and zero-based budgeting. Incremental budgeting is a budgeting method in which an organization bases its new budget off of the previous year's budget. In this form of budgeting, the organization assumes that the needs of the organization for the coming year will be very similar to the needs of the organization for the previous year; so the organization can just adjust the budget based on cost increases. Zero-based budgeting, on the other hand, is a budgeting method in which an organization creates a completely new budget. In this form of budgeting, the organization bases the new budget solely on what the organization believes it will need in the coming year without taking the previous year's budget into consideration.

Change management

Change management refers to a variety of different techniques that an organization can use in order to modify a particular aspect of how the organization operates with as little harm to the organization as possible. In most cases, an organization makes these operational changes either to adapt to changes in society or to improve the manner in which the organization operates overall. Change management is important because the environment around an organization is constantly changing and, as a result, the organization will have to be able to adapt. Since many of the organization's members may have difficulty adapting to social, economic, or other similar changes in the organization's environment, it is essential for the organization to be able to adapt without putting too much unnecessary stress upon the members of the organization. As a result, change management is important because it allows an organization to continue functioning normally while the organization implements changes.

Strategies
There are three major types of strategies that an organization might use in order to manage the organization's decision to implement changes. These three types of strategies include the empirical-rational strategy, the normative/re-educative strategy and the power-coercive strategy. Each strategy has its own advantages and disadvantages and the specific strategy that an organization should use in a particular situation can depend on a variety of factors, including how much the organization needs to change and what resources are available to relieve problems that may arise from the changes that the organization implements. The specific strategy that an organization chooses to use may also be heavily based on how much

time is available to make the changes and the level of risk associated with the members of the organization rejecting the change and refusing to make the necessary adjustments.

Empirical-rational strategy

The empirical-rational strategy of managing change assumes that people are ultimately interested in their own well being and, as a result, will be more likely to accept changes if they understand that those changes offer some sort of benefit. In other words, this strategy of managing change is based on either offering an incentive to each member of the organization that will need to take part in the change or convincing the members of the organization that the change will benefit not only the organization, but each individual within the organization as well. For example, if an organization is attempting to improve its image with the public, the organization might decide to use an empirical-rational strategy by offering a bonus to the employee that performs the largest amount of community service. The organization, by offering the bonus to the employee that performs the largest amount of community service, might be able to encourage more of their employees to take part in community service projects, which may in turn improve the organization's public image.

Normative/re-educative strategy

The normative/re-educative strategy of managing change is based on the concept that peer pressure is often an effective way to bring about change in an organization. Basically, this strategy assumes that people rely heavily on social interaction and, as a result, will therefore act according to the expectations of the rest of society. Using this strategy, an organization can implement changes by slowly changing the culture of the organization so that each individual will begin to accept the changes as social norms. For example, if an organization wants to change the process that they use to manufacture a particular product, but the employees of the organization have a set process that they have been using for many years to manufacture that product, the organization may decide to use a normative/re-educative strategy. By slowly introducing the new procedures through memos, posters and training, the organization can begin to convince the employees of the organization that the new process is the appropriate way to perform the task and that the old process is obsolete.

Power-coercive strategy

The power-coercive strategy of managing change is based on the concept that people will usually listen to authority figures and will ultimately do as they are told. This strategy works simply by making it clear that there are actually no other options available to the employees than the option that the management wants them to choose. In fact, under this strategy, if an individual refuses to accept the changes that the organization is attempting to bring about, the organization might punish the individual for not complying with the new policies. For example, if a large grocery store has to comply with a new local ordinance that prohibits the sale of eggs to anyone under the age of 18 during the month of October, that grocery store may use a power-coercive strategy by informing the staff that they must not sell eggs to anyone under the age of 18 during October. If an employee sells eggs to a minor during October, the manager may actually suspend or even terminate that individual's employment for failing to comply with the new law.

Advantages and disadvantages

The empirical-rational strategy is very effective for situations in which an organization has the resources available to offer the incentives necessary to make the changes more palatable or if the changes have an obvious benefit to the individuals who need to implement the change. However, it is much less effective for situations in which the organization lacks the resources to issue incentives substantial enough to influence members of the organization or the changes do not seem beneficial on the surface. The normative/re-educative strategy is useful for situations in which the managers and workers of the organization have a strong relationship and there is a lot of time available to implement the changes. It is not effective, however, in situations in which there is limited time available or the relations between management and staff are strained. The power-coercive strategy can be extremely useful for situations in which time is limited and the threat to the organization is more serious. However, this strategy can often cause unrest within an organization, especially if the members of the organization are accustomed to more freedom.

Structural changes

There are a variety of different structural changes that an organization might decide to implement at some point. Some of the most common include corporate restructuring, mergers and acquisitions, divestitures, workforce expansion/reduction and re-engineering. Corporate restructuring refers to a type of structural change in which an organization alters the way that tasks are distributed throughout the organization in order to make sure that each task is carried out as efficiently as possible. Mergers and acquisitions refer to a type of structural change in which two organizations unite into one organization. "Divestitures" refers to a type of structural change in which an organization eliminates a department, worksite, or other similar organizational unit. Workforce expansion/reduction refers to a type of structural change in which an organization increases or decreases the number of employees working for the organization. Re-engineering refers to a type of structural change in which an organization alters the way that each task is performed in order to make sure that each task is carried out as efficiently as possible.

Mergers and acquisitions

Mergers and acquisitions are actually similar in many ways, as both terms refer to a type of structural change in which two organizations join together to form a single organization. However, it is important to realize that the two terms are not exactly the same, as each term actually refers to a different way in which an organization's structure changes. A merger refers to a situation in which two or more organizations agree to "merge" into a single organization because both organizations will benefit from the merger. An acquisition, on the other hand, refers to a situation in which an organization purchases enough of another organization's stock to "acquire" control of the organization's operations. This can actually be an important difference to keep in mind because all of the organizations involved in a merger must agree to the merger in order for the merger to take place, while the organizations involved in an acquisition do not necessarily need to agree to the acquisition in order for the acquisition to take place.

Due diligence

The due diligence process refers to a series of activities that each organization involved in a merger or acquisition must conduct before the merger or acquisition actually takes place. These activities are related to gathering, reviewing, and distributing legal, financial and operational information for each organization involved in the merger or acquisition. The information that must be gathered and provided to the other organizations involved in a merger or acquisition include employment and financial documents, employee policies and procedures, information related to legal concerns such as current legal disputes or recent fines and violations, information related to contracts and licenses that the organization currently holds, information related to recent or ongoing labor/union concerns and other similar information. This information is

- 34 -

primarily designed to provide each organization involved in the merger or acquisition with a detailed idea of exactly how each organization stands at the time of the merger or acquisition.

Employee adaptation

There are a large number of different ways that an organization can help employees adapt to changes within the organization and the specific methods that an organization should use to help employees adapt can vary greatly from situation to situation. However, there are certain basic actions that an organization should take for virtually any situation in which a major change is taking place. First, the organization should provide employees with all of the information that they need to understand the change. This includes information related to what the change is, why the change is taking place, when the change is taking place, and how the change will affect the organization's employees. Secondly, the organization should inform employees of what they need to do or what they can do in order to implement the change with as little harm as possible. Finally, the organization should monitor how the employees within the organization are handling the change and address or at least respond to any employee concerns that may arise.

Business ethics

Business ethics refers to the practice of using a series of appropriate practices, procedures and behaviors to make sure that an organization functions in a socially acceptable fashion. In other words, business ethics refers to the process of making sure that each individual in an organization is performing their duties in a fair, proper and morally responsible manner. It is essential for any organization, regardless of the specific type of organization, to maintain a strong sense of what is appropriate and what is unacceptable throughout the organization. This is because an organization that continually conducts business in a questionable, unfair or even outright illegal manner will usually risk damaging its reputation, risk damaging its ability to find customers or suppliers, risk liability from unethical or unlawful practices, risk criminal charges related to unlawful or grossly negligent practices or may even risk the organization's ability to do business at all.

There are a variety of ways that an HR professional can establish and maintain a strong sense of ethics within an organization. The three most effective ways include establishing a corporate values statement, establishing a code of conduct and making sure that each individual follows the ethical codes set by the organization through HR audits. A corporate values statement is simply a declaration of the basic behaviors that the organization would like its employees to follow including behaviors such as promoting open communication, being a team player and treating fellow employees, customers and other individuals with respect and dignity. A code of conduct is actually a series of policies, procedures and practices that expands on the behaviors established by the corporate values statement in order to define exactly what is considered acceptable behavior and what is considered absolutely unacceptable. Finally, once an organization has established a corporate values statement and a code of conduct, the organization must make sure that the members of the organization follow the policies set by the organization through HR audits.

There are a variety of policies and procedures that an HR professional might have to establish in order to support ethical and legal corporate governance practices. Some of the most obvious examples include policies to protect employees that report unethical behavior; training programs to educate managers and executives regarding legal and ethical concerns; and checklists and review systems to make sure that the organization is documenting and reporting everything appropriately. Policies to protect employees that report unethical behavior such as confidentiality, the acceptance of anonymous reports and procedures for handling managers that punish employees that make reports can all support ethical and legal corporate governance practices. Training programs that educate managers and executives about legal and ethical concerns such as sexual harassment, standards for corporate responsibility, ethical requirements for senior financial officers and the legal concerns associated with fraud can also help support appropriate corporate governance. Finally, checklists and review systems that insure that all appropriate accounting practices are carried out, scheduled and unscheduled accounting audits and other similar reviews can all support appropriate corporate governance as well.

Functioning normally

Some of the basic types of functions that an organization must typically perform in order to function normally include accounting functions, employee functions, financial functions, IT functions, marketing and sales functions, operating functions, and research/development functions. Accounting functions include any task that keeps track of the financial resources of the organization. Employee functions include any task related to the organization's human resources. Financial functions include any task related to earning, managing, or spending capital. IT functions include any task related to the organization's computer systems or other technology. Marketing and sales functions include any task related to the promoting, distributing, and sale of the product by considering factors such as the product itself, the price of the product, the placement or location where the product is sold, and the promotion of the product. Operating functions include any task related to providing the product or service that the organization is attempting to sell. The research/development functions of the organization include any task that is related to designing new products or services.

Departmentalization

Departmentalization is the process in which an organization separates each position into a separate group. Each group, known as a department, contains a number of positions that have a specific similar characteristic or a group of similar characteristics. Most organizations form departments by separating jobs using a division method, a function method, or a matrix method. An organization using a division method will place each position within a department based on the geographical location of the position, the product to which the position is related, the type of tasks that are related to the position, the type of customer that will be using the end product or service that the position is designed to create and other similar characteristics. An organization using a function method will place each position within a department based on its overall purpose to the organization. Function departments include departments such as accounting, human resources, manufacturing, research and development and other similar departments. Finally, a matrix method uses both a division method and a function method to place each position into two departments.

Formalization

Formalization is the process in which an organization establishes rules, policies and procedures for each position or process within the organization. These rules, policies and procedures are designed to ensure that each employee completes the tasks necessary for the organization to continue functioning in the manner that the organization expects. In other words, formalization is the process of creating formal declarations or taking action to make

- 36 -

sure that each task within the organization is regulated and is therefore conducted in a standard fashion. This not only allows the organization to ensure that each task is carried out, but also allows the organization to ensure that each task is carried out correctly. However, it is important to note that it will become more difficult for the organization to adapt to change, for the organization to promote creativity and/or for the organization to allow reasonable flexibility as the organization becomes increasingly formalized.

Job specialization

Job specialization is the process in which an organization separates a particular goal into a series of specific tasks so that the organization can focus the resources that are available amongst those tasks. In other words, job specialization refers to the process in which an organization identifies all of the tasks that need to be completed for the organization to function normally and then assigns each of those tasks to a particular position. This process allows an organization to create complex products quickly. For example, a toy manufacturer might have an assembly line in which one individual works the machinery that cuts out the arms and legs for a teddy bear, one that works the machinery that places the stuffing in the teddy bear, and one that works the machinery that attaches the various parts of the teddy bear so the tasks necessary to complete the toy can be carried out without switching back and forth between tasks. It is important to note, however, that extremely specialized tasks will often seem repetitive and/or boring to employees.

Chain-of-command

The term chain-of-command refers to the specific way in which an organization distributes its authority and responsibility amongst the members of the organization. In other words, an organization's chain-of-command specifically defines which individuals are in charge of which departments, identifies the individuals that the department heads report to and specifies the employees for which each department head or manager is responsible. In most cases, the chain-of-command is designed to make sure that each individual only reports to one supervisor or manager and that each supervisor or manager has the authority to control the actions of each individual that reports to that supervisor or manager. However, it is important to note that certain organizations may actually have structures in which an individual may report to multiple supervisors and/or managers and it may be unclear which supervisor or manager has authority in a particular situation.

Span-of-control

The term span-of-control refers to the number of employees that report to a particular supervisor or manager. In other words, if a supervisor or manager were responsible for controlling and monitoring the activities of Jane, Jack, Daniel, Sam and Martin, the supervisor or manager's span-of-control would be five employees. The specific span-of-control for a particular supervisor or manager can vary greatly from organization to organization and from manager to manager depending on the needs and strategies of each organization and the skills and experience of each manager. However, it is important to note that the difficulty associated with managing a particular group of employees will increase as the size of the group increases so it is much more difficult for a manager to manage effectively if he or she has a large span-of-control.

Operational structures

The two main types of operational structures that an organization may use are organic and mechanistic. A mechanistic structure is any structure in which the operations of an organization are extremely well regulated and defined. Mechanistic structures are usually centralized, have a large number of departments, a large number of managers with very limited spans of control, have an extensive chain-of-command, are extremely formalized with a large number of policies and procedures and usually have a large number of extremely specialized tasks. An organic structure, on the other hand, is any structure in which an organization is loosely regulated and may be less defined. Organic structures are usually decentralized, have a small number of departments, have a small number of managers with each assigned a large span-of-control, have a short chain-of-command, have virtually no formalization so that only basic policies and procedures are established and usually have fewer specialized tasks than mechanistic structures.

Mechanistic and organic operational structures each have their own distinct advantages and disadvantages. As a result, the specific type of structure that is best suited for a particular organization can vary depending on the specific situation. If an organization wants or needs to maintain control of the individual processes and tasks that are performed by the various parts of the organization and the organization is in a business environment that is relatively stable, then it may be wise for the organization to use a structure that is more mechanistic. If the organization is in a business environment in which the organization needs to implement changes frequently and/or creativity is essential to the organization's success; then the organization may want to use a structure that is more organic. However, regardless of whether an organization is primarily mechanistic or primarily organic, it is impossible for an organization to be completely mechanistic or organic, as each organization needs some combination of the two operational structures in order to continue functioning.

Important terms

Mission Statement: A mission statement is a declaration of the general purpose for which a business or other organization has been created. In other words, it is a statement that indicates the broad mission that a company or organization has undertaken so that individuals within that company or organization as well as consumers and other outside individuals can easily identify the reason that the company or organization exists. For example, the mission statement of a hospital, since the basic purpose of a hospital is to help the sick or injured, might be "to promote the health and well-being of the general public in order for everyone to live longer, healthier lives."

Vision Statement: A vision statement is a declaration of the specific goals that a business or other organization wants to achieve at some point. For example, a hospital might want to become recognized as the number one health care provider in the region.

Goal: A goal is a particular objective that an individual or organization is attempting to achieve at some point in the future. For example, a business might set a profit goal of increasing their profits for the year by 25% over the profits of the previous year.

Business Metric: A business metric, also known as a performance metric or a key performance indicator, refers to a system of measurement for measuring a business' progress towards a particular goal. In most cases, a business metric is a group of statistics that a company can use to determine whether or not the company is moving towards achieving a particular goal. For example, a business that has set a goal of increasing their profits by 25% over the previous year may use profit/loss reports from the current year and compare those reports to the previous year to determine how close the company is to achieving that goal.

Liabilities: Liabilities refer to all of the financial costs that an organization must pay to another individual or organization. Liabilities include costs such as employee's wages, loan payments, taxes, and other similar costs. An organization's total liability is equal to the organization's total assets less the organization's total equity (Liability = Assets – Equity).

Assets: Assets refer to all of the resources that an organization owns. Assets may be tangible or intangible and include resources such as buildings, cash, equipment, land, inventory and other similar resources. An organization's total assets are equal to the sum of the organization's total equity and total liability (Assets = Liabilities + Equity).

Equity: Equity, which may also be referred to as owner's equity or in certain cases referred to as partners' equity or shareholder's equity, is the value of all of the resources that an organization owns less all of the costs that an organization must pay. Therefore, an organization's equity is equal to the organization's total assets less the organization's total liabilities (Equity = Assets – Liability).

Balance Sheet: A balance sheet is a financial statement that indicates the assets, equity and liabilities that an organization owns or owes at a specific point in time.

Income Statement: An income statement, also known as a profit and loss or P and L statement, is a financial statement that indicates the total amount of revenue that the organization has earned during a specific period, the total amount of expenses that the organization has incurred during that period and the total amount that the organization has earned or lost for the period after the organization's expenses have been subtracted from the organization's revenue.

Statement of Cash Flows: A statement of cash flows is a financial statement that indicates the amount of money that an organization has taken in during a particular period, the amount of money that an organization has paid out during a particular period, and the specific activities or products that the organization has earned money from or spent money on during the period.

Third-party vendor: A third-party vendor is an independent contractor or company that provides products or services for the organization, but is not directly related to the organization itself. In other words, a third-party vendor is an outside vendor that is under contract to perform a specific service for the organization, but does not work for a specific division of the organization or for another organization owned or operated by the organization. For example, a convenience store may have a contract with a soda company to deliver soda to the store and stock the store's coolers.

Request for proposal: A request for proposal (RFP) is a written invitation sent to third-party vendors requesting bids for a specific product or service. Organizations usually issue these requests in order to gather information about a particular product or service that the organization is considering outsourcing to a third-party vendor.

Centralization: Centralization refers to a process in which an organization places most or all of its decision-making authority with the organization's upper management. In other words, a centralized organization is an organization in which the organization's top executives make virtually all of the organization's decisions. Centralization allows an organization's upper management to have more control over the organization's day-to-day activities, but makes it more difficult for the organization to respond to issues quickly.

Decentralization: Decentralization actually refers to the opposite of centralization as it refers to a process in which an organization distributes all of its decision-making authority to employees throughout the organization. In other words, a decentralized organization is an organization in which some decisions are made by the organization's top executives, but employees throughout the organization also have some say in the organization's decision-making. Decentralization allows an organization to make decisions quickly, but reduces the amount of control that the upper management has over the organization's day-to-day decision-making.

Simple Structure: A simple structure is a type of organizational structure in which the organization's chain-of-command consists of one level of management so the chain-of-command is relatively flat. Simple structures are usually used in small organizations and are typically centralized, have virtually no departments, a small number of managers, each with a large span-of-control, have very little formalization, and very few specialized tasks. Simple structures are usually not practical for larger organizations.

Functional Structure: A functional structure is a type of organizational structure in which the organization's chain-of-command is shaped like a pyramid with a number of different levels of management. Functional structures are usually used in larger organizations and are typically centralized, have a large number of departments, have a large number of managers, each with a very limited span- of-control, have a lot of formalization and have a large number of specialized tasks.

Divisional Structure: A divisional structure is a type of organizational structure in which the organization's chain-of-command is separated into divisions based on a specific characteristic that differentiates that section of the organization from other sections of the organization. For example, an ice cream manufacturer may have a division that manufactures ice cream and a separate division that manufactures ice cream cones. Each division is usually managed by a divisional executive that reports to the organization's CEO. Divisional structures are typically decentralized and are usually only practical in large organizations.

Matrix Structure: A matrix structure is a type of organizational structure in which the organization has two overlapping chains-of-command so each employee actually reports to two supervisors or managers instead of one. A matrix structure resembles a grid, as each employee must report to the manager or supervisor in charge of the division and the manager or supervisor in charge of the department. Matrix structures are typically decentralized and are usually only practical in large organizations.

Workforce Planning and Employment

Discrimination

It may appear that discrimination is in fact illegal in every situation; however, this is actually not the case. The term "discrimination" only refers to the practice of making a decision regarding a person or thing based on the characteristics of that particular person or thing, which is actually a practice that most organizations perform legally on a daily basis. This is because discrimination is only unlawful if the employer's decision regarding a particular individual is based off a characteristic that is considered protected. For example, if an employer decides that the organization will only hire people under the age of 40, the employer is unlawfully discriminating against employees based on their age. On the other hand, if the employer decides that the organization will only hire people with a certain type of college degree and the college degree is actually required by law; or the knowledge associated with that degree is necessary to perform the tasks related to that particular position, the employer is discriminating based on the individual's characteristics and is performing the discrimination legally.

Disparate impact

Disparate impact is a type of discrimination in which an employer institutes a policy that appears to be reasonable, but the policy actually prevents individuals of a certain color, with certain disabilities, with a certain military status, of a certain national origin, of a certain race, of a certain religion or of a particular sex from receiving employment or any of the benefits associated with employment; such as promotions or pay. In other words, disparate impact refers to a policy that makes sense, but is actually unfair because it makes it more difficult for individuals of a certain group to receive the job or benefit. For example, a policy that states that individuals applying for an office job must be at least 5'10" and weigh at least 185 pounds may actually create a disparate impact if it makes it more difficult for individuals belonging to one of the protected groups, such as women, to get the job. This type of discrimination was first identified by the Supreme Court in Griggs v. Duke Power Co.

Disparate treatment

Disparate treatment is a type of discrimination in which an employer deliberately treats an individual differently because of that individual's age, color, disability, military status, national origin, race, religion, and/or sex. In other words, disparate treatment usually refers to any instance in which an employer uses a different set of procedures, expectations or policies than that employer would normally use simply because the individual belongs to a particular group. For example, a business that required each female employee to follow a strict dress code while the male employees of the business could wear whatever they like would be guilty of disparate treatment because the business is treating the employees differently based on each employee's sex. This type of discrimination was first identified by Title VII of the Civil Rights Act.

Civil rights legislation

CRA

The Civil Rights Act (CRA) of 1991 was designed to perform four primary functions, which are actually identified at the beginning of the document. The first function of the CRA is to declare specific rights that victims of discrimination may use in order to remedy the effects of discrimination. The second function of the CRA is to acknowledge and define the type of discrimination known as disparate impact. The third function of the CRA is to offer specific regulations and guidelines related to disparate impact cases. Finally, the fourth function that the CRA was designed to perform is to expand on the discrimination laws and regulations that were established before the Civil Rights Act of 1991 in order to offer more protection against discrimination. It is important to note that this fourth function of the CRA was primarily included to strengthen some of the equal opportunity laws that were not offering enough protection due to rulings made by the Supreme Court.

The Civil Rights Act of 1991 made a number of changes to Title VII of the Civil Rights Act of 1964 including expanding the protection offered by Title VII to cover congressional employees, expanding the protection offered by Title VII to cover foreign locations owned and/or operated by American businesses and creating a sliding scale for the maximum amount of damages for which a victim of discrimination could sue. The Civil Rights Act of 1991 also granted individuals or organizations accused of discrimination the right to a jury trial if a civil suit is brought against that individual or organization, placed the burden of proof for disparate impact cases on the victim of discrimination and granted individuals or organizations accused of discrimination the right to prove that a specific action or policy was necessary to the operation of the business and use that proof as a legal defense against accusations of disparate impact. The Civil Rights Act of 1991 also set other similar guidelines that define the specific types of actions that should be considered unlawful discrimination.

Title VII: Title VII of the Civil Rights Act, which was originally passed in 1964 and amended in 1972, 1978 and 1991, is primarily designed to prevent unlawful discrimination in the workplace. This section of the Civil Rights Act makes it unlawful to base hiring decisions or other similar decisions related to aspects of an individual's employment, such as the pay or benefits that the individual receives, on that individual's color, national origin, race, religion and/or sex. Title VII also makes it unlawful for an employer to discriminate against individuals that are pregnant, about to give birth or that have any other similar medical condition. Title VII of the Civil Rights Act applies to any employer that has more than 15 employees with the exception of religious organizations; which can choose to only hire individuals within that religion or to consider individuals of that religion for employment before individuals of other religions, and Indian reservations; which can choose to hire or consider Indians living on or near a reservation for employment before other individuals.

EEOC: The Equal Employment Opportunity Commission, or EEOC, was formed by Title VII of the Civil Rights Act in order to protect certain groups of individuals from unlawful discrimination. The EEOC is actually a federal agency that is designed to encourage equal employment opportunities, to train employers to avoid practices and policies that could cause unlawful discrimination and to enforce the laws included in the Civil Rights Act, Age Discrimination in Employment Act and laws included in other similar anti-discrimination legislation. The EEOC enforces the laws associated with the Civil Rights Act and other similar acts by attempting to obtain settlements from employers that have taken actions that the commission deems to be discriminatory. If the employer will not settle with the EEOC, the EEOC will then continue their attempt to enforce the law by filing a lawsuit against the employer on behalf of the victim of the discrimination.

ADEA

The Age Discrimination in Employment Act (ADEA), which was originally passed in 1967 and later amended in 1991, is designed to prevent discrimination against individuals over the age of thirty-nine. This act makes it unlawful for an employer to base hiring decisions or other similar decisions related to aspects of an individual's employment, such as pay or benefits, on the age of the individual if that individual is at least forty years old. This act applies to any business, employment agency, labor organization and state or local government agency with more than 20 employees. However, this act does not apply to individuals of age forty or over that do not meet the bona-fide occupational qualifications required to actually perform the tasks reasonably necessary to the business' operations; does not prohibit the termination of an individual's employment due to reasonable cause; does not apply to the employment of firefighters or police officers; or apply to the retirement of employees with executive positions or tenured educators under certain conditions.

Waiver of rights: Under the Age Discrimination in Employment Act, any individual may waive his or her right to protection from age discrimination by signing a waiver of rights, but there are certain requirements that the waiver must meet in order to be considered legal. First, the waiver must be written in a clear and concise manner and state that the individual should consult with an attorney prior to signing the waiver. Secondly, the employee must be allowed at least 21 days to consider the terms of the waiver and at least 7 days to change his or her mind and terminate the waiver after the individual has signed it. Finally, in order for any waiver of rights related to age discrimination to be considered valid, the waiver must offer some sort of consideration, such as pay or benefits, in addition to anything that the individual would normally receive.

Under the Age Discrimination in Employment Act an organization that wants to institute an early retirement program, an incentive program to encourage individuals to leave the organization or some other similar type of program, must make sure to meet certain requirements. First, the waiver must be written in a clear and concise manner, must state that the individual should consult with an attorney prior to signing the waiver, must allow the individual at least 45 days to consider the terms of the waiver and must allow the individual to have at least 7 days to change his/her mind after the signing it. In addition to these requirements, the employer must also inform the individual considering the waiver of the factors that make an individual eligible for the program, any time limits associated with the program, and the job titles and ages of everyone that is eligible or that has been chosen to take part in the program, as well as the ages of everyone that is ineligible or has not been chosen to take part in the program.

ADA
The Americans with Disabilities Act (ADA), which was passed in 1990, is designed to prevent discrimination against individuals with disabilities. This act makes it unlawful for an employer to base hiring decisions or other similar decisions related to aspects of an individual's employment, such as pay or benefits, on whether the individual is disabled or not. This act specifically requires any business, employment agency or labor organization with more than 15 employees to find or create a position that the disabled individual will be able to perform as long as creating that position will not cause the business significant financial or operational harm. This act also requires the business, employment agency or labor organization to make sure that the disabled individual has access to his or her place of employment unless making these changes will cause the business significant harm.

Rehabilitation Act of 1973
The Rehabilitation Act of 1973 is actually very similar to the Americans with Disabilities Act (ADA), as the Rehabilitation Act is designed to prevent discrimination against individuals with disabilities. However, the ADA is actually designed to expand on the protections granted by the Rehabilitation Act because the Rehabilitation Act only covered very specific organizations. In fact, the Rehabilitation Act was only designed to prevent discrimination against individuals with disabilities if those individuals were seeking employment in federal agencies or with federal contractors that

- 43 -

earned more than $10,000 a year from government contracts. It is also important to note that employers were not required under the Rehabilitation Act to make the organization's facilities accessible to individuals with disabilities so there was no legal remedy for an individual that was employed, but was unable to access his or her place of employment.

VEVRAA

The Vietnam Era Veteran's Readjustment Assistance Act (VEVRAA) is designed to prevent discrimination against veterans. This act makes it unlawful for federal contractors or subcontractors with $25,000 or more in federal contracts or subcontracts to base hiring decisions or similar decisions related to aspects of an individual's employment, such as the individual's pay or benefits, on the fact that the individual is a veteran. This act also requires federal contractors or subcontractors that meet these requirements to list any open positions with state employment agencies and requires these employers to institute affirmative action plans for veterans. However, in order for this particular act to apply, the veteran must have served for more than 180 days with at least part of that time occurring between August 5, 1964 and May 7, 1975 or the veteran must have a disability or group of disabilities that are rated at 10 percent or more and be eligible for compensation from the Department of Veteran Affairs or must have served on active duty for a conflict with an authorized campaign badge.

IRCA

The Immigration Reform and Control Act (IRCA) is designed to prevent discrimination that is based on an individual's nationality. This act makes it unlawful for an employer to base hiring decisions or other similar decisions related to aspects of an individual's employment, such as the pay or benefits that the individual receives, on that individual's country of origin or the individual's citizenship status as long as the individual can legally work within the United States. This act also makes it unlawful for an organization to intentionally hire individuals that cannot legally work in the United States and requires the organization to complete the I-9 form for all new employees. It is also important to note that this act specifically requires the employer to obtain proof of the employee's eligibility to work in the United States for the I-9 form, but the employee **must** be allowed to provide any document or combination of documents that are considered acceptable by the IRCA.

Meritor Savings Bank v. Vinson

The Supreme Court case known as Meritor Savings Bank v. Vinson is important because it is the first case that recognized sexual harassment as a form of unlawful discrimination. The case was brought against Meritor Savings Bank by Mechelle Vinson because the bank's vice president had created a hostile work environment through a series of repeated unwelcome sexual advances and acts. Prior to this case, the protections offered by Title VII of the Civil Rights Act of 1964 for discrimination based on sex had been related solely to economic or other types of tangible discrimination. However, the Supreme Court ruled in this case that Title VII was designed to prevent all types of "disparate treatment" and as such, actions that cause a hostile work environment for a member of a protected class constitute a form of unlawful discrimination.

UGESP

The Uniform Guidelines on Employee Selection Procedures (UGESP), which were passed in 1978, are actually a collection of principles, techniques and procedures that are designed to help employers and other organizations comply with Federal anti-discrimination laws. The primary purpose of these guidelines is to actually define the specific types of procedures that may cause disparate impact in more detail. In other words, the guidelines presented in the

- 44 -

UGESP were designed to make it clear which selection procedures would be considered illegal. The UGESP specifically relates to procedures that would cause disparate impact and is therefore designed to help employers and organizations avoid procedures that appear to be fair, but are actually unfair because they make it much less likely that an individual belonging to a protected class would actually be able to receive a particular position.

Executive Order 11246

An executive order is a written declaration made by the President of the United States that establishes a policy for how existing legislation should be enforced. Executive orders are legally binding and will be treated as law if the order remains in the Federal Registry for more than 30 days. Executive order 11246, which was published to the Federal Registry in 1965, was designed to make it clear that federal contractors were not only required to avoid employment discrimination, but were also required to take steps to make sure that equal opportunities were made available to individuals belonging to protected classes. This executive order clearly established the concept of affirmative action and required federal contractors with more than $10,000 in government contracts during a single year to implement affirmative action plans and federal contractors with $50,000 or more in contracts and 50 or more employees to file a written Affirmative Action Plan with the Office of Federal Contract Compliance Programs (OFCCP).

Originally, Executive Order (EO) 11246 only applied to employment discrimination that was based on an individual's color, national origin, race or religion. However, EO 11375, EO 11478, EO 13152 and EO 13279 amended the policy established by EO 11246 and changed the groups that were covered by the original order. EO 11375 added discrimination based on an individual's sex as a type of unlawful discrimination prohibited by EO 11246. EO 11478 added discrimination based on an individual's disabilities or age if that individual is over age forty as types of unlawful discrimination prohibited by EO 11246. EO 13152 added discrimination based on an individual's status as a parent as a type of unlawful discrimination prohibited by EO 11246. EO 13279 did not actually add to the list of protected classes included in EO 11246, but instead excluded federal contractors that were actually religious or community organizations providing services to the community from having to adhere to the policies established by the executive order.

AAP

Written Affirmative Action Plans (AAP), first established by Executive Order 11246, are required to include a variety of different information about a particular organization. The main purpose of an AAP, as established by a revision to 41 CFR Part 60-2 made in late 2000, is for an organization to establish a series of goals related to encouraging equal employment opportunities and to set forth a plan for how the organization plans to move towards and monitor their progress towards those goals. As a result, an AAP is required to include a list of action-oriented programs, an availability analysis of employees from protected classes, a section that designates the individual responsible for the organization's AAP, a job group analysis, an organizational profile, placement goals, a system for internal audits and reports related to analyzing barriers to equal employment opportunities and a utilization/incumbency analysis of the number of protected individuals employed by the company compared to the number of protected individuals available.

The availability analysis of an Affirmative Action Plan (AAP) includes information related to the number of individuals belonging to a protected class within a certain area that could be hired to fill a particular type of position. This analysis is actually a report of the estimated number of individuals for one of the protected classes that is externally available through the hiring process or internally available for that particular type of job from another department within the organization. The job group analysis of an AAP includes information related to the structure of job groups within the organization. In order to perform this analysis, the organization separates each job title into a separate group of related jobs and then determines the number of employees within each group. The organization preparing the report must also determine the appropriate Equal Employment Opportunity category code to associate with each job group.

The utilization analysis of an Affirmative Action Plan (AAP), sometimes referred to as an incumbency analysis, includes information that compares the number of available individuals belonging to a protected class within a certain area with the number of individuals belonging to a protected class that the organization has actually hired for a particular group of jobs. This report usually consists of a chart that shows the percentage of the local labor pool that is a member of a protected class within each job group compared with the percentage of employees that are members of a protected class that the organization actually employs for that job group. The analysis of equal employment opportunity barriers of an AAP is simply a report that identifies the procedure that the organization plans to use in order to monitor the effectiveness of its affirmative action plan. This report is designed to establish the specific system of internal audits and reports that helps the organization make sure that it is continually identifying and eliminating problems within the organization's employment system.

Placement goals

The placement goals section of an Affirmative Action Plan (AAP) is a list of the specific objectives that the organization hopes to accomplish in order to improve any problems that have been identified with the organization's AAP by the various analyses, audits or reports conducted by the organization. Usually, placement goals are necessary if the organization's utilization/incumbency analysis indicates that the percentage of individuals employed by the organization belonging to a specific protected class is less than 80% of the percentage belonging to the group of individuals with the highest percentage. For example, an organization that had 300 white applicants and hired 100 white employees and had 200 African-American applicants and hired 50 African-American employees would have hired 33% (100/300) of the white employees available and 25% (50/200) of the African American employees available. This particular organization would have to set placement goals for the organization because 25% is not equal to 80% or 4/5 of 33% (33% * 80% = 26.6%).

Action-oriented programs

The action-oriented programs section of an Affirmative Action Plan (AAP) should establish the specific procedures, policies and plans that the organization intends to use in order to meet the organization's placement goals; or that the organization intends to use in order to fix problems that have been identified by the organization's internal audits or reports. The information included in this section of the AAP must provide a detailed explanation of the procedure that the organization plans to use to make any of these changes to the organization's employment system and provide specific dates by which certain parts of the plan will be implemented and the progress that the organization intends to achieve by each specific deadline. It is also essential that the procedures and plans included in this section of the organization's AAP are actually different from plans introduced in previous years that have failed to deliver the desired results.

Designation of Responsibility

The designation of responsibility section of an Affirmative Action Plan (AAP) is simply a list of the names and titles of the organization's managers and/or HR professionals that are responsible for making sure that the organization's AAP is actually implemented, monitored and corrected as necessary. It is also important for an organization to identify which specific tasks each manager or HR professional will perform in regards to the organization's AAP.

Organizational Profile

The organizational profile section of an AAP is actually designed to expand on the information included in the organization's job group analysis. In fact, the organizational profile is required to contain information about the pay assigned to each job title within a specific job group, the number of males and females that hold each job title and the number of individuals of each ethnicity that hold each job title. The primary purpose of this section is to identify areas of the organization where there may be large differences in pay between people of different races or between men and women.

Discrimination claim

In order for an individual to file a discrimination claim, the claim must be made within a certain length of time from the time that the specific discriminatory act occurs. If the individual is filing in a state that has an equal employment opportunity enforcement agency, the individual must file his or her claim within 300 days of the specific incident of discrimination for which the individual is filing. If the individual is filing in a state that does not have an equal employment opportunity enforcement agency, the individual must file his or her claim within 180 days of the specific incident of discrimination for which the individual is filing. If the discrimination claim is not filed within the appropriate time limit, the Equal Employment Opportunity Commission (EEOC) will not investigate the claim.

In order for an individual to file a discrimination lawsuit, the individual attempting to file the suit must file a discrimination claim with the Equal Employment Opportunity Commission (EEOC) before filing the suit. Once the claim is filed, the individual will have to wait for notification from the EEOC. If the EEOC establishes that there is enough evidence to prove that the individual's employer has committed unlawful discrimination, the EEOC will attempt to reach a settlement with the organization that has been accused of discrimination. If the EEOC cannot reach a settlement, the EEOC may file a lawsuit on the victim's behalf. If the EEOC determines that there is not enough evidence to prove that discrimination has taken place, the EEOC will notify the individual that he or she has 90 days to file suit against his or her employer. If the individual does not file within 90 days from the date that the notification was issued, the individual forfeits his or her right to file any lawsuit related to that specific act of discrimination.

Amount of damages

The Civil Rights Act of 1991 establishes a sliding scale for the total amount of compensatory and punitive damages that an individual can receive from a discrimination suit. This sliding scale is based on the number of employees that an organization has and the maximum amount that an individual can be awarded increases as the size of the organization increases. If the individual is suing an organization with more than 15, but less than 101 employees, the maximum the individual can receive is $50,000. If the individual is suing an organization with more than a 100 employees, but less than 201 employees, the maximum the individual can receive is $100,000. If the individual is suing an organization with more than 200 employees, but less than 501 employees, the maximum the individual can receive is $200,000. Finally, if the individual is suing an organization with more than 500 employees, the maximum the individual can receive is $300,000. However, it is important to note that these limits **only** apply to compensatory and punitive damages.

- 47 -

Workforce planning

Workforce planning is an extremely important process in any organization because it is impossible for an organization to function if it does not have the appropriate staffing to perform the day-to-day tasks that are necessary for the success of the organization. The specific skills and knowledge that each individual needs in order to perform the tasks that keep the organization functioning normally can vary from organization to organization, from department to department and from position to position, so it is essential for the organization to make sure that they have the right number of people with the right skills at all times. However, the needs of the organization can change as the organization's size or environment changes and the organization needs to be able to identify the human resources that the organization has available now and the human resources that the organization will require in the future. As a result, workforce planning is extremely important because it allows an organization to identify its current and future staffing needs and allows the organization to develop a plan to obtain these needs.

Activities
There are a number of activities that an organization might perform during the workforce planning process. Some of the most common activities that an organization might perform include conducting staffing forecasts, establishing staffing goals and objectives, conducting job analyses and establishing plans to meet staffing goals and objectives. Many organizations begin by conducting a staffing forecast, which refers to any analysis that an organization can use to determine how its staffing needs might change. Once an organization has conducted a staffing forecast, the organization may set specific staffing goals and objectives that describe the current positions the organization needs to fill and the positions that the organization may need to fill in the future. After the organization has established its staffing goals and objectives, the organization should analyze each position to determine the specific qualifications that an individual would need in order to perform that position. Finally, once the organization has identified the positions and the qualifications required for each position, the organization can establish a plan to find and hire individuals to fill these positions.

Changing labor needs

Forecasting methods
The two main types of forecasting methods that an organization might use to evaluate the changing labor needs of the organization are qualitative forecasting methods and quantitative forecasting methods. Qualitative forecasting methods include any forecasting method that is based on the opinions or analyses of managers, experts in the industry, or other similar individuals. Quantitative forecasting methods, on the other hand, include any forecasting method that is based on actual data such as past trends or employee-to-output ratios that the organization can use to predict how their needs will change in the future. It is important to note that the difference between the two types of forecasting methods is simply that qualitative forecasting methods include any method that is based largely on an individual's knowledge and opinion of how the needs of the organization will change and quantitative methods include any method that is based largely on statistics or other similar mathematical data.

Qualitative forecasting methods
There are a number of different qualitative forecasting methods that an organization might use to evaluate the changing labor needs of the organization. Some of the most common qualitative forecasting methods include management forecasts and a variety of techniques

- 48 -

associated with expert forecasting. Management forecasts are a type of qualitative forecasting method in which the organization determines its future staffing needs by asking the managers of each department within the organization to discuss staffing needs at a meeting or to submit reports of the specific staffing needs that each manager feels he or she will need in the near future. Expert forecasting methods such as the Delphi method are actually a type of qualitative forecasting method in which the organization seeks the opinion of experts outside the organization from a variety of different sources. This allows the organization to obtain information about the effects of changes in the industry or changes in the specific organization from a variety of outside individuals and then form that information into a coherent report of how the organization's staffing needs might change.

Quantitative forecasting methods

There are a variety of quantitative forecasting methods that an organization might use to evaluate the changing labor needs of the organization. Some of the most common quantitative forecasting methods include historical ratios analyses, trend analyses, turnover analyses and a variety of probability models. A ratio analysis is a type of analysis in which an organization compares current employment ratios such as the number of employees required to produce a certain number of products with past ratios in order to determine how the ratios and staffing needs might change in the future. Trend analyses are similar to ratio analyses except that a trend analysis compares a single current employment variable such as the number of employees that the organization employs with a past employment variable instead of comparing two ratios. Turnover analyses are a type of analysis in which an organization examines the rate at which employees leave the organization during a given period and compares that rate to previous turnover rates. Finally, probability models allow the organization to chart and predict data related to changes in the organization.

Qualitative or quantitative forecasting method

There are a variety of factors that an organization might want to consider in order to decide whether to use a qualitative or quantitative forecasting method. The two most important factors to consider are: (1) how far in the future is the organization attempting to plan for, and (2) do the needs of the organization change at a steady rate. These two factors are important because they allow the organization to identify which methods will present the most accurate forecast. This is because qualitative methods are usually effective for short-term forecasts or for organizations that have staffing needs that are constantly changing and quantitative methods are usually more effective for long-term forecasts in organizations that have staffing needs that change at a relatively steady rate. However, since most organizations will have to make both short-term and long-term forecasts and there is always some level of variation in the level of staffing change within any organization, it is usually wise for an organization to use some combination of the two types of forecasts.

Job analyses

Job analyses can be used to identify a variety of different components related to the specific positions that the organization will require. The three main components that an organization usually identifies during a job analysis include job descriptions, job competencies and job specifications. A job description refers to a detailed breakdown of all of the specific tasks that an individual in a particular position will need to perform and the specific skills and knowledge that the individual will reasonably need in order to perform those tasks. A list of job competencies refers to a detailed breakdown of all of the broad skills and traits such as leadership ability that an individual in a particular position would need in order to be successful within a particular position.

Finally, a list of job specifications refers to a detailed description of all of the specific qualifications such as experience or education that an individual must have in order to perform the task.

Labor market analysis

A labor market analysis can be an essential part of any workforce planning process, as it allows an organization to evaluate the labor pool and determine how difficult it will be for the organization to find individuals that have the skills and knowledge necessary to fill the organization's empty positions. The potential employees that are available to an organization can vary greatly from situation to situation and from year to year, as there are a variety of different factors that may affect the availability of individuals that possess the skills and knowledge that the organization requires. As a result, it is essential for an organization to be able to identify the factors that may affect the organization's ability to find and hire individuals that have the appropriate skills and knowledge. A labor market analysis identifies factors that may be affecting the labor pool and how those factors may affect the organization's ability to find the staff that it needs.

There are number of different factors that may affect the labor pool from which an organization can hire. Some of the most common factors that an organization should consider include economic factors, industry factors, and labor market-specific factors. Economic factors include any factors that are related to the state of the economic environment including the salary and wages offered for similar positions in the same area, the number of individuals seeking employment in the area and other similar factors. Industry factors include any factors related to competitors within the labor market including factors such as the number of competitors entering the labor market, the hiring or downsizing activities of competitors within the market and other similar factors. Labor market-specific factors include any factors that are related specifically to the position itself such, as the number of individuals with the skills and knowledge necessary to fill the position, the number of individuals within a specific area that are interested in the position and other similar factors.

Recruiting process

The recruiting process, which refers to the procedures and strategies that the organization uses to encourage potential candidates to seek employment with the organization, is an essential part of any organization's staffing plan. This is because it is impossible for an organization to meet its staffing goals and objectives if the organization does not have a suitable labor pool from which it can hire individuals qualified to fill the staffing requirements of the organization. As a result, it is necessary for an organization to be able to use recruiting strategies that help develop the organization's labor pool so the organization can find qualified candidates to fill each position that is necessary for the success of the organization.

Types of methods

There are three main ways that an organization can recruit potential employees. These are external recruiting, internal recruiting and alternative recruiting. External recruiting refers to any recruiting strategy that attempts to encourage individuals from outside the organization to seek employment with the organization. This type of recruiting usually consists of strategies that stress the advantages of working for the organization, so individuals will understand the benefits associated with the organization and become interested in the organization. Internal recruiting refers to any recruiting strategy that attempts to encourage individuals within the organization to seek transfers or promotions into vacant positions that the organization needs to fill. Finally, alternative recruiting refers to the process of finding individuals that may not necessarily become employees of the company, but are individuals such as interns, telecommuters, temps and other similar individuals that can perform specific tasks for the organization.

Filling positions from within

There are a variety of different recruiting strategies that an organization might use to find qualified individuals from within the organization to fill vacant positions. Some of the most common strategies include internal job announcements, job bidding and promotion/succession plans. Internal job announcements are simply job postings that are only available to individuals within the organization or that are made available to individuals within the organization before they are made available to the general public. Internal job announcements are usually posted as new positions become available. Job bidding is a process in which individuals within the organization can inform the organization that they are interested in transferring to another position regardless of whether that position is available or not. Finally, a promotion/succession plan strategy is a method in which an organization keeps a chart or a list that details each employee, each employee's skills and training, and the specific positions that each employee is actually qualified to fill. Under this strategy, the organization can fill these positions by offering promotions or additional training to these qualified individuals.

Filling positions from outside the organization

There are a variety of different places outside an organization from which an organization can recruit new employees. Some of the places that organizations commonly use in order to find new employees include job listings and advertisements, career fairs and employment-related organizations/centers, and word-of-mouth recruiting. Job listings and advertisements found in magazines, newspapers, on the organization's website, on employment websites and other similar sources can all be good places for an organization to find new employees. Career fairs and employment-related organizations/centers, such as career placement offices, employment agencies, job fairs, labor unions, open houses, professional organizations, unemployment offices, universities, and other similar career-oriented locations can all be extremely useful for an organization that is attempting to recruit new employees as well. Finally, word-of-mouth recruiting through employee referrals, suggestions made by former employees, and other similar individuals can also be useful for an organization attempting to expand its labor pool.

Many organizations will target their recruiting efforts in places such as job listings, career fairs and employment offices in order to increase the number of candidates that are available for employment. However, in certain situations these sources may not provide enough candidates and the organization may have to seek out more unusual places to find the employees that the organization needs. As a result, an organization may decide to search for employees in unusual locations or by using unusual methods such as passing out fliers, looking for employees in religious organizations, using employees from prison work programs, looking for individuals leaving vendors and suppliers that may make good employees, offering sign-on bonuses and a variety of other similar methods.

Filling a position in a foreign country

In order to fill a position in a foreign country an organization must recruit employees from one of three main groups. These three main groups are separated based on the country from which the employees are recruited and include host-country nationals, parent-country nationals, and third-country nationals. Host-country nationals are individuals that are from the foreign country in which the position is located. For example, if an organization based in the United States hires an individual from France for a position located in France, the individual would be considered a host-country national. Parent-country nationals, also known as expatriates, are individuals that are from the country in which the organization is based. For example, if an organization based in the United States hires an individual from the United States for a position located in France, the individual will be considered a parent-country national. Third-country nationals are individuals that are from any country other than the country in which the organization is based or the country in which the position is located.

The four main types of staffing strategies that an organization can use to fill positions in a foreign country are geocentric strategies, ethnocentric strategies, polycentric strategies and regiocentric strategies. Geocentric strategies include any strategy in which the organization hires the individual that is best for the position without considering the costs or disadvantages associated with the country from which the individual is arriving. Ethnocentric strategies include any strategy in which the organization hires its general staff from the country in which the foreign office is located, but all of the management positions for the foreign office are filled by parent-country nationals. Polycentric strategies include any strategy in which the organization fills its general staff and management positions by hiring host-country nationals. Regiocentric strategies include any strategy in which the organization moves managers from offices in nearby countries to fill empty positions within the foreign office.

Hiring a host-country national

There are certain advantages and disadvantages associated with hiring host-country nationals that an organization should consider before making a hiring decision. First, host-country nationals will almost always be more familiar with the culture and attitudes of the country in which the position is located than individuals from other countries. This allows host-country nationals to help the organization establish effective relations with customers and suppliers within the foreign country. In addition, it is usually less expensive to hire a host-country national because the organization does not need to pay for all of the costs associated with bringing an individual in from another country. However, at the same time, host country nationals will usually be less familiar with the culture, attitudes and common practices of the country in which the organization is based, which may lead to problems if the organization's operations or compensation does not live up to the employee's expectations.

Hiring a parent-country national

There are certain advantages and disadvantages associated with hiring parent-country nationals that an organization should consider before making a hiring decision. First, parent-country nationals are usually familiar with the culture and attitudes of the country in which the organization is located, which allows them to relate better with individuals at the organization's headquarters. In addition, the organization may train parent-country nationals at the organization's headquarters prior to sending the individual overseas, which allows the organization more control over the individual's training and the operations of the foreign department as a whole. However, parent-country nationals will usually be less familiar with the culture, attitudes and expectations of the country in which the position is located, which may make it difficult for the organization to relate with individuals in the foreign country. It is also usually much more expensive to hire a parent-country national because all of the costs associated with sending an employee overseas.

<u>Hiring a third-country national</u>

There are certain advantages and disadvantages associated with hiring third-country nationals that an organization should consider before making a hiring decision. First, in certain cases, a third-country national may be familiar with the culture, attitudes and expectations of the country in which the position is located and/or the culture, attitudes and expectations of the country that the organization is based. This is because the organization may be hiring the individual from a country with a similar culture to the organization or a similar culture to the country in which the position is located. This can be extremely useful if the organization has a manager or employee stationed in a country near the country in which the position is located as the individual may be familiar with the culture of the organization and the culture of the foreign country. In addition, it is usually less expensive to transfer or hire a third-country national from a nearby country than it is to hire a parent-country national. However, these advantages only apply if the individual is from a country close to the foreign country.

<u>Measuring effectiveness</u>

There are a variety of different business metrics that an organization might use in order to measure the effectiveness or efficiency of a recruiting strategy. Three of the most common effectiveness/efficiency metrics for recruiting include the quantity of applications, the cost per hire and the time to fill. The quantity of applications simply refers to the number of employment applications that the organization has received for a particular position or group of positions. The cost per hire refers to the estimated amount that the organization spends on recruiting for each employee that is hired by the organization. The time to fill refers to the number of days that a specific position remains open before the organization is able to hire an individual to fill the open position.

Screening process

There are a variety of different screening tools that an organization may decide to use during the screening process. The screening tools that are most commonly used include employment applications, resumes and interviews. Employment applications usually include any form designed by an employer that requires an individual to fill out information related to the individual's personal information, previous experience, education and other similar information. Resumes are usually a page to two page written lists of all of the experience, education, and/or references that may qualify an individual for a particular position. The term resume does not usually refer to a pre-made form that is filled out, but rather a document that was designed and written by the individual seeking employment. Finally, interviews used for screening refer to any meeting with an applicant that is designed to determine whether an individual should be considered further or not.

Hiring process

There are a variety of different selection tools that an organization may decide to use during the hiring process. The selection tools that are most commonly used include interviews, pre-employment tests, and realistic job previews. Interviews at the selection stage of the hiring process refer to any meeting with an applicant that is designed to determine if an individual should receive the position or not. Pre-employment tests include any written examination that is administered prior to hiring an employee that is designed to evaluate the applicant's specific skills and knowledge. Finally, a realistic job preview (RJP) refers to any activity that helps give the applicant an idea of the specific day-to-day tasks and responsibilities that the individual will have to perform. A realistic job preview may include activities such as watching videos about the organization, observing current employees or other similar presentations of the job actually being performed.

Types of validity

The three main types of validity that an HR professional may have to evaluate in order to determine if a screening or selection tool is valid are construct validity, content validity, and criterion validity. A screening or selection tool will be considered to have construct validity if the tool actually assesses whether or not the individual possesses the specific traits that have been shown to indicate success within a particular position. In other words, the screening or selection tool must test for specific characteristics that can be shown as indicators of job performance in order to be considered valid in this sense. A screening or selection tool will be considered to have content validity if the tool actually assesses whether or not the individual possesses the skills and knowledge necessary to perform the tasks associated with a particular position. Finally, a screening or selection tool will be considered to have criterion validity if the tool can be used to reasonably predict how an individual will behave in the work place based on the individual's score on a written or verbal test.

The two types of criterion validity that an HR professional may have to evaluate in order to determine if a screening or selection tool is valid are concurrent validity and predictive validity. A screening or selection tool will be considered to have concurrent validity if it can be proven that the individual's score on a written or verbal test indicates that the individual currently possesses the desired trait or will behave in the desired fashion at the time the test is taken. For example, a test might be considered valid if the individual's score on the test indicates that the individual remains calm in stressful situations; and the individual actually remains calm during a stressful situation that the organization places the individual into at the time of the test. A screening or selection tool will be considered to have predictive validity if it can be proven that the individual's score on a written or verbal test indicates that the individual will possess the desired trait or will behave in the desired fashion at some point in the future.

References

The two main types of references that an organization would normally need to check are educational references and employment references. Educational references refer to any certifications, degrees, diplomas, professional licenses, scholarly awards or any other similar documents that can be used to prove the individual's knowledge of a particular field. Educational reference checks may be used to ask universities or certification organizations for specific information about the individual's performance, such as the individual's grades, but most educational reference checks are only used to verify the individual's education and the dates that each degree, certification or license was earned. Employment references refer to any individuals such as previous employers, co-workers or customers that can be used to verify that the individual actually has experience in a particular field. During an employment reference check an organization will usually ask previous employers and co-workers for information related to an individual's performance on the job, in addition to verifying information about the individual's position, pay and length of time with the previous employer.

Criminal record

It is important for an organization to check an individual's criminal record because, in many situations, individuals that have caused problems in the past will often end up causing similar problems in the future. As a result, it is important for an organization to be able to find out whether or not an individual has been convicted of a crime and, if that individual has been convicted, determine how those crimes relate to the position itself. In many cases, even if an individual has been convicted of a crime, the specific crime that the individual committed may not be relevant to how the individual will perform in a particular position and the organization may still decide to hire the individual. However, in other cases, the organization may find specific crimes or a history of past acts such as violent crimes, theft, or substance abuse that may make it clear that an individual is not suited for the position. Ultimately, criminal record checks are important because they help protect the organization from unnecessary damage or liability caused by the organization's employees.

Employment contract

There is a wide range of different information that can be included in an employment contract. Each organization will usually tailor its employment contracts to the specific needs of the organization. However, all employment contracts should include information related to the position that the individual is being offered, the specific tasks and responsibilities that the individual will be expected to perform, the date that the employee will start and the duration for which the contract will remain in effect, the compensation and benefits that the individual will receive for taking on the position and an explanation of the specific situations in which the contract can be voided and the employee's employment terminated. Some employment contracts may also include contact information for the employee and the employer, nondisclosure agreements that prevent the individual from releasing the organization's confidential information, non-solicitation agreements that prevent the individual from trying to convince customers or suppliers to continue buying from or selling to the individual after the contract has elapsed and a variety of other similar agreements or information.

Employee orientation

An employee orientation, also known as an on-boarding program, is a program that is designed to help make sure that each new employee becomes an effective member of the organization. Usually, the first step to any effective employee orientation is to make sure that the employee will have all of the resources that he or she will need to perform his or her job as soon as the individual starts work. This means that resources such as tools or workspace should be setup before the individual's first day on the job. On the individual's first day, most organizations will provide individuals with a formal introduction that explains the organization's mission, objectives, and values. Once the individual has a basic understanding of the organization, most organizations will then provide the individual with an introduction to his or her specific position and/or department by introducing the individual to his or her co-workers and supervisors, by showing the individual around the facilities, by explaining the department's rules and guidelines, by explaining the department's goals and by identifying places to find help.

Employment termination

The two main types of employment termination are voluntary termination and involuntary termination. Voluntary termination refers to any type of employment termination in which the employee ends his or her employment by his or her own choice. In other words, voluntary termination simply means that the employee decided to stop working for the organization and informed the organization that he or she was terminating his or her employment agreement. Involuntary termination, on the other hand, refers to any type of employment termination in which the organization decides to end the employee's employment, regardless of whether the employee wishes to stay with the organization or not. Involuntary terminations are usually used in situations in which the employee has been performing poorly or inappropriately or in situations in which the organization's staffing needs have changed.

Human Resource Development

Human resource development, which may also be referred to as talent development, refers to the process by which an organization attempts to modify the behavior, skills and knowledge of the employees of the organization in order to achieve the goals of the organization. In other words, human resource development is a term used to describe all of the practices, procedures and policies that an organization uses to make sure that each employee is able to perform their duties and responsibilities as effectively as possible. There are a variety of different methods, techniques and strategies that an organization can use in order to develop the organization's human resources. All of these methods are ultimately used in order to make sure that each employee is actually helping the organization to meet its specific needs and goals

Types

The three main types of development that are usually associated with human resource development are career development, learning and development, and organization development. Career development includes any activity that is related to an employee's professional progress within an organization such as activities related to encouraging the individual to seek promotions or other positions within the organization for which he or she may be well-suited. Learning and development, which is more commonly referred to as training, includes any activity that is related to teaching an employee the specific skills and knowledge that are required to effectively perform the tasks associated with his or her position. Finally, organization development includes any activity that helps establish the system of methods and tools that allows the organization's employees to carry out their duties and responsibilities in as effective a manner as possible. For example, the installation of a new computer system that allows employees to complete certain tasks much more efficiently than they would normally be able to is an example of an activity that might be considered part of an organization development strategy.

Copyright Act of 1976

The Copyright Act of 1976 is designed to prevent individuals from stealing original works and/or claiming original works as their own. This act specifically prohibits any individual other than the copyright holder from creating works based on the original work, duplicating the original work, reproducing the original work, selling or renting copies of the original work and performing or displaying an original work in any format without the expressed permission of the copyright holder. The protections offered by the Copyright Act apply to any original work that is in a tangible form and therefore includes any written, musical or visual work, such as a book or screenplay, a written or recorded song or a movie. In most cases, the original author of the work is considered to be the copyright holder and as a result, these protections are granted to the original author.

In most cases, the original creator of a work is considered to be the copyright holder under the regulations set by the Copyright Act of 1976. However, there are actually two situations in which another individual or organization may actually hold the copyright to a particular work. The first situation in which another individual or organization may hold the copyright to a particular work is when an employee creates an original work for a specific organization. In this case, the organization that employs the individual is automatically assigned the copyright to the work because the individual was paid to create the work for the organization. The second situation in which another individual or organization may hold the copyright to a particular work is when an organization hires an independent individual specifically for the purpose of creating that work. In this case, the organization that hires the individual to create the work is automatically assigned the copyright because the independent individual was paid to create the work for the organization.

Public domain

A work that is considered to be public domain is a work that has no official copyright holder and any individual can therefore use the work without permission. It is important to note that there are usually two ways that a work becomes public domain. The first way that a work can become public domain is if the original copyright expires. A copyright is only valid for 70 years after the death of the work's original author or for 95 years from the first publication or 120 years from the creation of the work if the work was commissioned by another individual or organization. The second way that a work can become public domain is if the work was created by a federal agency. This is because any work created by the federal government is automatically considered to be public domain.

Fair use

The legal concept of fair use establishes an individual or organization's ability to use certain parts of a copyrighted work without permission under certain conditions. In other words, there are certain situations in which it is legal for an individual or organization to use a copyrighted work even if that individual or organization does not own the copyright to that work. However, there are certain broad requirements for the use of a copyrighted work that the individual or organization must meet for that use to be considered fair use. First, the individual or organization must only use a limited portion of the original work and must make sure that each use of the original work does not have a significant impact on the market value of the original work. Second, the portion of the original work that is used by the individual or organization must be used to critique the work, comment on the work, be used for news-related purposes, or be used for teaching purposes and should generally be used for educational or nonprofit uses.

U.S. Patent Act

The U.S. Patent Act is designed to prevent individuals from stealing inventions and/or claiming inventions created by other individuals as their own. This act specifically prohibits any individual other than the patent holder from producing the invention, using the invention, offering the invention to other individuals or selling the invention unless the individual receives permission from the patent holder. The protections granted by the U.S. Patent Act only apply to inventions within the United States or to inventions entering the United States. As a result, this act does not apply to actions taken in other countries unless those actions result in the invention entering the United States. It is also important to note that even though this act grants the patent holder the ability to prevent other individuals from producing, using, offering or selling the invention, it does not actually offer any specific recourse for handling patent infringement.

Types of patents
The three types of patents that an individual or organization may hold in the United States are design patents, plant patents, and utility patents. Design patents are patents that are designed to protect new, original, and/or ornamental designs related to the manufacturing of a specific item. Design patents are valid for 14 years from the date that the patent is filed. Plant patents

are patents that are designed to protect new types of asexually reproducing plants that an individual or organization has created or discovered. Plant patents are valid for 20 years from the date that the patent is filed. Utility patents are patents that are designed to protect new or improved machinery, new or improved processes and new or improved products. Utility patents are valid for 20 years from the date that the patent is filed.

ADDIE Model

The ADDIE Model is a set of instructional design guidelines that are commonly used by organizations to develop human resource development (HRD) programs. This model consists of five separate steps and each step is identified by one of the letters in the term "ADDIE." In other words, the "A" in ADDIE represents the Analysis step, the first "D" in ADDIE represents the Design step, the second "D" in ADDIE represents the Development step, the "I" in ADDIE represents the Implementation step, and the "E" in ADDIE represents the Evaluation step. Each step of the model establishes a basic set of guidelines and procedures that an individual or organization can follow to develop a training or instructional program piece by piece. This procedure is commonly used in human resource development because it is a simple but effective way of creating a training program. However, it is important to note that the ADDIE model can actually be applied to a variety of different fields and does not necessarily need to be used only for training programs.

"A"
The "A" in ADDIE stands for Analysis, which is the first step described by the ADDIE Model. In this step of the process, the individual or organization tries to define the problem that the individual or organization is attempting to solve in as much detail as possible. In other words, during this step of the process, the individual or organization attempts to identify the specific goals and objectives that the organization wants to achieve through the training program and the specific knowledge, skills and abilities that are required in order to achieve those goals. In most cases, the individual or organization will conduct this step of the process by creating questions, such as why is the program being developed, will the program be used to improve performance or eliminate performance problems, how long will the organization have to implement the program and a variety of other similar questions that the organization can then answer.

"D"
The first "D" in ADDIE stands for Design, which is the second step described by the ADDIE Model. In this step of the process, the individual or organization attempts to design a plan to achieve the goals and objectives set during the analysis phase. In other words, during the design step of the process the individual or organization creates a series of documents that each describe the specific strategies that the individual or organization intends to use to solve the problem, improve overall performance or achieve some other similar type of goal. In order to design this plan, the individual or organization must attempt to identify strategies that will provide the knowledge, skills and abilities necessary to achieve the goal in a logical fashion.

"D"
The second "D" in ADDIE stands for Development, which is the third step described by the ADDIE Model. In this step of the process the individual or organization will actually develop a series of tools that can be used to carry out the strategies that were identified and planned out during the design step of the process. This is the phase of the process in which the organization actually creates or obtains the specific program materials such as activities, exercises, handouts and other similar training tools that are required to implement the

organization's training strategy. This is also the phase in which the individual or organization will develop instructional guides that will help each skill trainer or instructor to understand the procedure for teaching the specific information that the employees need to know.

"I"

The "I" in ADDIE stands for Implementation, which is the fourth step described by the ADDIE Model. In this step of the process the individual or organization will actually use the materials created during the development stage to put the program into action. However, most organizations begin this phase of the process by testing the program through a pilot program that is only used to train a certain section of the organization before actually implementing the program throughout the organization. This is because pilot programs allow the organization to identify problems with the program's strategies and make changes to these strategies as necessary before the program is actually implemented. Once the organization is relatively certain that the program will function as expected, the organization can put that program into action.

"E"

The "E" in ADDIE stands for Evaluation, which is the fifth and final step described by the ADDIE Model. This part of the process actually occurs throughout the entire model as the individual or organization must make sure that the objectives, plans, strategies and the overall program itself are logical and well defined before acting upon each of those objectives or strategies. This step of the process primarily refers to an ongoing evaluation of the results of the program and is therefore the step in which the organization determines if the program has achieved the desired result or not and, if not, what changes can be made to the program or what additional programs must be added in order to achieve the desired result.

Needs analysis

It is important for an organization to perform a needs analysis before designing a training program for several different reasons. First, by using a needs analysis an organization can accurately identify problems that the organization may have not known about without an analysis. Secondly, even if the organization is aware of a particular problem prior to the analysis, it can be extremely difficult for the organization to identify the cause of that specific problem without conducting an analysis. Third, and most importantly, it is impossible for any organization to design an effective training program without first identifying the specific knowledge, skills and abilities that are required to achieve the organization's goals or that are required to correct a problem in a particular area of the organization. As a result, a needs analysis can be an essential part of the training development process because it ultimately allows the organization to identify and gather information about problems within the organization, so the organization can identify potential solutions to these problems.

There are a variety of different steps that an organization might take during a needs analysis. Most organizations begin by collecting data related to the performance of each part of the organization. This information is usually gathered from surveys, interviews, observations, skill assessments, performance appraisals and other similar methods. Once this information is collected the organization will then attempt to identify problems within specific areas of the organization or identify areas that can be improved upon through human resource development. Once the organization has identified all of the areas that may require attention, the organization will usually attempt to identify solutions that may solve the problem or improve the performance of that particular area. Finally, after the organization has identified a series of potential solutions the organization can identify the advantages and disadvantages of each solution and choose the plan that seems to provide the greatest benefit for the lowest cost.

Teaching a particular skill

There are a variety of different methods that an organization can use to teach a particular skill, area of knowledge or ability. Some of the most common training methods that an organization may use include case studies, demonstrations, group discussions and lectures. A case study is a type of training method in which the individual has the opportunity to apply certain skills, information or abilities to a real-life situation. In other words, a case study allows the individual to learn how to perform a task or use a piece of information through practice. A demonstration is a type of training method in which an instructor **shows** an individual or group of individuals how to perform a particular task. A group discussion is a type of training method in which a group of individuals learns a particular skill, ability, or piece of information by discussing that skill or the application of that particular skill. A lecture is a type of training method in which an instructor **tells** an individual or group of individuals how to perform a particular task.

Pilot program

There are a variety of different ways that an organization can implement a pilot program and the specific steps that an organization might use to implement a specific pilot program can vary greatly from organization to organization. However, most organizations begin the process by identifying a test group that will act as a suitable representation of the organization as a whole. This test group should consist of individuals that need to learn how to perform the specific task or improve the specific ability that the training program has been designed for and should include members of management so these members can see how the training program works firsthand. Once the organization has identified the pilot group, most organizations will then attempt to decide whether part of the program or the entire program should be tested. Usually, it is better to test the entire program, but the costs or problems associated with implementing the entire program for a small group may prevent the organization from administering the entire program. Finally, the organization can implement the program and evaluate the results.

Training instructors

There are a variety of factors that an organization should consider before choosing a training instructor for a training program. The most important factors to consider for any training instructor, regardless of the specific program, are the instructor's ability to teach and the instructor's knowledge of the subject. The instructor's ability to teach refers to the individual's ability to actually convey his or her knowledge of a particular subject to other individuals. In other words, an instructor not only needs to know a subject, but also has to be able to teach information about that subject to other employees. An instructor's ability to teach can usually be measured by assessing the individual's ability to present and communicate information clearly, the individual's ability to involve trainees in his or her instruction and the individual's ability to present information in a logical and effective manner. The instructor's knowledge of the subject simply refers to how much the instructor knows about the subject, the amount of experience that the instructor has with the subject and the instructor's ability to demonstrate the subject.

Organization development

There are a variety of different processes associated with organization development and, as a result, there are a variety of different reasons that an organization may decide to implement a particular organization development strategy. Organization development is primarily intended to improve the organization's ability to identify and solve problems within the organization in order that the organization can ultimately continue to function as effectively as possible. This means that organization development usually focuses on developing the organization's internal systems for decision-making, systems for program development, systems for promoting progress towards organizational goals, systems for identifying problems, systems for handling problems that have been identified and other similar internal systems. As a result, organization development refers to an approach that does not necessarily target one specific area of the organization, but instead refers to an approach that attempts to improve every part of the organization by constantly modifying the way the organization operates.

Organizational culture

Organizational culture refers to the system of beliefs and values that has been established in a particular organization and the way that individuals within the organization act based upon those values. In other words, organizational culture refers to the work environment that the employees and managers of the organization have created and continue to create as time passes. Most organizations attempt to modify or control the culture within the organization to some degree in order to make sure that the employees of the organization remain motivated. The culture of a particular organization is usually heavily influenced by the specific experiences of the members of the organization and by the outside environment surrounding the organization. As a result, it can sometimes be difficult for an organization to control its own culture, especially when prominent figures in the organization become unhappy or outside influences begin placing a great deal of stress on the organization's employees.

Change management vs. organization development

Change management and organization development are two systems that are very closely related. In fact, organization development, in many ways, is actually a type of change management. This is because organization development refers to a series of processes and methods that can be used to modify the way that a particular aspect of the organization functions, so that the organization as a whole will function more effectively. Change management refers to a series of processes and methods that an organization can use to modify the way that a particular aspect of the organization functions with as little harm to the organization as possible. As a result, both systems are related to implementing change within the organization and, in many cases, organization development strategies may be used to help with the change management process and change management strategies may be used to minimize the risk of a negative impact associated with implementing the changes made through organization development.

Kurt Lewin's change process theory

The two primary sources of change identified by Kurt Lewin's change process theory are the environment and the individual's needs. According to Kurt Lewin's change process theory an individual changes the way he or she functions due to the environment around the individual or due to his or her specific needs. Changes that occur due to the environment include any changes that occur due to an external factor affecting the individual, such as in the case of an individual changing the way that he or she performs a particular task in order to comply with the organization's request to perform the task more quickly. Changes that occur due to the individual's needs, however, are changes that occur due to an internal factor affecting the individual, such as in the case of an individual changing the way that he or she performs a particular task so that he or she can receive the satisfaction associated with completing the task more quickly.

According to Kurt Lewin's change process theory, the three stages of change that an organization will usually need to go through are unfreezing, moving, and refreezing. Unfreezing refers to the first stage of the change process in which the organization attempts to remove the barriers that may prevent the change from occurring by making it clear to the organization's members that the change is necessary and that it must happen immediately. Moving refers to the second stage of the change process in which the organization attempts to actually implement the change and attempts to make sure that each individual makes the change. Finally, the refreezing stage refers to the third and final stage of the change process in which the change becomes a normal part of the organization's functions and the organization attempts to determine whether that change has produced the desired result or not. If the organization decides that the change has not produced the desired result, the organization will usually begin the process again and introduce new changes to reach the desired result.

Implementation theory

Implementation theory refers to the study and application of the specific methods and strategies that an organization can use during the change process to bring about desired modifications within the organization. In other words, implementation theory refers to the process in which an organization identifies a set of specific processes that the organization can use to implement changes to specific aspects of the organization and then implements those changes in order to ultimately change the way the organization functions overall. As a result, implementation theory is actually an essential part of organization development, as it is the part of the process in which the organization identifies the specific tools necessary to bring about the change and actually uses those specific tools to begin the unfreezing, moving and refreezing stages of the change process within the organization.

Interventions

Organization development intervention
An organization development intervention is a specific strategy that describes the plan that an organization intends to use to bring about a particular change within the organization. In other words, if an organization has already identified a particular problem or area that needs to be improved upon within the organization, the specific strategy that the organization uses to fix that problem or improve that area is known as an organization development intervention. Organization development interventions include any action that can be used to influence a specific part of an organization and, as a result, there are a variety of different types of organization development interventions that an organization may decide to use. However, the three most common types of interventions that an organization will normally

use are human process interventions, sociotechnical interventions, and techno-structural interventions.

Human process interventions

A human process intervention is a type of organization development strategy in which an organization attempts to improve its overall performance by changing the way that the members of the organization interact. Some specific examples of human process interventions include the use of incentive programs, the use of diversity programs and the use of team building activities. Incentive programs that encourage individuals with the appropriate knowledge and skills to enter the organization, encourage individuals to stay with the organization and/or encourage individuals to perform up to or exceed the expectations of the organization can all help address problems within the organization. Diversity programs that place employees with different backgrounds into teams with each other can help to improve the ability of the organization to function as a whole by making it easier for each member of the organization to work together. Finally, team building activities that encourage individuals within the organization to communicate and function effectively in groups can help to teach each individual what they need to do in order to move the organization towards a particular goal.

Sociotechnical interventions

A sociotechnical intervention is a type of organization development strategy in which an organization attempts to improve its overall performance by changing the way that a particular group functions within the organization. Most sociotechnical interventions are specifically related to changes made within the organization that are designed to make a particular group more self-sufficient. Some specific examples of sociotechnical interventions include job enrichment, job rotation and process improvement. Job enrichment refers to the practice of meeting new needs or un-addressed needs in the organization by giving a particular individual or group more authority and more responsibilities than that individual or group had previously. Job rotation refers to the practice of periodically changing the specific tasks that each individual or group within the organization has to perform in order to make sure that each individual or group is capable of performing a variety of tasks for the organization rather than one single task. Finally, process improvement refers to a strategy in which the organization attempts to analyze and change the way that a group performs a particular task.

Techno-structural interventions

A techno-structural intervention is a type of organization development strategy in which an organization attempts to improve its overall performance by changing the way that work is performed within the organization. Techno-structural interventions are usually related to changes within the organization that are designed to make sure that a specific process or piece of technology is used as efficiently as possible. One of the best examples of a techno-structural intervention is total quality management. Total quality management is actually a strategy in which an organization attempts to maintain the highest level of quality possible for the output produced by each specific task carried out by the organization. In most organizations, total quality management is implemented by using a series of procedures that are designed to establish a quality-oriented organizational culture and a system for monitoring and controlling the quality of each task performed by the organization.

Flexible work arrangements

Many organizations offer flexible work arrangements to employees in order to ensure that each employee can function as effectively as possible. This is because virtually every employee has a number of responsibilities outside of work that can create undue stress for the individual if he or she does not have the time available to address his or her responsibilities. Flexible work arrangements such as flexible scheduling programs, childcare programs, health programs, and other similar programs can help employees find the time and/or the resources necessary to handle family issues and other external issues that may affect the individual's performance. As a result, an organization may choose to provide flexible work arrangements to employees because these programs allow employees to balance their work and personal responsibilities, so that each employee can continue to perform up to the expectations of the organization.

Diversity programs

A diversity program can be an extremely useful tool for any organization. However, organizations operating within multiple countries may find that diversity programs are not only useful, but essential. This is because organizations operating within multiple countries will usually have employees from very different cultures and an employee from one country may not understand the cultural beliefs or behaviors of an employee from another country. This can lead to a number of difficult issues if these cultural differences are not addressed as an employee from one country may find the actions or beliefs of an individual from another country to be ridiculous or even offensive. As a result, diversity programs are extremely important in these situations as they allow the organization to encourage teamwork and understanding between individuals of different cultures, so that these individuals can function effectively together.

There are number of issues that may arise if an organization implements a diversity program or other similar program for locations spread out between multiple countries. Some of the most common issues that may arise include language issues, timing issues and cultural issues. Language issues refer to any problems that may arise because the language of the employees in a particular country or area is different from the language of the country or area in which the organization is based. These issues can cause serious problems because a program is only effective if the employees can actually understand the information associated with the program. Timing issues refer to any problems that may arise from trying to initiate a program or changes to a program in multiple locations at once. These issues can cause serious problems if certain program tasks need to be performed immediately or simultaneously with other program tasks in order for the program to work correctly. Finally, cultural issues refer to any problems that may arise from the different cultural beliefs of the employees in each country.

Repatriation programs

Repatriation programs can be extremely important for any organization that fills foreign positions with parent-country nationals. This is because most parent-country nationals will only take a foreign position if they believe the position will help further their career. As a result, it is essential for an organization to establish a program that can clarify exactly how taking the position will help the individual's career and ensures that individuals can return to the organization's base at a later time. A repatriation program is vital to this process as it provides information about the positions that will be available to the individual when they return to the parent country, provides information about the benefits and pay that the individual can expect when he or she returns, provides notifications of any changes that have occurred to the opportunities available to the individual and actually provides assistance for the individual when he or she returns to the organization's parent country.

Quality management

William Edwards Deming
William Edwards Deming was one of the first individuals to actually discuss quality management in detail and, as a result, he introduced a variety of different concepts to the field of quality management. In fact, two of Deming's concepts actually form the basis for many of the quality management strategies used today. The first of these concepts was the idea that the quality of a product or service can only be decided by the consumer. In other words, even if an organization thinks that a particular product or service is of a high quality, that particular product or service will not sell if the customer believes that the product or service is of a low quality. As a result, it is important for an organization to base a quality assessment on the characteristics that a consumer would look for in a specific product or service. The second concept introduced by Deming was his 14-point system, which established a series of guidelines for quality management and introduced the idea that an organization's top management is ultimately responsible for quality control.

Joseph Moses Juran
Joseph Moses Juran expanded on a few of the concepts proposed by William Edwards Deming and introduced a number of his own concepts to the field of quality management. The first of these concepts was the idea that quality is determined by the consumer, but the needs of the organization have to be considered as well. In other words, Juran agreed with Deming that an organization had to assess the needs of the consumer in order to determine the quality of a product, but he made it clear that an organization must form processes and practices that would meet those needs without harming the organization. The second concept introduced by Juran was the Juran Trilogy in which Juran established three stages that an organization should go through during the quality management process, including the quality planning stage, the quality control stage and the quality improvement stage. Finally, Juran introduced the idea that the Pareto Principle could be applied to quality control and therefore 80% of the quality problems within an organization are actually related to 20% of the possible causes.

Juran Trilogy
The Juran Trilogy, which was established by Joseph Moses Juran, identifies three stages that an organization must go through during the quality management process in order to ensure that the organization can achieve the highest level of quality possible. The first stage of the Juran Trilogy is the quality planning stage, which is the stage in which the organization should identify the consumer's needs and work to implement practices and processes to meet those needs. The second stage of the Juran Trilogy is the quality control stage. In this stage of the process, the organization should monitor the quality achieved by each practice or process and make sure that the result meets the needs of the organization and the needs of the consumer. The third stage of the Juran Trilogy is the quality improvement stage. This stage of the process actually occurs throughout the quality management process and is the stage in which the organization attempts to solve quality problems or make specific processes more efficient by changing the way that certain practices and processes are used.

Pareto analysis system

The Pareto analysis system, which was originally designed by Vilfredo Pareto, is a decision-making model that assumes that approximately 80% of the benefits that an organization receives from a particular task are a result of 20% of the effort that the individuals within the organization put into that particular task. However, in a quality control context, a Pareto analysis usually uses a second assumption made by the Pareto system, which is that 80% of the problems within the organization are typically caused by approximately 20% of the potential causes. In most cases, the Pareto analysis system is applied to quality control using a Pareto chart. A Pareto chart is a type of bar chart that displays each factor that may be related to a particular problem, how frequently each of those factors actually causes the problem, and arranges each factor from most frequent to least frequent. This is important because an organization, by identifying and charting the potential causes of a quality control issue, can identify the most influential factors and focus their quality control efforts on those factors.

Philip B. Crosby

Philip B. Crosby introduced a number of concepts to the field of quality management and ultimately attempted to change the way that organizations handled quality control. One of the most important concepts introduced by Crosby was his "Zero Defects" philosophy, which established the idea that the goal of any quality management program should be a product or service with no defects, rather than a product or service that meets an acceptable level of quality. This philosophy is actually part of "Philip Crosby's 14 Step Quality Improvement Process" and is based on the idea that an organization should encourage its employees to work towards creating the best possible product rather than creating a product that is only acceptable. Another extremely important concept introduced by Crosby was his "doing it right the first time" (DIRFT) principle, which established four basic principles for quality management, including the notion that quality can be defined as conformance to requirements, defect prevention is the best way to approach quality control, the goal of quality should be no defects and quality can be measured by the price of non-conformance.

Philip B. Crosby's "doing it right the first time" (DIRFT) principle established four basic rules for how an organization should approach quality management. The first rule of the principle states that quality should be defined as conformance to requirements. In other words, an organization must identify and set specific requirements for each end product and the end product can be considered to be an acceptable product if it meets the requirements set by the organization. The second rule of the principle states that defect prevention is the best way to approach quality control. This rule actually refers to the foundation of the DIRFT principle, as it proposes the idea that an organization should find ways of preventing quality issues instead of using practices and procedures that fix problems over and over again.

The third rule of the principle states that the goal of any organization should be "zero defects." In other words, an organization should implement processes and procedures to make sure that all products meet the requirements set by the organization rather than accepting processes or practices that produce products that do not meet all of the desired requirements, but are considered "acceptable." The fourth rule of the principle states that quality can be measured by the price of non-conformance. This simply means that quality should be measured in terms of how much the organization will save by making sure that a task is done right the first time instead of performing the task multiple times.

Dr. Kaoru Ishikawa

Dr. Kaoru Ishikawa introduced a variety of different concepts to the field of quality management. One of the most important concepts introduced by Ishikawa was the idea that the quality management process does not end once the product has been produced. Instead, Ishikawa suggested that an organization should be concerned with the quality of the product or service after that product or service reaches the customer in order to make sure that the customer is happy with the product and will return to purchase more from the organization in the future. If an organization determines that the customer is unhappy with a product; then it is the responsibility of the organization to identify the problem and find a way to fix it. In addition to his concepts relating to an ongoing quality management process, Ishikawa also helped to introduce the widespread use of charts, diagrams and other similar tools in quality assessment. In fact, Ishikawa actually designed a chart specifically for the purpose of assessing quality known as a cause and effect diagram.

Cause and effect diagram

A cause and effect diagram is a figure that an organization can use to represent the factors that may be causing a particular problem or the factors related to achieving a particular goal. This type of diagram is usually used so an organization can easily view each factor, analyze each factor and decide the appropriate course of action. A cause and effect diagram, which is also known as a fishbone or Ishikawa diagram, consists of a center line with a series of lines branching off of the center line so the lines form a tree or fishbone-like figure. The problem or goal that the organization is attempting to address is identified on the center line of the figure and the categories that may lead to the desired goal or be related to the problem are identified at the end of each line that branches off of the main line. Smaller lines then branch off of each category line, which identify specific factors that may have a negative or positive impact on the goal or problem.

Six Sigma's DMAIC process

DMAIC, which actually stands for Define, Measure, Analyze, Improve, and Control, is a five-stage process. In the first stage of the DMAIC process, the organization defines the specific requirements that the end product must meet in order to meet the needs of the consumer and the needs of the organization. The organization also defines the process that the organization plans to use in order to meet these requirements during this stage of the process. In the second stage of the DMAIC process, the organization measures the effectiveness of the process by gathering information about the type and number of defects found in each area of the organization or batch of products. Once this information is collected the organization can analyze the information and identify some solutions that may eliminate the defects that have been identified. After the organization has identified a series of possible solutions, the organization can choose the best solution and improve the process by implementing the solution. Finally, the organization can continue to control the process by making sure that everyone is carrying out the process correctly.

Learning organization

A learning organization is a type of company in which the employees of the company are encouraged to develop their knowledge, skills and abilities, so the organization as a whole will ultimately perform more effectively as the business environment changes. In other words, a learning organization is simply an organization that attempts to encourage individuals to learn the knowledge, skills and abilities that are required for the organization to adapt and remain competitive and/or profitable. Learning organizations attempt to encourage this development through initiatives that promote the open exchange of ideas, initiatives that reward individuals for exceptional performance, initiatives that reward or simply allow employees to try out new ideas and apply those ideas to solve problems within the organization or improve the way that certain tasks are performed and other similar initiatives.

Peter Senge

According to Peter Senge, the five disciplines that are essential to a learning organization are mental models, personal mastery, shared vision, systems thinking and team learning. Mental models refer to an individual's need for an understanding of the assumptions, beliefs and other similar factors that affect an individual's perception and the way that an individual acts based on those perceptions. Personal mastery refers to an individual's need to have a specific area of expertise and be able to further his or her knowledge of that area through additional learning. Shared vision refers to the need of the organization for a culture that encourages employees to work towards a common goal. Systems thinking refers to the idea that an organization and the individuals within the organization must be able to identify patterns and predict how those patterns might change in the future. Finally, team learning refers to the idea that the members of a team must be able to openly exchange ideas with each other and must all put in as much effort as possible so the team can achieve its goals.

Knowledge management

Knowledge management is a system of specific initiatives, practices, procedures and processes that an organization uses to make sure that each member of the organization knows or can access all of the information necessary to effectively perform his or her duties and responsibilities. In other words, knowledge management is the practice of making sure that each employee within the organization has the knowledge that he or she needs to perform his or her job. Knowledge management can be extremely important for any organization, as most organizations have a number of different employees working in a number of different departments at different times and each employee may have important information that other employees working at other times or in other departments may not have. As a result, knowledge management is not only designed to make sure that each individual within the organization has the same basic training, but also to make sure that each individual has access to information from other departments or information entered by other employees, so employees do not need to perform the same task multiple times.

Andragogy and pedagogy

Andragogy and pedagogy are similar in some ways as they both study how individuals learn. Andragogy is the study of how **adults** learn and is a science that focuses heavily on finding ways to make it easier to teach adults. Pedagogy, on the other hand, is the study of how **children** learn and is a science that focuses heavily on finding ways to make it easier to teach children. Even though both fields are closely related and it may appear that they are very similar, they are actually two very different fields. This is because studies have found that children and adults actually learn in different ways and while one method may be effective for teaching a child, that same method may be significantly less effective or even useless for teaching an adult. As a result, it is important for an instructor or organization to understand the differences that exist between teaching children and teaching adults so the instructor or organization can identify the teaching methods that will be most effective.

Malcolm Knowles

According to Malcolm Knowles, there are five assumptions that can typically be made about adult learners. The first assumption, which refers to an adult's motivation to learn, is that adult learners are internally motivated to learn by understanding why they need to learn. The second assumption, which refers to an adult's self-concept, is that adult learners want to direct their own learning. The third assumption, which refers to an adult's experience, is that adult learners want to apply what they already know as they learn and use their experience to help others learn. The fourth assumption, which refers to an adult's readiness to learn, is that adult learners are willing to learn if what they learn will help them in some way. The fifth assumption, which refers to an adult's orientation to learning, is that adult learners learn so that they can apply their knowledge to current problems rather than learning information that may or may not be useful at some point in the future.

Learning styles

A learning style refers to the specific way in which an individual learns most effectively. In other words, each individual is different; so the specific way that each individual learns information is different as well and certain teaching methods will therefore be more effective than other teaching methods. An individual's learning style is simply the method of learning that is most effective for that particular individual. The three main learning styles that an individual may use are auditory, tactile and visual. Most individuals will learn more effectively through one of these styles than they would be able to through one of the other two styles. As a result, it is important for an organization to understand how to use each learning style and to make sure that each training program is designed to take different learning styles into consideration, so the program will help each member of the organization learn the material necessary as efficiently as possible.

Auditory learner

An auditory learner is an individual that learns more effectively by hearing information rather than seeing it or using it. As a result, auditory learners usually learn most effectively by hearing spoken descriptions or instructions such as an individual might hear in a lecture or group discussion, by hearing a demonstration of a particular sound such as an alarm or a sound that might indicate a particular problem with a piece of machinery or by listening to his or her own words as the individual reads aloud. However, auditory learners usually have difficulty learning simply by using a particular object without verbal instructions or learning by reading about a particular subject if the individual cannot hear the written words spoken aloud. There are a variety of learning activities that may make it easier for an auditory learner to learn a particular subject. Some of the more common activities include listening to audiotapes, attending group discussions, attending lectures and other similar activities that allow the individual to hear the information.

Tactile learner

A tactile learner is an individual that learns more effectively by touching or using something related to a particular piece of information rather than hearing it or seeing it. As a result, tactile learners usually learn most effectively by actually using a new tool or process, by actually being able to touch or move an object related to something that the individual is attempting to learn or by physically applying the information in a controlled situation. However, tactile learners usually have difficulty learning through verbal instruction such as one might receive in a lecture or from a supervisor attempting to explain how a particular task should be performed and have difficulty learning with visual methods such as reading a handout. There are a variety of learning activities that may make it easier for a tactile learner to learn a particular subject. Some of the more common activities include practicing techniques, applying information through role-playing, applying the information in simulations and other similar activities that allow the individual to learn through a "hands-on" approach.

<u>Visual learner</u>

A visual learner is an individual that learns more effectively by seeing information rather than hearing it or using it. As a result, visual learners usually learn more effectively by seeing the information on a board or in a book, by seeing a representation of the information in a picture or diagram or by taking detailed notes and then rereading those notes. However, visual learners usually have difficulty learning through verbal instruction such as one might receive in a lecture or from a supervisor attempting to explain how a particular task should be performed and have difficulty learning by simply performing a task without written instructions or handouts. There are a variety of learning activities that may make it easier for a visual learner to learn a particular subject. Some of the more common activities include taking and reading notes, reading the information on a flashcard or handout, seeing the information in a book, watching videos or presentations related to the information and other similar activities that allow the individual to see the information.

Learning curve

A learning curve is a representation of the rate at which an individual learns. This representation is referred to as a curve because the rate will almost always form a curve on a graph since the rate at which a particular individual learns a particular subject will begin to change over time. Learning curves can be extremely useful tools for instructors, human resource professionals, managers, and other individuals within an organization that are attempting to plan or evaluate a training program because they allow an individual to identify patterns in the way that individuals learn. This can be extremely important because sudden changes in the learning curve may indicate that a new training program is working effectively or that a new training program or another change in the work environment is actually slowing down the learning process.

There are a variety of different learning curves that a particular organization might encounter and it is rare for two separate curves to be completely identical. However, there are certain curve patterns that an organization will typically encounter. Some of these typical curve patterns include negatively accelerating learning curves, plateau learning curves, positively accelerating learning curves and S-shaped learning curves. A negatively accelerating curve is a curve that starts out increasing quickly but eventually begins to increase more slowly over time. A plateau learning curve is a curve that starts out increasing quickly but stops increasing around a certain point. A positively accelerating learning curve is a curve that starts out increasing slowly but eventually begins to increase more rapidly over time. An S-shaped learning curve is a curve that starts out increasing slowly but over time increases more quickly and then slows down again so the curve has an "S" shape.

Training program

Environmental factors

There are a variety of different environmental factors that may play a role in how effective a particular training program will be. Some of the most important factors relate to the training facility. Factors related to the facility such as airflow, noise, seating and temperature can all have a large effect on whether an individual will be able to effectively learn or not. This is because most individuals will have difficulty remaining focused on the subject that they are attempting to learn if the location has poor ventilation, is too loud or distracting, does not have enough seating or the seating is arranged in a way that certain individuals cannot see or hear what is going on and/or if the temperature in the location is too hot or too cold.

Measuring effectiveness

Three of the most common types of metrics that an organization might use to measure the effectiveness of a training program include cost-benefit measures, financial measures and production measures. Cost-benefit measures refer to any metrics that an organization can use to compare the advantages associated with a training program with the disadvantages or costs associated with the program. Cost-benefit measures are usually identified through a cost-benefit analysis and the specific measures that an organization can use will vary from program to program. Financial measures refer to any metrics that an organization can use to measure the effect that the training program has had on the organization's financial resources. Financial measures include metrics such as return on investment, profit margins and cash flow. Production measures refer to any metrics that an organization can use to measure the effect of the training program on the organization's amount or quality of production. Production measures include metrics such as the number of items produced per day, the number of items produced that do not meet specifications and the amount of orders filled per day.

Kirkpatrick's Levels of Evaluation

Donald Kirkpatrick identified four different factors or "levels" that should be considered in order to evaluate the effectiveness of a training program or other similar type of program. The first level that Kirkpatrick identified is the Reaction level in which the organization evaluates the program by measuring each employee's reaction to the program through surveys, questionnaires, interviews and other similar methods. The second level that Kirkpatrick identified is the Learning level in which the organization evaluates the program by testing each employee to determine whether or not the individual learned the skills or knowledge that the program was designed to teach. The third level that Kirkpatrick identified is the Behavior level in which the organization evaluates the program by monitoring each employee's behavior to make sure that each individual is actually using the information that he or she learned from the program. The fourth and final level that Kirkpatrick identified is the Results level in which the organization evaluates the program by measuring the organization's progress towards the goal that the organization originally hoped to achieve by implementing the program.

Brinkerhoff's Stages of Evaluation

Robert Brinkerhoff's Six Stages of Evaluation refers to a six-step process that an organization can use to ensure that a program is effective. The first stage of the process is the goal setting stage in which the organization identifies the specific problem that the program is going to address and sets the specific goals that the organization hopes to achieve as a result of the program. The second stage of the process is the program design stage in which the organization designs the program in order to achieve the goals set in the first stage of the process. The third stage of the process is the program implementation stage in which the organization implements the program in order to determine whether the program actually accomplishes the goals the organization set out to achieve or not. The fourth stage of the process is the immediate outcomes stage in which the organization tests each employee in order to determine whether or not the program succeeded in teaching the information that the program was designed to teach. The fifth stage of the process is the intermediate outcomes stage in which the organization monitors each employee's behavior in order to make sure that each individual is actually applying the information that the program taught. The sixth and final stage of the process is the impacts and worth stage in which the organization measures the value of the program based on the organization's progress towards the goals that the program set out to achieve versus the cost of implementing the program.

Seating styles

- Banquet-style seating is a type of seating arrangement in which round tables are carefully distributed throughout the program or meeting room. Each seat is positioned around one of these round tables so that each individual attending the program or meeting can sit around the table and see the other individuals around the table or turn to see a trainer, lecturer, or other similar individual. Banquet-style seating is usually used for training programs that want to encourage teamwork or group discussion.
- Chevron-style seating is a type of seating arrangement in which desks, small tables or chairs are arranged in small lines at either side of the room. Each line is angled so the individuals in the line can easily discuss information with the people beside them or with the people in the line in front or behind them while still being able to see the trainer, lecturer, or other similar individual. Chevron-style seating is usually used in narrow rooms, for large groups or for programs or meetings that include both lecture and discussion.
- Boardroom-style seating, also known as conference-style seating, is a type of seating arrangement in which a large table is placed in the center of the program or meeting room. Each seat is positioned around the large table so that each individual attending the program or meeting can sit around the table and see everyone else at the table. Boardroom-style seating is usually used for large discussions, meetings, or management training programs.
- U-shaped-style seating is a type of seating arrangement in which three long, narrow tables are placed at three sides of the room with at least one side of each table touching one side of another table so the three tables create a "U" formation. Each seat is positioned around one of these three long tables so each individual has a clear view of everything going on in the center of the room, a clear view of the instructor or other similar individual, and a clear view of everyone at each table. U-shaped-style seating is usually used for training programs that have a combination of presentations, lectures, discussions, etc.
- Classroom-style seating is a type of seating arrangement in which long, narrow tables or lines of desks are arranged across the program or meeting room. Each seat is positioned around one of the long, narrow tables positioned across the room or the desks are positioned in lines so individuals can sit at the table or desk, see the instructor or other similar individual and have a surface to take notes or fill-in handouts. Classroom-style seating is usually used for large groups and/or for presentations or lectures.

- Theatre-style seating is a type of seating arrangement in which chairs are arranged in lines across the room. Each chair is positioned so the individual can see what is going on at the other side of the room. Theatre-style seating is usually used for large demonstrations, lectures, films, presentations and other similar activities that involve large groups.

Career development

The six stages of career development are assessment, investigation, preparation, commitment, retention, and transition. The assessment stage is the first stage of the career development process in which an individual attempts to assess his or her own strengths and weaknesses. The investigation stage is the second stage of the process in which an individual investigates the world around him or her in order to find careers that the individual may want to pursue. The preparation stage is the third stage of the process in which an individual attempts to prepare for his or her chosen career by setting goals and learning new information, skills and abilities. The commitment stage is the fourth stage of the process in which an individual attempts to find a job and commit to his or her chosen career. The retention stage is the fifth stage of the process in which an individual will attempt to maintain his or her current career through additional networking and training. Transition is the final stage of the process, in which an individual transitions from one career to another.

Individuals
There are a variety of different methods that an organization can use to further an individual's career development. Some of the career development methods commonly used by organizations include; coaching programs, employee counseling and support programs and training workshops. Coaching programs are programs that are designed to provide each employee with a specialist or group of specialists that can help the employee learn new skills or understand how to handle work-related problems or situations related to certain tasks. Employee counseling and support programs are programs that are designed to provide employees with help if the employee is experiencing problems inside or outside of work that may be affecting the individual's performance or the individual's ability to seek other opportunities within the organization. Training workshops that offer employees the opportunity to learn the knowledge and skills associated with other positions within the organization can also be extremely helpful as they allow individuals to expand their knowledge outside of what is specifically necessary for their current position.

Manager's role
There are a variety of different methods that a manager or supervisor can use to further an individual's career development. Some of the career development methods commonly used by managers or supervisors include coaching, counseling, mentoring and evaluating. Managers or supervisors can coach employees by teaching employees how to perform new tasks, how to handle certain problems outside of the scope of their current position and by helping them develop communication, leadership and other similar skills. Managers or supervisors can counsel employees by offering employees advice or emotional support for problems occurring inside or outside the organization. Managers or supervisors can act as mentors by helping employees apply for promotions, suggesting employees for promotions and offering guidance about other positions and how to reach those positions. Finally, managers or supervisors can help further an individual's career by evaluating the individual and offering an accurate opinion of the individual's strengths and weaknesses.

Management vs. leadership development

Management development refers to the process by which an organization attempts to make sure that a particular individual has all of the knowledge, skills and abilities necessary to effectively manage a particular department or functional area of the organization. In other words, management development includes any activity related to training an individual to become a manager or supervisor. Leadership development, on the other hand, refers to the process by which an organization attempts to make sure that a particular individual has all of the knowledge, skills and abilities necessary to effectively lead. In other words, leadership development includes any activity related to developing an individual's leadership skills. Basically, the difference is that management development is designed to teach an individual how to make sure each function is carried out as expected, while leadership development is designed to teach an individual how to predict change within the business environment, identify the way the organization needs to change to meet those needs and encourage other individuals to meet the changing needs of the organization.

Performance management

Performance management refers to the process by which an organization attempts to make sure that each individual, team, and department within the organization functions as expected. In other words, performance management includes any activity related to evaluating and improving the performance of individuals, teams and departments within the organization. Performance management actually plays an essential role in human resource development, as it is impossible for an organization to function effectively if the tasks necessary for the organization's operations are not consistently carried out as expected. Human resource development is designed to provide the organization with individuals that have the skills and knowledge necessary for the organization to achieve its goals. Performance management is designed to evaluate whether the members of the organization are helping the organization achieve those goals or not. As a result, even though performance management and human resource development are two separate processes, they both work together to identify and eliminate performance problems so the organization can continue to function normally and ultimately continue to make progress towards it goals.

Process
The performance management process can vary from organization to organization, but most organizations use a process that consists of three basic steps. The first step of the process that most organizations use consists of establishing the goals that the organization wants to achieve; identifying the tasks and skills required to achieve those goals; and informing employees of the appropriate way to carry out tasks and responsibilities in order to achieve these goals. This step is usually carried out by the organization's executives, decision-makers, and HR professionals through goal setting, needs analysis, the creation of corporate value statements and a code of conduct and other similar processes. Once the organization has set goals and informed employees of the appropriate way to carry out each task, the organization's supervisors and managers need to monitor the tasks performed by each employee, identify and document performance problems and inform employees of the problems and the appropriate way to fix these problems. Finally, at the end of each year or other set period, the organization needs to conduct in-depth appraisals of the performance of each employee.

Appraisals

Performance appraisal

The four main types of performance appraisals are behavioral appraisal methods, comparison appraisal methods, essay/narrative appraisal methods, and rating appraisal methods. Behavioral appraisal methods are methods that identify the most important tasks related to each position, the specific way that the employee is expected to behave in order to perform that task and establish a system of descriptions that describe how effectively or ineffectively the individual behaved. Comparison appraisal methods include any appraisal methods that compare the performance of an employee with the performance of other employees. Essay/narrative appraisal methods include any appraisal methods in which a manager or supervisor needs to describe an employee's performance in writing. Rating appraisal methods include any appraisal methods that use a checklist or scale to rate the individual's performance.

Behavioral appraisal

There are a number of behavioral appraisal methods that an organization might use. The most common behavioral appraisal method is a method known as BARS. BARS, which stands for Behaviorally Anchored Rating Scales, is an appraisal system in which an organization analyzes the job description for a particular position and attempts to identify the tasks that must be performed by an individual in that position for the organization to function effectively. Once the organization has identified the specific tasks associated with a position, the organization can identify the specific way that the individual should behave in order to perform each task. For example, if communication is identified as a necessary skill for a management position, the organization may determine that an individual in that position must be able to keep others "in the loop." The organization will then design a series of statements that describe how effectively or ineffectively the individual behaved and rank each of these statements. Performance evaluators can then choose the statement that best describes the employee's behavior.

Comparison appraisal

There are a variety of different comparison appraisal methods that an organization might use. The three most common comparison appraisal methods are the forced distribution method, the paired-comparison method and the ranking method. The forced-distribution method, which is also known as forced ranking, is a method where performance evaluators rank employees using a bell curve, so the majority of employees within the organization will receive an average score and only a very small group will receive extremely high or extremely low performance scores. The paired-comparison method is a method in which performance evaluators compare the performance of each member of a specific group with the performance of each other member of the group. The ranking method is a method in which performance evaluators rank each employee based on performance from the most effective performing employee to the least effective performing employee.

Essay/narrative appraisal

There are a variety of different essay/narrative appraisal methods that an organization might use. The three most common essay/narrative appraisal methods are the critical incident method, the essay method and the field review method. The critical incident method is a method in which performance evaluators document each performance problem related to a particular employee that occurs during a set performance period so the evaluator can discuss the problems with each employee during the performance appraisal at the end of the period. The essay method is a method in which performance evaluators write a short essay for each employee that describes the employee's performance during the performance period. The field review method is a method in which an individual other than the employee's direct supervisor or manager performs the appraisal and writes down a series of assessments and observations about that particular employee's performance.

<u>Rating appraisal methods</u>
There are a variety of different rating appraisal methods that an organization might use during a performance appraisal. The two rating appraisal methods that are most commonly used by organizations are the checklist method and the rating scale method. The checklist method is a method in which the organization creates a series of statements with each statement describing a certain level of performance. The performance evaluator can then check a box next to the statement that best describes the individual's performance in each performance area. The rating scale method is a method in which performance evaluators rate an individual's performance on a point scale. For most organizations, this means that performance evaluators using this method rate each employee's performance on a 1 - 3, 1 - 4, 1 - 5 or 1 - 10 scale with lower numbers representing poor performance and higher numbers representing superior performance.

Other employee legislation

<u>Employee Polygraph Protection Act</u>
The Employee Polygraph Protection Act of 1988 was designed to protect individuals seeking employment from being required to submit to polygraph tests. This act specifically forbids any private employer from basing any hiring decision on the results of a polygraph test unless the individual is seeking a position that involves working with pharmaceuticals, involves working in an armored car, or involves working as a security officer. This act also does not apply to any government agency or to any federal contractor or subcontractor with FBI, national defense and/or national security contracts. If an employer requires an individual to submit to a polygraph test and the position is not related to one of these specific areas, the employer may be subject to fines of up to $10,000.

<u>Fair Credit Reporting Act</u>
The Fair Credit Reporting Act, which was passed in 1970, is designed to prevent individuals and organizations from misusing information about an individual's credit or background. This act specifically requires agencies that collect and distribute credit or background information, known as consumer reporting agencies, to adhere to strict guidelines regarding how credit and other similar information should be maintained and when credit and other information may be released to other individuals or organizations. This act also requires consumer reporting agencies to verify and correct mistakes on an individual's credit record if there is a dispute, requires consumer reporting agencies and any other agency conducting a credit or background check to verify that an individual or organization requesting information has a legitimate need for the information before the agency releases the information and places limits on the length of time that negative information may be kept on record. In addition, this act specifically requires employers to notify the individual that a background or credit check will occur and requires the organization to provide additional information related to the check in certain situations.

According to the Fair Credit Reporting Act, there are several situations in which an employer must provide information related to a background or credit check to the employee or potential employee that is being checked. First, if an employer is seeking a background or credit check, the employer must notify the individual that his or her background or credit will be checked and the employer must receive written consent from the individual before

- 77 -

proceeding with the check. Second, if the employer decides to take a negative action against the individual based on the information that the employer received from a background or credit check, the employer must issue a pre-adverse action disclosure that includes a copy of the background or credit report, explains the actions that the employer is taking based on that information, explains the individual's right to dispute the decision and describes the appropriate manner in which to dispute the decision. Finally, if the employer makes a final decision, the employer must notify the individual of his or her rights under the Fair Credit Reporting Act.

Fair and Accurate Credit Transactions Act

The Fair and Accurate Credit Transactions Act, passed in 2003, is an amendment to the Fair Credit Reporting Act that is designed to help protect consumers and employees from identity theft and protect employers from the problems associated with employee misconduct. This act specially grants consumers the right to receive one free copy of their credit report from the three major consumer reporting agencies each year, defines strict use and distribution guidelines for consumer reporting agencies and anyone using or selling the information provided by those agencies and requires employers to destroy any credit report or other similar report after the employer has made a decision based upon the information included in the report. This act also establishes that an employer is not required to notify an employee prior to a credit or other similar check if the employee is suspected of misconduct, is suspected of violating a company policy or is suspected of violating a state or federal law and the check is related to an investigation of the misconduct or violation.

Congressional Accountability Act

The Congressional Accountability Act, which was passed in 1995, is designed to extend many of the protections offered by other employment acts to employees of the legislative branch of the United States government. This act establishes that every employee working for Congress is entitled to the same rights and protections that other employees would receive under the employment acts and laws specifically identified by the Congressional Accountability Act as applying to employees of Congress. The Congressional Accountability Act identifies 11 major federal employment acts and laws that apply to employees of Congress including the Age Discrimination in Employment Act, the Americans with Disabilities Act, the Civil Rights Act, Chapter 71 of Title 5, Chapter 43 of Title 38, the Employee Polygraph Protection Act, the Fair Labor Standards Act, the Family and Medical Leave Act, the Occupational Safety and Health Act, the Rehabilitation Act and the Worker Adjustment and Retraining Notification Act.

WARNA

The Worker Adjustment and Retraining Act (WARNA), which was passed in 1988, is designed to make sure that employees have an opportunity to seek other employment before their employment is terminated as part of a mass layoff or plant closing. This act requires employers with 100 or more full-time employees to notify each employee or their union representatives in writing of a pending mass layoff or plant closing at least 60 days prior to the actual event. This act also applies to employers with 100 or more employees that work either full or part time if those employees work for a total of 4000 hours or more in an average work week. However, it is important to note that WARNA does not apply to plant closings or mass layoffs that are a result of a national disaster or are the result of unforeseeable business circumstances and WARNA does not apply to plant closings if the organization has a reasonable expectation that they will receive funding to keep the plant open if they do not announce the plant closing.

Mass layoff: A mass layoff is identified by the Worker Adjustment and Retraining Act (WARNA) as an event in which a plant does not actually close, but a large number of employees lose their employment due to the event. According to WARNA, a layoff is considered to be a mass layoff, if during a 90-day period 500 or more employees, or 50 or more employees if those employees make up 33% or more of the organization's workforce, will lose their jobs permanently, lose their jobs for more than six months or receive at least a 51% reduction in the number of hours that they are allowed to work per month for six months or more. However, employees that have worked for the organization for less than 6 months in the past year and employees that work less than 20 hours a week for the organization are not included for the purposes of determining whether or not a layoff should be considered a mass layoff.

Plant closing: A plant closing is identified by the Worker Adjustment and Retraining Act (WARNA) as an event in which an organization closes a single facility or a group of facilities located at the same site and a large number of employees working at the facility or site lose their employment as a result. According to WARNA, an organization must give notice 60 days prior to the time that a plant will be closed permanently or temporarily, if 50 or more employees will lose their jobs permanently, lost their jobs for more than six months or receive at least a 51% reduction in the number of hours that they are allowed to work per month for six months or more if the organization decides to relocate the individual to another facility or site. However, employees that have worked for the organization for less than 6 months in the past year and employees that work less than 20 hours a week for the organization should not be included for the purposes of determining whether the organization is required to give notice or not.

Fair Credit Reporting Act

The Fair Credit Reporting Act, which was passed in 1970, is designed to prevent individuals or organizations from misusing information about an individual's credit or background. This act specifically requires agencies that collect and distribute credit information, known as credit reporting agencies, to adhere to strict guidelines regarding how credit and other similar information should be maintained and when credit and other information may be released to other individuals or organizations. This act also requires consumer reporting agencies to verify and correct mistakes on an individual's credit record if there is a dispute, requires consumer reporting agencies and any other agency that conducts credit or background checks to verify that an individual or organization requesting information has a legitimate need for the information before the agency releases the information and places limits on the length of time that negative information may be kept on record.

Total Rewards

Definition

The concept known as total rewards refers to all of the compensation and benefits that the members of an organization receive for performing the tasks related to each individual's specific position. In other words, the concept known as total rewards refers to all of the different ways in which an organization encourages employees to perform work for the organization. It is extremely important for an organization to have an effective total rewards program for two main reasons. First, it is impossible for an organization to function without employees, so each organization must make sure to implement total reward programs that encourage employees to join the organization and stay with the organization. Secondly, there are a number of legal concerns associated with the minimum amount of compensation that an individual can receive for a certain amount of work and it is therefore essential that an organization takes these concerns into consideration to avoid unnecessary fines or litigation.

Types of rewards

The two main types of rewards that an organization may use to compensate employees are monetary compensation and non-monetary compensation. Monetary compensation refers to any tangible reward that an organization provides to pay an individual for his or her work. This type of compensation includes rewards such as salary and wages, paid sick days, paid vacation time, retirement plans, stock options, and any other similar rewards that **have** a specific monetary value. Non-monetary compensation refers to any intangible reward that an organization provides to encourage an individual to perform work for the organization. This type of compensation includes rewards such as better assignments, employee-of-the-month awards, flexible scheduling, special privileges and other similar rewards that **do not have** a specific monetary value.

Monetary compensation

An organization can issue monetary compensation to employees through direct compensation or indirect compensation. Direct compensation refers to any monetary compensation that the organization pays directly to the employee for performing work for the organization. This method of compensation includes any money that an individual receives from the organization for his or her salary or wages and includes any bonuses, overtime, or any other special pay that an individual receives for actually performing work for the organization. Indirect compensation refers to any monetary compensation that an organization pays to a third party on the employee's behalf or pays to the employee without the employee having to perform work. Indirect compensation includes benefits such as health insurance, paid sick days, paid vacation time, retirement plans, stock options and any other type of compensation that is not directly related to the amount of work that an individual performs.

Total rewards philosophy

A total rewards philosophy is a statement that establishes the principles that an organization plans to use as the basis for the organization's total rewards program. In other words, a total rewards philosophy is a short statement that an organization develops to clearly state the goals that the total rewards program should achieve and to establish the basic way in which the organization plans on achieving these goals. A total rewards philosophy can be extremely useful, as it allows an organization to create a basic set of guidelines that the organization could use to design the total rewards program. A total rewards philosophy can also be extremely important if the organization needs to modify its total rewards program, as a total rewards philosophy helps the organization identify the specific values and goals that the total rewards program should take into consideration.

Types

The two types of total reward philosophies that an organization may decide to use are entitlement philosophies and performance-based philosophies. An entitlement philosophy is a type of total reward philosophy in which an organization issues rewards based on the length of time a particular employee has been with the organization. In other words, an entitlement philosophy assumes that an individual is entitled to certain rewards because of his or her seniority or that the individual is entitled to certain rewards because he or she has spent a certain length of time in a specific position. Entitlement philosophies encourage individuals to stay with the organization, but do not necessarily encourage individuals to perform in an effective way. A performance-based philosophy, on the other hand, is a type of total reward philosophy in which an organization issues rewards to individuals that perform as expected or better than expected. Performance-based philosophies focus on programs that encourage individuals to perform more effectively rather than programs that encourage individuals to stay with the organization.

Total rewards strategy

A total rewards strategy is a plan that an organization uses to design a total rewards program. Most total rewards strategies are based off the organization's total rewards philosophy and are primarily designed to establish the framework for how the organization will distribute the resources allocated for the program. In other words, an organization's total rewards strategy simply refers to the various ways that the organization will use its resources to encourage individuals to work for the organization. A total rewards strategy can be an extremely important part of an organization's rewards planning process, as it allows the organization to design a total rewards program that will encourage individuals to join the organization and stay with the organization without exceeding the resource limits of the organization. Most organizations only have a very limited number of resources that they can allocate to a total rewards program. Therefore, it is essential for the organization to find ways of attracting employees to and keeping employees with the organization using the resources that are available.

There are a variety of different factors that an organization must consider in order to design an effective total rewards strategy. The four main factors that an organization should consider include the competitive environment, the economic environment, the labor market and the legal environment. The competitive environment refers to the effect that the organization's competition will have on the organization's ability to allocate resources to the total rewards program. For example, if an organization's competitors are offering a specific product at a price that is far lower than the organization's prices, the organization may have to reduce the amount of funds allocated to its total rewards program in order for the organization be able to afford to reduce the price of the product. The economic environment refers to the effect that the economy has on the organization's cost of labor. For example, as the cost of living increases in a particular area the cost of labor will also usually increase as well. Finally, the labor market refers to the availability of skilled employees. The legal environment refers to taxes and regulations.

Job evaluation

It is important for an organization to conduct a job evaluation during the total rewards planning process for two major reasons. First, a job evaluation allows the organization to identify the positions that are most important to the success of the organization in order that the organization can make sure to assign higher rewards to positions that are more valuable to the organization and lower rewards to positions that are less valuable to the organization. This allows the organization to focus its resources on keeping individuals that are essential to the success of the organization. Secondly, a job evaluation allows the organization to determine whether there should be a difference in pay between two positions or not. For example, an organization may be evaluating the tasks performed by an administrative assistant and a secretary within the organization. If the evaluation determines that the organization's administrative assistants are actually performing the same tasks as the organization's secretaries and the positions require the same skills, the two positions may actually be similar and therefore, should receive equal pay even though they have different titles.

Employee or independent contractor

It is important for an organization to determine whether an individual is an employee of the organization or an independent contractor for several different reasons. First, an organization is required to pay half of an employee's social security tax and is required to withhold federal and state taxes from an employee's pay, but is not required to pay any taxes on behalf of an independent contractor. Secondly, an organization is required to pay overtime, on-call pay and other similar special pay to an employee under certain conditions, but is not required to pay any special pay to an independent contractor. Finally, many of the legal protections granted to employees do not cover independent contractors because they are not considered to be employees of the organization. Instead, they are considered to be independent individuals under contract. As a result, it can be important for an organization to determine if an individual should be considered an employee or an independent contractor because the responsibilities of the organization will vary depending on how the individual is classified.

IRS Standards

According to the IRS, there are three groups of factors that an organization should consider in order to determine whether an individual should be considered an employee or an independent contractor. These three groups of factors relate to the organization's behavioral control over the individual, the organization's financial control over the individual and the type of relationship between the organization and the individual. The organization's behavioral control refers to the ability of the organization to control how the individual conducts his or her work for the organization. The organization's financial control refers to the ability of the organization to control how much the individual will ultimately profit or lose from performing his or her work. The type of relationship refers to whether the individual is under contract or not and, if the individual has a contract, whether or not that contract forms a permanent arrangement that makes it difficult for the individual to perform work for other organizations.

DOL standards

According to the Department of Labor (DOL), there are seven factors that an organization should consider in order to determine whether an individual should be considered an employee or an independent contractor. First, the organization should consider whether it is attempting to form a permanent relationship with the individual or if it is attempting to form a temporary relationship with the individual. Second, the organization should consider the importance of the task to the organization and the extent to which the organization could function without someone performing that particular task. Third, the organization should consider how much control it has over the individual. Fourth, the organization should consider how much the individual has invested in the facilities and equipment used to perform the work. Fifth, the organization should consider whether the individual is required to make decisions related to competing with other competitors in an open market or if the organization makes these decisions. Sixth, the organization should consider whether the individual operates independently of the organization or not. Finally, the organization should consider the individual's risk of profit/loss.

Important legislation

Davis Bacon Act

The Davis Bacon Act, which was passed in 1931, is designed to prevent employees working in the construction industry from receiving substandard wages. This act requires any employer in the construction industry with $2,000 or more in federal contracts or any employer in the construction industry with $2,000 or more in federal funding to pay each employee working at the construction site a wage equal to or greater than the prevailing wage for the area in which the construction site is located. The prevailing wage for a particular area is defined as the wage of an individual performing a similar local job. This act is important because it is the first act to actually establish a regulation related to the minimum amount that an organization could pay an employee.

Walsh-Healy Public Contracts Act

The Walsh-Healy Public Contracts Act, which was passed in 1936, is primarily designed to prevent employees working under government contract from receiving substandard wages. This act requires any employer with $10,000 or more in federal contracts to pay each employee working for the organization a wage equal to or greater than the prevailing wage for the area in which the work is performed. The prevailing wage for a particular area is defined as the wage of an individual performing a similar local job. This act also required employers covered by the act to pay overtime pay equal to 1 ½ times an individual's regular wage for each hour that an individual works in excess of 8 hours in a day or for each hour in excess of 40 hours in a week. In addition to establishing wage regulations, this act also prevents employers covered by the act from hiring children under the age of 18 or from hiring individuals convicted of a crime. It also requires the employer to make sure that the employee's workplace meets certain safety and sanitation standards.

FLSA

The Fair Labor Standards Act (FLSA), which was passed in 1938, is primarily designed to prevent employees from receiving substandard wages and to prevent organizations from employing children except in very specific situations. This act specifically established regulations related to the minimum wage that an employee could be paid, regulations related to the situations in which an employer would be required to pay an individual overtime or on-call pay, regulations related to keeping payroll records and regulations related to the minimum age that an individual needs to be in order to perform certain types of work and the hours that a particular individual can work if he or she is below age 16. The regulations established by the Fair Labor Standards Act usually apply to all employers with at least two employees that have $500,000 or more in annual sales or any employer that engages in interstate commerce of any kind. However, it is important to note that this act does not apply to employers that are covered by another labor standard law specific to their industry.

Minimum wage regulations: The Fair Labor Standards Act (FLSA) established a number of regulations designed to prevent employees from receiving substandard wages. One of the most important protections established by the FLSA is the federal minimum wage. The federal minimum wage is the smallest amount that an employer can pay an individual for each hour of work. Employers are required to pay at least the amount specified by the federal minimum wage to any nonexempt employee. An employee will be considered exempt from this provision of the Fair Labor Standards Act if the individual receives a weekly salary of at least $455, if the employee works in a profession that is not covered by the FLSA or a profession that is identified as exempt from the minimum wage provision of the FLSA or if the employer has received special permission to pay less than the minimum wage as part of a Department of Labor program.

Paying more than the federal minimum wage: There are two situations in which an organization may have to pay an employee more than the federal minimum wage. First, if the individual has worked more than 40 hours in a single week and is in a position covered by the Fair Labor Standards Act, the individual is entitled to overtime pay for each additional hour over 40 hours. Secondly, an employer may be required to pay more than the minimum wage if the minimum wage for the state in which the organization's employees are located is higher than the federal minimum wage. This is because most states have their own minimum wage laws and the organization is required to adhere to the labor laws of the state in which its employees work. However, it is also important to note that most states have their own list of exemptions and requirements, so a particular organization may be part of an industry that is covered by the Fair Labor Standards Act but not by the regulations set by state law.

Overtime regulations: The Fair Labor Standards Act established a number of regulations designed to prevent employees from receiving substandard wages. One of the most important protections offered by the act relates to overtime pay. This regulation defines overtime pay as 1 ½ times the regular wage that an employee would normally receive and establishes that overtime pay must be paid to any nonexempt individual that works more than 40 hours in a single week. It is important to note for the purposes of overtime pay, the number of hours that an individual has worked in a given week does not include hours paid for vacation time, sick leave, paid holidays, and other similar pay that an individual receives when work is not actually performed. It is also important to note that certain states may have overtime regulations in addition to those established by the Fair Labor Standards Act.

On-call regulations: The Fair Labor Standards Act established a number of regulations designed to prevent employees from receiving substandard wages. One of the specific wage regulations established by the act is related to on-call pay. This regulation requires an employer to pay an employee his or her regular wages if the employee is required to wait at the job site and is required to be ready to perform work as it becomes available. This pay must be paid to the employee even if the individual is not actually performing work as he or she waits. In other words, this regulation requires an employer to pay any employee that is on-call at the job site. However, it is important to note that this regulation does not apply to individuals that are on-call at any location other than the job site.

Record keeping regulations: The Fair Labor Standards Act established a series of regulations that require employers to record specific information related to an employee's personal information, an employee's pay period and an employee's pay. The specific personal information that an employer must record includes information such as the employee's name, address, occupation and the individual's date of birth if the individual is 18 or younger. The specific pay period information that an employer must record includes the specific day and time in which the pay period begins, the date that payment is issued for the period, the total hours worked by the individual each day and the total number of hours worked for the period. The specific pay information that an employer must record includes the total regular pay that an individual receives per day, the total overtime pay that an individual receives for the period, the regular wage of the employee if the employee worked overtime, the total pay that the individual received for the period, any deductions such as tax withholdings from the individual's pay and any additions such as bonuses.

Child labor standards: The Fair Labor Standards Act established a series of child labor regulations that are designed to prevent children from entering the workforce before they are mature enough to do so, prevent children from working in hazardous environments, prevent children from working for long periods and prevent children from working instead of attending school. These regulations prohibit employers from employing anyone under the age of 14 unless the individual is working for a parent or for a farm and prohibit employers from hiring individuals under the age of 18 for any kind of work that is deemed hazardous by law. These regulations also prevent individuals under the age of 16 from working in any manufacturing or mining-related job, working during school hours, working more than 3 hours a day or 18 hours a week during a school week or 8 hours a day and 40 hours a week during a non-school week and working before 7:00am or past 7:00pm during the school year or working before 7:00am or past 9:00pm during the summer.

Portal-to-Portal Act

The Portal-to-Portal Act, which was passed in 1947, is actually an amendment to the Fair Labor Standards Act that is designed to define the difference between compensable time and time that is not compensable. In other words, this act is designed to set specific criteria for the situations in which an employer needs to pay an employee and for the situations in which an employer does not need to pay an employee. As a result, this act specifically requires an employer to pay an employee covered by the Fair Labor Standards Act for any time in which the employee is performing a task related to his or her particular position, including travel time if that time is not part of the individual's regular commute and any time that the individual spends waiting to begin work by request of the employer. However, the employer is not required to pay the employee for regular commuting time or any other period in which the individual is not performing a task required by the position or specifically requested by the employer.

Equal Pay Act

The Equal Pay Act, which was passed in 1963, is primarily designed to prevent wage discrimination based on an individual's gender. This act specifically requires an employer to provide equal pay to both men and women that are performing similar, if not identical, tasks unless the employer can prove that there is an acceptable reason for the difference in pay between the two individuals other than their gender; such as a difference in merit, a difference in seniority, a difference in the quantity or quality of work performed and other similar reasons. This act also establishes the specific criteria that must be considered to determine whether a particular position is similar or not. This includes the effort necessary for the tasks related to the position, the level of responsibility associated with the position, the skills required to perform the position and the working conditions associated with the position.

ERISA

The Employee Retirement Income Security Act (ERISA), which was passed in 1974, is designed to protect individuals from benefit plans that are operated using questionable methods. This act requires an employer, or the benefit plan administrator working for an employer, to provide information about the benefits, system for obtaining benefits and financial reports associated with a benefit plan to any employee participating in the plan. This act also requires a benefit plan to allow any individual over the age of 21 that has performed at least 1,000 hours of work for the organization to participate in the plan. In addition to these regulations, this act also specifically holds benefit plan administrators responsible for designing and operating benefit plans that are in the best interest of the plan's participants. It is important to note that this act does not actually require an organization to establish a benefit plan, but instead requires any private organization that chooses to establish a benefit plan to follow these regulations.

OWBPA

The Older Worker Benefit Protection Act (OWBPA), which was passed in 1990, is an amendment to the Age Discrimination in Employment Act that is designed to prevent employers from unfairly refusing benefits to individuals over a certain age. This act prohibits an employer or benefit plan administrator from preventing an individual from participating or continuing to participate in a benefits program due to the individual's age if the individual is covered by the Age Discrimination in Employment Act. In fact, this act establishes that an employer may only set a maximum age limit or reduce an individual's benefits due to age in situations in which the age limit or age-related reduction can be shown to significantly reduce the costs associated with implementing the benefit plan. The act also specifically establishes that an employer may implement a plan or system that is based on seniority as long as the plan does not require an individual to leave the program after a certain age.

REA

The Retirement Equity Act (REA), which was passed in 1984, is an amendment to the Employee Retirement Income Security Act (ERISA) that is designed to establish a number of benefit plan regulations in addition to those originally established by the ERISA. These regulations are primarily designed to protect spouses from losing their benefits after a plan participant's death or after a divorce, but also include regulations to strengthen the protections offered by the ERISA. Some of the specific protections established by the REA include regulations that specifically prohibit benefit plan administrators from considering maternity/paternity leave as a break in service in regards to an individual's right to participate in a plan or become vested in a plan, regulations that require pension plans to automatically provide benefits to a spouse in the event of the plan participant's death unless a waiver has been signed by both the spouse and the participant and regulations that lowered the age at which an employer had to allow an individual to participate in a pension plan.

Pension Protection Act

The Pension Protection Act, which was passed in 2006, is an amendment to the Employee Retirement Income Security Act (ERISA) that is designed to protect individuals from pension plans that do not actually have enough funding to pay out all of the retirement benefits that have been promised to employees. This act specifically requires any employer that establishes a pension plan to make contributions in amounts large enough to ensure that the pension plan is not under funded and requires employers to offer at least three investment options in addition to the employer's own stock if the employer's stock is offered as part of a benefit plan. This act also allows employers to include employees in an organization's 401(k) program with or without the permission of the individual as long as the individual has the right to opt-out of the plan.

COBRA

The Consolidated Omnibus Budget Reconciliation Act (COBRA), which was passed in 1985, is an amendment to the Employee Retirement Income Security Act (ERISA) that is designed to make sure that employees leaving an organization or employees that have had their hours reduced below the minimum necessary to participate in a group health insurance plan still have access to the health insurance offered by the employer. This act requires any employer with at least 20 employees to offer an employee the opportunity to continue his or her coverage if the individual terminated his or her own employment, the individual's hours were reduced below the participation limit or if the employer terminated his or her employment, unless the individual was terminated for gross misconduct. This act also requires any employer with at least 20 employees to offer an employee's spouse or dependents access to the health insurance offered by the employer if specific qualifying events occur. If an employee, spouse or dependent chooses to continue coverage, the employer may require the individual to pay the full insurance premium.

Qualifications: The Consolidated Omnibus Budget Reconciliation Act (COBRA) is designed to make sure that employees and/or their families still have access to the health insurance plan offered by an employee's former employer. However, in order for an employee's spouse or dependent to be covered under COBRA, a specific qualifying event must occur. An employee's spouse or dependent will be covered under COBRA if the employee terminates his or her own employment, the employee's hours are reduced below the participation limit, the employer terminated his or her employment unless the individual was terminated for gross misconduct, the employee and the spouse become legally separated or divorce and the employee is eligible for COBRA coverage, the employee becomes eligible for Medicare and the employee is eligible for COBRA coverage, or if the employee dies and the employee was eligible for COBRA coverage. An employee's dependent will also be eligible for COBRA coverage if the dependent loses his or her dependent child status according to the rules established by the insurance plan.

Eligibility: The Consolidated Omnibus Budget Reconciliation Act (COBRA) is designed to make sure that employees and/or their families still have access to the health insurance plan offered by an employee's former employer. However, COBRA coverage only lasts for a set amount of time after a qualifying event occurs. If an employee, spouse, or dependent claims coverage because the employee has terminated his or her own employment, the employee's hours have been reduced below the participation limit, the employer terminated the employee's employment unless the individual was terminated for gross misconduct, or the dependent lost his or her dependent child status, the individual may receive insurance coverage from the employer for up to 18 months. If an employee's spouse or dependent claims coverage because the employee is eligible for Medicare and is eligible for COBRA coverage, the individual may receive coverage for up to 29 months. If an employee's spouse or dependent claims coverage for a divorce or the death of the employee, the individual may receive coverage for up to 36 months.

HIPAA

The Health Insurance Portability and Accountability Act (HIPAA), which was passed in 1996, is an amendment to the Employee Retirement Income Security Act (ERISA) that, in addition to addressing certain privacy concerns, is designed to make sure that employees and their families have access to health insurance coverage even if they have a preexisting medical condition. This act specifically prohibits an employer from refusing to cover an individual under the employer's health insurance plan or charging the individual a higher rate for the plan because of a preexisting medical condition. However, this act allows the employer or the employer's health care provider to refuse coverage of any costs directly related to the preexisting condition for a period of 12 months for individuals that enrolled during a normal enrollment period or 18 months for individuals that enrolled during a late enrollment period if the individual was not previously covered by another health insurance plan.

Privacy protections: In addition to making sure that employees have access to health insurance coverage, HIPPA is designed to protect the privacy of health information that could be linked to a specific individual. This act requires any organization handling health information that could be used to identify a particular individual to conduct a series of activities to safeguard information that the Department of Health and Human Services (HHS) has identified as protected health information (PHI.) These activities include creating a written plan for protecting the privacy of PHI, implementing procedures to protect and prevent the misuse of PHI, training employees regarding the privacy requirements set by the HIPAA act and other similar activities related to protecting an individual's personal health information.

MHPA

The Mental Health Parity Act (MHPA), which was passed in 1996, is designed to prevent health plan providers from setting limits on mental health benefits that are stricter than the limits the provider has set for other health benefits. This act specifically prohibits a health plan provider from setting a financial cap on the amount that the health plan provider will pay for mental health benefits if that cap is lower than the financial cap the provider has set for other benefits. This act applies to any health plan provider providing coverage for an employer with at least 51 employees, but only if the regulations set by this act will not result in a 1% or greater increase in the costs of the provider. It is also important to note that health plan providers are not required to offer mental health benefits and providers may set other limits related to mental health coverage as long as there is no specific payout limit.

FMLA

The Family Medical Leave Act (FMLA), which was passed in 1993, is designed to protect employees that need to take a temporary leave of absence, from losing their employment or benefits as a result of the leave. This act specifically requires an employer to allow each employee up to 12 weeks of unpaid leave during a 12-month period if the individual is unable to work due to a serious health condition, the employee needs to care for an immediate family member with a serious health condition or if the individual needs to care for his or her newly born or newly adopted child. This act also requires an employer to allow the individual to retain his or her current health coverage if the individual is receiving coverage from the employer. Once the leave period has ended, the employer is required to allow the individual to take back his or her original position.

Requirements: The Family Medical Leave Act (FMLA), which was passed in 1993, is designed to protect employees that need to take a temporary leave of absence due to a serious health condition or qualifying family event, from losing their employment or benefits as a result of the leave. This act applies to any employer with at least 50 employees and applies to any public or educational agency. However, for an employee to be covered by this act, the employer must employ at least 50 employees that work within 75-miles of the worksite at which the individual taking the leave is employed at unless the individual is employed by a public agency or an educational agency. The employee taking the leave must also have worked at least 1,250 hours during the 12 months prior to the leave and must have worked for the employer for a period of at least 12 months.

The Family Medical Leave Act only protects an individual if that individual is taking his or her leave to care for a newly born or newly adopted child, if the individual is caring for a family member with a serious health condition or if the individual cannot work because he or she is suffering from a serious health condition. According to the Family Medical Leave Act, a serious health condition is "an illness, injury, impairment, or physical or mental condition" that incapacitates an individual. A condition that incapacitates an individual specifically refers to any condition in which an individual must receive treatment while staying at an inpatient care facility such as a hospital or any condition that may prevent the individual from working and performing other daily tasks for at least three days for which an individual must receive continuing treatment.

USERRA

The Uniformed Services Employment and Reemployment Rights Act (USERRA), which was passed in 1994, is designed to protect individuals that serve in the military from losing their employment or being denied employment. This act specifically prohibits an employer from refusing to hire an individual that is a member of the military or is about to become a member of the military, prohibits an employer from refusing to allow an individual to retake his or her previous position after a leave of absence to serve for the military and prohibits an employer from refusing to promote an individual or refusing to offer the individual certain benefits because of his or her military status. This act also requires an employer to inform all employees of these regulations by posting the regulations in a location that can be viewed by all employees or by informing employees of these regulations in another similar fashion.

Compensable factors

A compensable factor is a specific characteristic of a position that an organization can use to determine the value of that particular position. In other words, compensable factors are specific job requirements that an organization considers important and the organization will therefore, compensate individuals based on their ability to meet these requirements. Compensable factors are commonly used by organizations during a job evaluation, as they act as an easy way for an organization to compare the requirements of a variety of different positions. As a result, there are a variety of compensable factors that an organization may consider. Some of the most common compensable factors relate to an individual's knowledge, skills and abilities. These factors include characteristics related to a particular position such as the experience required, the level of education required, the level of responsibility required, the knowledge of specific technology or processes required and other similar characteristics.

Job evaluation techniques

The two main types of job evaluation techniques that an organization may use to determine the value of a particular position are non-quantitative techniques and quantitative techniques. Non-quantitative techniques, also referred to as whole job methods, are techniques that are designed to evaluate the skills and abilities associated with a particular position and assign a value to that position based on whether the position appears to require more or less skill than other jobs within the organization. Quantitative techniques, also referred to as nontraditional techniques or factor-based methods, are techniques in which an organization assigns a specific value to each factor in a series of compensable factors that the organization identifies as important. The organization can then evaluate each position, determine how many compensable factors are required for the position and can assign a value to the position by using a mathematical formula.

Non-quantitative job evaluation techniques

There are a variety of non-quantitative job evaluation techniques that an organization may use to determine the value of a particular position. The three most common non-quantitative job evaluation techniques are the classification method, the pricing method and the ranking method. The classification method is a technique in which an organization separates positions into categories based on the tasks that are related to each position. Each category is then listed in order of its importance to the organization and each position can be assigned pay based on the importance of its category. The pricing method, also known as the slotting method, is a technique in which an organization assigns a value to a new position or a position that has recently changed that is equal to the value of a similar position or category that already exists. Finally, the ranking method is a technique in which an organization ranks each position from lowest to highest based on how the skills and abilities required to perform the position compare with those associated with other positions.

Quantitative job evaluation techniques

There are a variety of quantitative job evaluation techniques that an organization may use to determine the value of a particular position. The most common quantitative job evaluation techniques are the factor comparison method and the point factor method. The factor comparison method is a technique in which an organization identifies a series of compensable factors and establishes a ranking system that can be used to measure how much of a particular compensable factor, such as education, is required for a particular position. Each factor ranking is assigned a specific dollar value and the value of the position is determined by adding the total dollar value for the rank of each factor that is required for the position. The point factor method is actually a very similar technique to the factor comparison method, but it assigns a point value to each factor rank instead of a dollar value and the pay for the position is determined by comparing the total amount of points to a chart.

Pay structures

A pay structure is the compensation system that an organization uses to determine the appropriate base pay for a particular position. In other words, a pay structure refers to a list that separates each job into a category based on its value to the organization so the organization can easily identify a range for each individual's base pay. Pay structures are an essential part of any organization's total rewards program, as they allow the organization to establish a guide for the appropriate hourly wage or salary that an individual should start at and how much that wage or salary should be allowed to increase. This is because a pay structure actually allows the organization to assign specific base pay minimums and maximums to each category, so the organization can determine the base pay for a specific individual using a well-defined system instead of arbitrarily choosing a base pay.

Process

The process that an organization goes through in order to create a pay structure can vary greatly from organization to organization, but most organizations begin the process by conducting a job evaluation for each position. Once an organization has evaluated each position within the organization and assigned a value to each position, the organization can separate each position into a category based on the position's value to the organization. The organization will usually then gather information from salary surveys and other similar sources to determine the market median for each category, which is the wage that an individual would receive if he or she was at the midpoint of a similar pay category for another organization. Finally, the organization can develop a pay range for each category to define exactly what the minimum and maximum base pay for each category should be.

Base pay

There are a variety of factors that an organization should consider in order to determine the appropriate base pay for a new employee. Three of the most important factors that an organization should consider are the value of the position to the organization, the education and experience of the individual taking the position and the demand for individuals able to fill the position. The value of the position to the organization refers to the value that the organization identified during the job evaluation process, based on the importance of the position to the organization. The education and experience of the individual taking the position refers to the knowledge, skills and abilities that the individual has beyond the minimum requirements necessary to perform the position. The demand for individuals able to fill the position refers to the ability of the individual to seek employment with another organization and the ease or difficulty that the organization would have in replacing the employee.

Differential pay

There are a variety of different types of differential pay that an organization may use to encourage individuals to perform unusual or unpleasant work. Some of the most common types of differential pay include hazard pay, on-call pay, and shift pay. Hazard pay is a type of differential pay that an organization pays to an individual for performing dangerous or extremely unpleasant work such as handling chemicals, working in extremely harsh environments or working in environments in which the individual may risk exposure to disease, infection, or radiation. On-call pay is a type of differential pay that an organization pays to an individual if he or she is required to report to work on extremely short notice. Shift pay is a type of differential pay that an organization pays to an individual for working unusual hours, such as working an evening shift or working an overnight shift.

Variable pay programs

There are a variety of different variable pay programs that an organization may decide to implement. Some of the most common variable pay programs include individual incentive programs, gain-sharing programs and profit sharing programs. An individual incentive program is a type of variable pay program in which an organization pays an employee a specific amount or a percentage of his or her base pay if the employee achieves a specific goal set by the organization. A gain-sharing program is a type of variable pay program in which an organization encourages an individual to reach a certain financial goal by offering the individual a percentage of the money that the organization earns or saves from achieving that goal. A profit sharing program is a type of variable pay program in which an organization encourages an individual to help the organization achieve a certain amount of profit by offering the individual a percentage of the profit if the organization reaches the goal.

Differential pay vs. variable pay

Both differential pay and variable pay refer to a type of special pay that is used to encourage individuals to perform work for an organization. However, they are actually two completely different kinds of pay. This is because differential pay is used specifically in situations in which an organization needs to encourage an individual to perform a task that most individuals do not want to perform. Variable pay, on the other hand, is used specifically in situations in which an organization wants to accomplish a particular goal and the individual may be persuaded to perform more effectively if he or she will receive a reward for his or her work. As a result, the difference between the two types of pay is that differential pay is given to an individual in order to make sure that an essential task is performed while variable pay is awarded to an individual for achieving a specific organizational goal.

Broad-banding

Broad-banding is a type of pay structure design in which an organization creates a very small number of broadly defined pay grades and separates all of the jobs within the organization into these broad pay grades. For example, an organization that has decided to use a broad-banding pay structure design may separate all of the jobs in the organization into three categories such as general staff, management, and executives. Organizations usually choose to use a broad-banding approach in order to encourage teamwork and/or eliminate some of the problems that arise from perceived differences in status between different pay grades. In fact, this is actually the primary advantage of broad-banding, as broad-banding encourages employees to focus on performance instead of activities related to achieving promotions or other similar advancement.

Wage compression

Wage compression refers to any situation in which an organization hires an employee at a wage that is more than the amount that employees with similar skills already with the organization receive for a similar position. In other words, if a new employee is hired for a position that is similar to a position held by a currently employed employee and the new employee receives higher pay even though both employees have similar skills, then the organization is causing wage compression. It is important for an organization to avoid wage compression as much as possible because it can easily lead to a variety of staffing and performance problems. This is because wage compression, even though it encourages some individuals to join the organization, will ultimately cause the employees already employed by the organization to become dissatisfied and unmotivated. In fact, some employees may even leave the organization due to wage compression, since the discrepancy in pay may cause individuals to believe that their pay is arbitrarily determined and is not based on merit, seniority, or other similar factors.

Compa-ratio

A compa-ratio is a mathematical formula that is used to compare a specific employee's pay with the pay that an employee in a similar position that is receiving pay at the middle of the pay range would receive. A compa-ratio is expressed as a percentage and can be determined by dividing the employee's base salary by the midpoint salary for the employee's pay range (base salary / midpoint salary = compa-ratio.) For example, if an individual is in a pay grade that ranges from $25,000 to 45,000 a year and the individual receives $30,000 a year, the midpoint of the range is equal to ($25,000 + 45,000) / 2 or $35,000 and the compa-ratio is equal to $30,000 / $35,000, which is equal to 0.857 or 85.7%. Compa-ratios are primarily used by an organization in order to compare an employee's current pay with the pay of other employees in similar positions, so the organization can determine whether the individual is receiving a fair amount of pay for his or her seniority, performance and other similar characteristics.

Salary survey

A salary survey is an assessment of the compensation and benefits that are currently offered by organizations in a particular labor market. In other words, a salary survey is a collection of information related to how each organization encourages employees to work with the organization in the current economic environment. In many cases, a salary survey will specifically consist of information related to a particular industry or market and how organizations within that industry or market encourage employees to work for the organization. These surveys are usually conducted by individuals or other third parties outside the organization and are usually an essential part of an organization's total rewards planning process. This is because a salary survey allows an organization to identify changes in the current labor market that may have an impact on the effectiveness of the organization's total rewards strategy.

<u>Types</u>
There are a variety of different types of salary surveys that an organization may use. Three most common types of salary surveys are commissioned surveys, government surveys and industry surveys. A commissioned survey is a type of salary survey that an organization obtains by hiring an individual or firm outside the organization to prepare the survey. Commissioned surveys are typically expensive and are usually only used when an organization needs very specific information related to the labor market. A government survey is a type of salary survey that is prepared by a government agency such as the Bureau of Labor Statistics. Government surveys can usually be obtained without cost to the organization, but the information is usually less specific than the information included in other types of surveys. An industry survey is a type of salary survey that is prepared by the members of a particular industry. Industry surveys are usually relatively inexpensive and typically provide information that is more specific than the information provided by government surveys.

OASDI

The Old Age, Survivors, and Disability Insurance (OASDI) program, which was established by the Social Security Act (SSA) of 1935, is designed to offer benefits to employees that have retired or become disabled. This program requires employees to pay a percentage of their income to the federal government and requires employers to match the contributions made by their employees. As employees make these contributions to the fund, they will receive social security credits. Each employee may receive up to four social security credits a year based on the amount that he or she pays into the fund. If an individual becomes completely disabled for a period of at least five consecutive months or retires at age 62 or older, the individual is entitled to receive a certain portion of his or her previous earnings from the social security program. In order for an individual to receive retirement benefits from social security, the individual must have at least 40 credits before retiring.

Federal-State Unemployment Insurance Program

The Federal-State Unemployment Insurance Program, which was established as part of the Social Security Act of 1935, is designed to offer benefits to employees that have lost their employment. This program requires employers to pay a state unemployment insurance (SUI) tax to help individuals that are seeking employment after losing a position. The specific tax rate that an employer has to pay and the specific requirements for an employee to be eligible for unemployment benefits vary from state to state. However, most states require an individual to work for a specific period of time prior to claiming unemployment and require an individual to actively seek employment while he or she is receiving benefits. If an individual is eligible for unemployment, the individual may receive a portion of his or her previous pay for up to 26 weeks. It is important to note, however, that most states will not allow an individual to claim any unemployment benefits if the individual was terminated due to the individual's own actions.

Medicare program

The Medicare program, which was established by an amendment made to the Social Security Act in 1965, is designed to offer health insurance coverage to elderly and/or disabled individuals. This program consists of four benefit areas referred to as parts and each part offers a specific type of coverage to the individual. The first part of the Medicare program is Medicare Part A, which covers an individual's inpatient care including any hospital stays and home nursing that the individual needs as long as that nursing care is not part of an individual's rehabilitation. Medicare Part B covers an individual's outpatient care including physicals, vaccinations, and other similar outpatient services and tests. Medicare Part B also covers the costs associated with certain medical equipment, such as wheelchairs. Medicare Part C is actually an alternative to Medicare Part A in which an individual may choose to be covered by a private Medicare insurance plan instead of the Part A plan offered by the federal government. Finally, Medicare Part D offers a variety of different prescription drug plans that an individual may choose.

Requirements
There are certain requirements that an individual must meet in order to be covered by the Medicare program. However, it is possible for an individual to be eligible for certain parts of the program even though the individual is ineligible for other parts. In order for an individual to be covered by Part A, the individual must be at least 65 years old and must be eligible to receive social security or railroad retirement benefits. An individual may also be eligible to receive benefits from Medicare Part A if the individual has been disabled for a period of at least 24 months or the individual has a qualifying disability and is eligible to receive social security disability benefits. In order for an individual to be covered by Part B, the individual must be at least 65 years old or be eligible for Medicare Part A under the disability provision. In order for an individual to be covered by Part C or Part D, the individual must be eligible for Medicare part A and must be currently covered by Part B.

Compensation and benefits

Corporate Officers
The specific compensation and benefits that a particular organization would normally provide to compensate a corporate officer can vary greatly from organization to organization. Most organizations provide corporate officers with an extremely competitive annual base salary, benefits equivalent or superior to what other employees within the organization would typically receive, perquisites, stipends to cover expenses associated with attending corporate meetings and stock options or other similar incentives based on the individual's or organization's performance.

Skilled Professionals
The specific compensation and benefits that a particular organization would normally provide to a skilled professional can vary drastically from organization to organization and from position to position. However, most organizations provide skilled professionals with higher compensation, benefits equivalent or superior to what other employees within the organization would typically receive, stipends or reimbursements to cover expenses associated with professional development and/or increased access to company resources.

Individual working in a foreign country
There are a number of different factors that might effect the compensation and benefits that an organization would have to provide to an individual working in a foreign country. Three of the most common factors influencing the compensation and benefits of an organization's employees in

- 94 -

a foreign country are local compensation practices, local laws and local taxes. Compensation practices can vary greatly from country to country or even from region to region and certain types of compensation may be acceptable and competitive in certain areas while the same compensation may be seen as inadequate, offensive or may even be illegal in other areas. The laws regulating compensation and benefits can also vary greatly from country to country so different types of compensation and benefits may be required in different countries. Finally, the taxes that an organization is required to pay on behalf of an employee will vary from country to country, which may affect the amount that the organization can afford to pay for a specific employee.

Benefits
The two main types of benefits are voluntary benefits and involuntary benefits. Voluntary benefits are benefits that an organization chooses to implement in order to achieve some sort of specific goal such as encouraging individuals to join the organization and/or stay with the organization. Voluntary benefits include 401(k) plans, dental insurance plans, health insurance plans, profit sharing plans, vacation pay and any other similar benefits that an organization is not required to implement. Involuntary benefits, on the other hand, are benefits that an organization is required to implement by a local, state, or federal law. Involuntary benefits include social security, unemployment insurance, unpaid family leave, worker's compensation and any other similar benefits that an organization is legally required to implement.

Voluntary benefits
The three main types of voluntary benefits are deferred benefits, health and welfare benefits and work-life balance benefits. Deferred benefits refer to any benefits that an individual does not receive immediately, but instead receives at some future point. Deferred benefits are usually specifically related to planning for an individual's retirement. Health and welfare benefits refer to any benefits that help an individual and/or his or her family pay for medical costs or any benefits that help with any other cost associated with an unexpected emergency or event. Health and welfare benefits are usually provided in the form of insurance. Work-life balance benefits refer to any benefits that allow an individual to perform the day-to-day activities that the individual must perform outside of work to function normally. In other words, work-life balance benefits are benefits that allow an individual to "balance" the individuals' work responsibilities with his or her other responsibilities. Work-life benefits are usually related to time-off or flexible hours.

Executive compensation program
In most cases, an organization will decide that an executive compensation program is necessary because the organization is having difficulty keeping the organization's executive positions filled. This difficulty may be the result of a variety of different issues including extremely competitive compensation for executives in today's market, the difficulty associated with finding individuals with the skills and knowledge required to operate a large organization effectively and/or any problems associated with a particular organization's image that may make it difficult to attract individuals to the organization. All of these problems can make it extremely difficult for an organization to fill its executive positions and nearly impossible for an organization to keep these positions filled if the organization's executives do not receive benefits that are similar or better than the organization's competitors. As a result, an effective executive compensation program can be essential to a large organization as it helps the organization attract individuals to executive positions and helps ensure that those individuals will stay in those positions.

Important terms

Base Pay: Base pay refers to the standard amount that an individual receives for performing work for an organization before any special pay is added. In other words, an individual's base pay is the regular wage that the individual receives per hour or the regular salary that the individual receives per pay period.

Differential Pay: Differential pay is a type of special pay that organizations pay to employees on top of their base pay in order to encourage individuals to perform certain tasks that they would normally be unwilling to perform. Differential pay is usually paid to employees for performing unpleasant or unusual work such as working in hazardous environments, working more than 40 hours in a week, or working overnight shifts.

Variable Pay: Variable pay, also known as incentive pay, is a type of special pay that organizations pay to employees on top of their base pay to encourage individuals to help the organization achieve certain goals. Variable pay is usually paid to employees that meet a certain performance goal such a selling a certain number of products.

Pay Grade: A pay grade, also referred to as a job grade or a step, is a pay category that consists of a series of positions with each position having a similar value to the organization. In other words, each position within a pay structure is separated into a pay category based on its value to the organization and each pay category in a pay structure is referred to as a pay grade.

Pay Range: A pay range refers to a set of base pays that are equal to or greater than the minimum base pay and less than or equal to the maximum base pay that an individual can typically earn for a particular pay grade.

Pay Range Spread: A pay range spread refers to a percentage that is used to describe the size of a specific pay range. A pay range spread can be determined by using the formula: (maximum – minimum) / minimum = spread.

Annual Review: An annual review is a yearly evaluation of an individual's pay in which an organization decides whether or not an individual should receive additional pay for his or her performance or seniority. Annual reviews are used to increase an employee's pay either by using a performance system that rewards individuals with a percentage raise based on the individual's level of performance or a seniority system that assigns a specific increase to each individual based on the individual's time with the organization.

Cost of Living Adjustment: A cost of living adjustment, also known as a cost of living increase, is an automatic increase that an organization assigns to each employee's pay to adjust the pay issued by the organization for changes related to inflation or changes related to increases in local costs. A cost of living adjustment is usually a flat percentage increase added to each individual's pay.

Defined-Benefit Plan: A defined-benefit plan is a type of retirement plan in which an organization promises that an individual will receive a specific amount of money each month after the individual retires. The specific amount that an individual receives per month is usually determined using a formula that takes the individual's monthly pay and the individual's length of time with the company into consideration.

Defined Contribution Plan: A defined contribution plan is a type of retirement plan in which an organization contributes a specific amount of money into an account. The money that is placed into the account may be in addition to the individual's pay or taken out of the individual's pay. As money is placed into the account, the money is invested in order to offer a larger retirement benefit to the individual at the time he or she retires. However, since there is always some risk associated with any investment, the amount that a specific individual will receive upon retirement with a defined contribution plan can vary greatly.

Cash Balance Plan: A cash balance plan is a type of retirement plan in which an organization promises an employee that he or she will receive a set amount of money at the time the individual retires. Most organizations determine this set amount by establishing a specific amount that the account should increase by each month and calculating the amount that the account would have when the individual retires. The organization can then determine the amount that it needs to deposit into the employee's cash balance plan account annually, with interest taken into consideration, to make sure that the account has the appropriate balance at retirement.

Simplified Employee Pension Plan: A simplified employee pension plan is a type of retirement plan in which both the organization and the employee can make contributions to an individual retirement account (IRA). Organizations contributing to an employee's IRA can either match the amount that the employee contributes to the account or establish a set contribution rate.

Health Maintenance Organization Program: A health maintenance organization (HMO) program is a type of health care insurance that is used to minimize the costs associated with expensive procedures and examinations by encouraging employees to take part in activities that would prevent employees from requiring and/or receiving expensive procedures or examinations. Most HMO programs control the individual's access to expensive procedures and examinations by requiring an employee to choose a primary care physician that must approve any special procedures or examinations.

Preferred Provider Organization Program: A preferred provider organization (PPO) program is a type of health care insurance that is used to minimize medical costs by requiring an individual to seek care from a specific network of health care facilities and physicians. Most PPO's actually allow an individual to seek care from outside the network as well, but the individual will usually be responsible for a much larger portion of the costs related to the medical care than he or she would be responsible for if the individual used a provider within the network.

Perquisites: A perquisite, also known as a perk, is a type of executive benefit in which any of a number of different luxuries are purchased or paid for by an organization for an executive's use. Perquisites include benefits such as club memberships, company cars, entertainment packages, personal security, tax preparation and counseling services, vacation trip opportunities and a variety of other similar benefits.

Severance Packages: A severance package, which is sometimes referred to as a golden parachute, is a type of executive benefit in which an executive is guaranteed to receive a certain amount of money or stock if he or she is terminated. Severance packages may be paid immediately in one payment upon the individual's termination or may be paid over a period of time.

Stock Options: A stock option is a type of executive benefit in which an executive receives stock automatically under certain conditions or has the ability to purchase stock at a discount or set rate.

Qualified Stock Options: A qualified stock option, also referred to as an incentive stock option, is a type of stock option in which employees are allowed to purchase stock, but executives are not allowed to purchase stock. Employees that purchase qualified stock are not required to pay tax on the funds used to purchase the stock until the stock is sold. Employers will not be able to take a tax deduction on qualified stock options in most situations.

Nonqualified Stock Options: A nonqualified stock option is a type of stock option in which both employees and executives are allowed to purchase stock. Employees or executives that purchase nonqualified stock are required to pay taxes at the time the stock is purchased and may have to pay additional taxes when the stock is sold. Employers will usually be able to take a tax deduction for nonqualified stock that is issued to employees or executives.

Phantom Stock: Phantom stock refers to a type of benefit in which an organization issues shares to an executive or other individual, but the shares do not actually represent the individual's ownership in the organization. In other words, phantom stock will pay dividends as if the individual owned shares of common stock and may be sold or converted under certain conditions, but the individual does not receive voting rights as he or she would with other types of stock because phantom stock does not actually grant the individual any official ownership in the organization.

Restricted Stock: Restricted stock refers to a type of benefit in which an organization issues shares to an executive or other individual without requiring the individual to actually pay for those shares. Restricted stock is usually only issued to individuals if they meet specific conditions, such as achieving a specific performance goal or staying with the organization for a specific period of time.

Host-Country Nationals: Most organizations will typically provide host-country nationals filling foreign positions with compensation and benefits similar to that of individuals in other comparable positions within the country that the position is based.

Parent-Country Nationals: Most organizations will provide parent-country nationals with a weekly salary and benefits similar to that of individuals in other comparable positions in the country in which the organization is based, payments or reimbursements for housing and living costs, bonuses and stipends for issues or achievements associated with the foreign assignment and tax payments.

Third-Country Nationals: Most organizations will provide third-country nationals with a weekly salary and benefits similar to that of individuals in other comparable positions in the country in which the organization is based or the country that the individual is from, payments or reimbursements for housing and living costs, bonuses and stipends for issues associated with the foreign assignment and tax payments.

Employee and Labor Relations

Constructive discharge

The legal concept known as constructive discharge refers to a common law protection offered by certain states that holds an employer responsible for the work environment in which an employee works. This common law specifically holds an employer responsible if an individual terminates his or her employment because the employer has created a hostile work environment. In other words, a constructive discharge is a situation in which an employer creates a work environment that is so threatening and/or ultimately unpleasant that the individual has no choice, but to terminate his or her employment. The specific requirements that a situation must meet in order for an individual to claim a constructive discharge varies from state to state. An individual that believes that he or she has been the victim of a constructive discharge may bring a lawsuit against his or her former employer.

Defamation

The legal concept known as defamation refers to a common law protection that holds an employer responsible for any communication that unfairly affects an individual's reputation. This common law specifically holds an employer responsible if an individual is adversely affected by a statement made by the employer through any medium, if that statement is untrue or unrelated to the individual's performance. In other words, if an employer lies or releases information that is completely unrelated to an individual's ability to perform a task, such as the individual's sexual orientation, and that information prevents the individual from receiving a specific benefit, such as a position with another organization, the employer may be held liable for any damage caused by the false or unrelated information.

Employment-at-will

The legal concept known as employment-at-will refers to a common law protection that allows an employer or an employee to terminate an employment agreement at any time. This common law specifically allows an employee to terminate his or her employment at any time for any reason and allows an employer to terminate the employee's employment at any time for any reason as long as the individual is not terminated in violation of any other employment law or public policy. However, it is also important to note that the employment-at-will protection may not apply if there is a contract between the employee and the employer that would prevent the termination, or if there is a policy established by the employer that would prevent the employer from terminating the employee without going through a specific procedure first.

Expressed and implied contracts

The two main types of contracts that may prevent an employer from terminating an employee are expressed contracts and implied contracts. An expressed contract is a written document created by the employer or a verbal statement made by the employer or one of the employer's representatives that establishes the specific arrangement that exists between the employee and the employer. An expressed contract can prevent an employer from terminating an individual's employment if the contract guarantees the individual employment or states that the individual may only be terminated under very specific circumstances. An implied contract is a written

- 99 -

document created by the employer, a verbal statement made by the employer or one of the employer's representatives or an activity that the employer consistently performs that establishes a policy for the appropriate procedure that must be followed for an individual to be terminated. An implied contract can prevent an employer from terminating an individual's employment if the contract establishes a standard action that the employer must take before terminating the employee such as following a disciplinary process or identifying a just cause.

Good faith and fair dealing

The legal concept of good faith and fair dealing refers to a common law protection that holds an employee and/or an employer responsible for upholding the agreement established by an expressed or implied employment contract. This common law specifically requires each individual involved in a particular employment contract to act in a way that will allow the agreement to be carried out as agreed upon by the employer and the employee. In other words, an employee must be able and willing to perform the tasks associated with the contract and the employer must be able and willing to provide the compensation and benefits that the employer promised to the employee in exchange for his or her work. As a result, an employee that lies about his or her experience, education, skills and other abilities or background information may be held liable for his or her false statements and an employer that lies about the benefits that the individual will receive or deliberately prevents the employee from claiming those benefits may be held liable.

Promissory estoppel

The legal concept known as promissory estoppel refers to a common law protection that holds an employer responsible for promises that the employer makes. This common law specifically holds an employer responsible if the employer promises an employee a particular reward in exchange for the employee taking a particular action and the employee takes the action, but the employee never actually receives the reward from the employer. In other words, if an employer promises a specific reward to an employee for performing a specific task or taking a specific action and the employee takes the action, then the employer must provide the reward to the employee. It is important to note that the protections offered by the common law concept of promissory estoppel are similar to the protections offered by the common law concept of good faith and fair dealing except that an employer may be held liable for not carrying out a promise that the employer made to an employee even if the promise was made in good faith.

Respondeat superior

The legal concept known as respondeat superior, which literally means, "let the master answer," refers to a common law protection that holds an employer responsible for the actions of the employer's employees as they are performing tasks for the employer. This common law specifically holds an employer responsible for any civil offense committed by an employee while the individual is performing work for the employer if the offense is related to the employee's standard responsibilities. In other words, an employer may be held liable for any actions taken by the employer's managers, supervisors and/or employees if one of these individuals commits an act that is a violation of civil law while performing his or her standard responsibilities. It is also important to note that, in certain situations, an employer may be held liable under respondeat superior even if the employer was unaware of the employee's actions.

Discrimination charges

There are a variety of different reasons that an organization may want to settle a discrimination charge before the charge can be investigated by the Equal Employment Opportunity Commission (EEOC) or investigated by a state or local Fair Employment Practices Agency (FEPA). One of most common reasons for an organization to settle a discrimination charge is so the organization can avoid the financial costs associated with defending itself. This is because the financial costs associated with defending an organization such as court fees, lawyers' fees, the amount that the organization may have to pay if the court finds that discrimination has taken place and other similar costs can all be extremely expensive for the organization. As a result, an organization may want to settle a discrimination charge, even if the organization has not actually committed an act of unlawful discrimination, because the settlement may cost less than the organization would have to pay to defend itself in court.

Another common reason for an organization to settle a discrimination charge is so the organization can avoid or minimize the damage to its reputation. This is because any charge of discrimination, regardless of whether the charge has any basis or not, will affect the organization's reputation with its employees, customers and vendors as each individual hears about the charge and questions the organization's practices and procedures. As a result, an organization may want to settle a discrimination charge to avoid any media coverage or rumors that may damage the organization's reputation, may damage the organization's employee relations and ultimately make it more difficult for the organization to function normally.

An organization may also want to settle so the organization can avoid the EEOC or FEPA investigation itself. This is usually because an organization can avoid devoting the time or resources associated with providing the information necessary for the investigation by settling the charge before the investigation begins. It is also important to note that in certain situations, an organization may also wish to avoid an investigation because the organization has actually committed unlawful discrimination or the organization believes that an individual or group within the organization may have committed unlawful discrimination. As a result, the organization may want to avoid an investigation that will only reveal additional information about questionable activities within the organization.

Front pay to a complainant

In most cases, an employer will not be required to provide an individual with front pay, but will instead be required to offer the individual the opportunity to take or return to a specific position within the organization or required to offer the individual another similar remedy if the court decides that the employer has committed unlawful discrimination. However, there are three specific situations in which a court may award a complainant front pay. The first situation in which an individual may be awarded front pay is if the original position that the individual was interested in is no longer available and there is no other similar position available. The second situation in which an individual may be awarded front pay is if the employer has shown a consistent pattern of discrimination and has made little or no attempt to eliminate the activities leading to the discrimination. The third and final situation in which an individual may be awarded front pay is if the individual would be subjected to an ongoing hostile work relationship with the employer.

Organizational climate

Organizational climate refers to the way that individuals within an organization perceive the organization in which they work and how those perceptions effect how each individual feels about that organization. In other words, organizational climate refers to how each employee feels about his or her work environment and the organization as a whole. The current organizational climate can be an important factor to monitor in any organization because the way that employees within a particular organization feel about the organization can greatly affect the ability of the organization to retain employees and motivate the employees that the organization retains. It is important to realize that the climate of a particular organization is primarily based off the perceptions of the organization's employees. As a result, it can often be extremely difficult for an organization to control its own climate because of all of the different factors that effect how the organization's employees perceive the organization.

Organizational culture

An organization's culture and an organization's climate are very closely related, but are actually two separate parts of an organization. This is because an organizational culture refers to the beliefs and values that the employees and managers of an organization have established and the way that those individuals act based on those beliefs and values. An organizational climate, on the other hand, refers to the way that individual's perceive the organization and the way individuals feel about the organization based on those perceptions. In other words, organizational culture refers to the work environment that the members of the organization have created and the climate refers to how the members of the organization feel about that environment. As a result, the terms organizational culture and organizational climate describe two different elements of an organization that are closely related because the organizational climate within a particular organization depends heavily on the organizational culture that exists within the organization.

Employee involvement strategies

It is possible for a particular strategy to be used as both a communication strategy and an involvement strategy because the amount of employee involvement within an organization is closely related to the amount of employee communication. This is because strategies that encourage communication between an organization's employees and the organization's management will often allow employees to have more input in the organization's decision-making and ultimately allow employees to become more involved in the organization's operations as a whole. However, this does not necessarily mean that every strategy is both a communication strategy and an involvement strategy. In fact, a strategy that allows a manager to communicate important information to employees without allowing each employee to respond to or discuss the information may be considered a communication strategy, but it cannot be considered an involvement strategy. At the same time, a strategy that allows an individual to have more control over a particular task may be an involvement strategy without being a communication strategy, as it does necessarily encourage an individual to communicate.

Open-door policy

An open-door policy is an employee involvement/communication strategy in which an organization encourages employees to share information or suggestions with managers or

- 102 -

supervisors by assuring the employees of the organization that they will not be adversely affected by what they say. Open-door policies are designed to establish effective communication between managers, supervisors and employees by removing the barriers that prevent or discourage an employee from discussing important issues with his or her immediate supervisor or manager. As a result, the primary advantage of an open-door policy is that it allows the organization to identify issues within the organization and potential solutions to issues within the organization that may have gone unnoticed without information from the organization's employees. It is important to note that there is a major disadvantage to an open-door policy, as there are certain situations in which a manager or supervisor may need to release information that will adversely affect an employee in order to handle an issue that has been reported.

MBWA

The Management by Walking Around (MBWA) strategy is simply a communication and involvement method in which an organization encourages employee communication and employee involvement by making managers and supervisors readily available. Under this strategy, an organization makes its managers and supervisors more readily available by encouraging managers and supervisors to "walk around" so they can check on the progress of each employee, discuss questions or concerns and ultimately handle any problems that the employee or the manager identifies. This particular strategy may appear to be extremely straightforward and relatively obvious, as most organizations attempt to make sure that managers and supervisors are actually monitoring the progress of the employees under their supervision. However, it is still important for an organization to make sure that its managers and supervisors are continually "managing by walking around" because it is very easy for a manager or supervisor to get caught up in other activities and miss important issues that should have been identified and handled.

Progressive discipline

Progressive discipline refers to a discipline system in which an organization modifies its response to a particular behavioral issue based on the severity of the issue and how often the issue has occurred in the past. In other words, progressive discipline refers to a process in which an organization identifies a particular behavioral problem, assesses the severity of the problem, determines whether or not the problem has occurred before and takes a specific disciplinary action based on the organization's assessment. As a result, the primary purpose of this system is to create different responses for different situations. This can be extremely important because each situation is different and two separate behavioral problems may require two completely different responses if the two problems affect the operations of the organization in different ways. Progressive discipline addresses this need for varying disciplinary responses by allowing an organization to make sure that a response to a particular behavioral problem is not overly severe and that repeat offenders are punished more severely than first-time offenders.

The specific disciplinary stages that an organization will use in a progressive discipline system can vary greatly from organization to organization. Most organizations use a five-stage disciplinary process. The first stage in this process is the coaching stage in which the organization discusses the behavioral issue with the individual. A first stage response is usually used if the issue is relatively minor and/or if the issue is the individual's first offense. The second stage in this process is the first warning stage, also known as the counseling stage, in which the organization will issue a verbal warning to the individual regarding the undesirable behavior. The third stage in this process is the second warning stage, also known as the formal warning stage, in which the organization will issue a written warning to the individual regarding the undesirable behavior. The fourth stage in this process is the disciplinary action stage in which the organization suspends the individual or takes other similar action. The fifth stage is the termination stage in which the organization terminates the individual's employment.

Behavioral issues

There are a variety of different behavioral issues that an organization may need to address and, as a result, there are a number of different ways that an organization can respond in a specific situation. Most behavioral issues can be addressed simply by creating a policy that identifies the undesirable behavior, provides an in-depth definition of which actions should be considered part of that undesirable behavior and provides an in-depth explanation of the disciplinary action that will be taken if an individual takes one of the actions described in the policy. In the case of absenteeism, an organization should establish a clear absentee policy that informs members of the organization exactly how much sick time is allowed, the appropriate manner in which to use that sick time, what uses will be considered excessive and/or inappropriate and the action that the organization will take if an individual is absent on a regular basis. In the case of insubordination, a code of conduct that defines certain general behaviors that are unacceptable may be sufficient to handle these issues.

Arbitration

The two main types of arbitration are compulsory and voluntary arbitration. Compulsory arbitration is a form of arbitration in which two or more parties involved in a particular dispute are required by law to seek arbitration. Compulsory arbitration is usually the result of a specific clause in a contract or the result of a court order. Voluntary arbitration, on the other hand, is a form or arbitration in which two or more parties involved in a particular dispute decide to seek arbitration in order to solve the dispute before it goes to court. Voluntary arbitration usually occurs because the parties involved in a particular dispute cannot come to an agreement, but all of the parties involved would like to avoid investing the time and money required for a lawsuit.

Types of arbitration decisions

The two main types of arbitration decisions that may result from a particular arbitration are binding and non-binding. A binding decision is a decision in which all of the parties involved in a particular dispute are legally required to accept the arbitration decision and each party is required to take any specific actions, such as paying remedies, which are required by the decision. Once a binding decision is made, the decision is final and no party involved in a binding arbitration decision can take any further legal action based on the specific dispute covered in the decision. A non-binding decision, on the other hand, is a decision in which all of the parties involved in a particular dispute are **not** required to accept the arbitration decision and each party may decide to take or decide not to take the specific actions required by the decision. As a result, a non-binding decision is merely the opinion of the arbitrator regarding how the particular dispute should be resolved and any party involved in the dispute may take further legal action.

Mediation process

The mediation process can vary greatly depending on the specific situation. However, in most cases, the mediation process begins with the parties involved choosing an independent and impartial mediator. Once the parties have chosen a mediator, the mediator establishes the format of the mediation process by answering questions such as what is being disputed, who is actually involved in the dispute, when will the negotiations take place, where will the negotiations take place, and how will the negotiations be conducted. Once the format of the mediation process has been established, the parties involved in the dispute will meet, the mediator will explain the format and explain the purpose of the meeting and the parties will present information related to each side of the dispute. After all of the parties involved have presented the facts related to the dispute, the mediator will attempt to help each party identify solutions to the dispute and come to a compromise. Finally, each party will sign a written document agreeing to the compromise if a compromise was reached.

Constructive confrontation

Constructive confrontation, which was originally designed by Guy Burgess and Heidi Burgess, is a mediation method that is designed to address complicated disputes in which all of the parties involved are unwilling to consider alternative solutions. This method assumes that most disputes that seem to be irresolvable may be resolved if the parties involved address the secondary issues involved in a particular dispute first and then move on to the main issues present in the dispute itself. In other words, in a complicated dispute, it is possible for factors that are not related to the primary issue of the dispute itself to play a role in whether or not the dispute can be resolved. As a result, the constructive confrontation method suggests that the parties involved in a particular dispute should identify problems that are not directly related to the primary issue that is being disputed, such as disagreements related to the dispute resolution method that is being used, and eliminate or minimize the effects of those problems so a compromise may be reached.

Important legislation

Sherman Antitrust Act
The Sherman Antitrust Act, which was passed in 1890, is designed to prevent organizations from restricting free trade. This act specifically prohibits any individual or organization from entering into a contract that would significantly restrict the ability of other individuals or organizations to trade or engage in commerce. This act also specifically prohibits any individual or organization from taking any action that would form a monopoly and grants the courts the authority to issue injunctions to halt actions that would allow a particular individual or organization to monopolize a particular type of trade. This act applies to any organization unless there is a specific law protecting the organization from being considered a monopoly. Under this act, if a particular individual or organization is suspected of forming a monopoly, a government attorney or the district courts have the authority to initiate an investigation and take appropriate action.

Clayton Act
The Clayton Act, which was passed in 1914, is designed to explain the prohibitions established by the Sherman Antitrust Act in more detail and to establish regulations protecting certain organizations from being considered monopolies under the Sherman Antitrust Act. This act specifically defines some of the trade-restrictive activities that should be considered illegal due to the regulations established under the Sherman Antitrust Act including exclusive dealings, price discrimination, mergers and any other similar activities if those activities actually prevent other individuals or organizations from competing. This act also specifically establishes that agricultural organizations and unions are exempt from the regulations established by the Sherman Antitrust Act

and that court injunctions may only be used to settle a labor dispute if there is a threat of property damage.

Railway Labor Act

The Railway Labor Act, which was passed in 1926 and amended in 1936, is designed to prevent railroad and airline strikes from causing significant trade and transportation problems. This act specifically establishes that airline and railroad employees have the right to unionize and strike if the strike is related to a major contract dispute. However, this act requires the employees involved in an airline or railroad union to seek alternative dispute resolution methods including arbitration and mediation before initiating a strike. This act also allows the president to declare a national emergency if an airline or railroad strike is significantly affecting trade and transportation within the United States. If the president declares a strike to be a national emergency, all strikers involved in that particular strike must return to work for a period of 90 days.

Norris-LaGuardia Act

The Norris-LaGuardia Act, which was passed in 1932, is designed to protect the right to unionize. This act specifically grants employees the right to form unions and initiate strikes. In addition to granting the right to unionize, this act also specifically prohibits the court system from using court injunctions to interfere with any nonviolent union activity and specifically prohibits employers from forcing employees to sign "yellow-dog" contracts. A "yellow-dog" contract refers to any contract that prohibits an employee from joining a union or any contract that requires an employee to agree that the employee will be terminated if it is discovered that he or she is a member of a union or intends to become a member of a union.

NLRA

The National Labor Relations Act (NLRA), also known as the Wagner Act, is designed to grant certain rights to unionized workers or employees that want to unionize. This act reaffirms some of the protections established by the Norris-LaGuardia Act, as it specifically grants employees the right to form unions and establishes that all employees covered by this act have the right to join a union and take part in union activities. This act also specifically establishes that all employees have the right to take part in any activity related to a collective bargaining process with their employer regardless of whether they are a member of a union or not. However, the regulations established by this act do not apply to employees that are covered by the Railway Labor Act or to employees working on a farm or for other agricultural employers. The regulations established by this act also do not apply to managers, supervisors, independent contractors, immediate family of the employer and any other individuals that may make labor decisions on behalf of an employer.

Strike situations: According to the National Labor Relations Act (NLRA), there are certain situations in which a strike should be considered legal and certain situations in which a strike should be considered illegal. The National Labor Relations Act establishes that a strike should be considered lawful if the members of the union refuse to work because they are seeking an increase in their benefits, compensation or are seeking an improvement related to their work environment. A strike should also be considered lawful if the members of the union refuse to work because their employer is using an unfair labor practice. A strike should be considered unlawful, on the other hand, if employees refuse to work even though they are covered by a contract with a no-strike clause, if employees refuse to work in order to assist the union in defending an unfair labor practice committed by the union or if the actions taken by the employees during the strike can reasonably be expected to result in property damage or harm to any person.

Labor practices: The National Labor Relations Act (NLRA) identifies five types of employer practices that should be considered unfair labor practices. First, the NLRA establishes that it is unfair for an employer to interfere in the activities of a union or prevent employees from taking any action related to forming or joining a union. Second, the NLRA establishes that it is unfair for an employer to take any action that would allow the organization to control a union or offer special attention and/or preferential treatment to a particular union. Third, the NLRA establishes that it is unfair for an employer to discriminate against any employee because he or she is a member of a union or takes part in any lawful union activity. Fourth, the NLRA establishes that is it unfair for an employer to discriminate against any employee because he or she has filed charges with the National Labor Relations Board or has taken part in any investigation. Fifth, the NLRA establishes that it is unfair for an employer to refuse to bargain with a union representing the employer's employees.

LMRA

The Labor Management Relations Act (LMRA), also known as the Taft-Hartley Act, identifies a number of union practices that should be considered unfair labor practices. First, the LMRA establishes that it is unfair for a union to force an employee to join or take part in a union or force an employee to accept a particular representative. Second, the LMRA establishes that it is unfair for a union to refuse to bargain with the representative of an employer or restrict the ability of an employer to negotiate a contract and enforce that contract. Third, the LMRA establishes that it is unfair for a union to call for an employer to discriminate against employees that are not part of a particular union or that speak out against a union. Fourth, the LMRA establishes that it is unfair for a union to encourage individuals outside the organization to take part in a secondary boycott or encourage employers to enter into a hot cargo agreement. Finally, the LMRA establishes that it is unfair for a union to charge unreasonably high membership fees.

NLRB

The National Labor Relations Board (NLRB) is a federal agency that is designed to protect the right of employees to choose whether they want to be represented by a union or not and is designed to handle activities related to investigating and preventing employers and unions from taking part in unfair labor practices. The National Labor Relations Board can take a number of actions related to employer unfair labor practices including requiring employers to rehire or return positions to employees that were affected by an unfair labor practice, requiring employers to resume negotiations with a union and disbanding unions that are controlled by an employer. The National Labor Relations Board may also take a number of actions related to union unfair labor practices including requiring unions to refund membership fees with or without interest to union members that have been charged unreasonable fees, requiring unions to resume negotiations with an employer and requiring unions to accept the reinstatement of any employee if the union specifically discriminated against that employee.

Organizing process for unions

In order for a union to be recognized as the official representative of a certain group of employees, the union must go through a four-step organizing process. First, a group of employees interested in joining the union or the union itself must establish that the members of the organization are interested in being represented by the union. Second, the group of employees or the union itself must have employees sign authorization cards to prove that the employees of the organization are interested in being represented by a union. Third, the union must inform the employer that the employees of the organization have requested to be represented by the union and that the union requests that the employer recognize the union as their representative. If the employer refuses to recognize the union as a representative, the union may file a petition with the NLRB. Once the union has been recognized by the employer, the fourth and final step is to have the NLRB conduct an election to confirm that the employees actually want to be represented by the union.

Picketing

The three types of picketing that are specifically allowed by the National Labor Relations Board while a particular union is campaigning are informational picketing, organizational picketing and recognitional picketing. Informational picketing refers to an activity in which employees assemble or march with signs near a worksite in order to inform the public that the employees of the organization are not represented by a single authority that will speak on their behalf. Organizational picketing refers to an activity in which employees assemble or march with signs near a worksite in order to encourage other employees to support a union. Recognitional picketing refers to an activity in which employees assemble or march with signs near a worksite in order to convince an employer to recognize that a particular union represents the majority of the employer's employees.

Picketing during a dispute
The types of picketing that are specifically allowed by the National Labor Relations Board while a union is in the middle of a dispute with an employer are common situs picketing, consumer picketing, and double breasting picketing. Common situs picketing refers to an activity in which employees assemble or march with signs near a worksite that is used by both the employer that the union is picketing against and other employers. Common situs picketing is legal as long as the signs make it clear that there is a specific employer the union is picketing against. Consumer picketing refers to an activity in which employees assemble or march with signs near a worksite in order to inform the public that any products and services being offered by the employer are being offered while there is a work dispute. Double breasting picketing refers to an activity in which employees assemble or march with signs near a nonunion worksite operated by the employer that the union is picketing against. However, double breasting picketing is only legal in certain situations.

Union decertification process

In certain cases, the employees of a particular organization may decide that the union acting as their official representative is not representing their interests effectively. In these cases, the employees of the organization may actually choose to remove the union's status as their representative through a process known as decertification. In order to begin the process, the employees of the organization must create a petition and obtain the signatures of no less than 30% of the organization's employees. Once the petition has the required number of signatures, the employees of the organization may file the petition with the National Labor Relations Board (NLRB) for review. If the NLRB determines that the petition has the required number of signatures and that the petition has not been filed within 12 months of the date that the union was certified as the representative of the organization's employees, the NLRB will hold a decertification election. If 50% or more of the organization's employees vote to decertify the union, the union will no longer be considered as a representative of the organization's employees.

Union deauthorization process

In certain cases, the employees of a bargaining unit may decide that the union acting as their official representative has put a security clause in place that is not in their best interest. In these cases, the employees of the bargaining unit may actually choose to remove that specific security clause through a process known as deauthorization. In order to begin the process, the employees of the bargaining unit must create a petition and obtain the signatures of no less than 30% of the unit's employees. Once the petition has the required number of signatures, the employees of the unit may file the petition with the National Labor Relations Board (NLRB) for review. If the NLRB determines that the petition has the required number of signatures, the NLRB will hold a deauthorization election for the entire union. If 50% or more of the union's members vote for deauthorization, the union's security clause will be considered null and void.

Collective bargaining process

The National Labor Relations Act (NLRA) specifically requires any party involved in a collective bargaining process to negotiate in good faith. As a result, it is important for both unions and employers to be aware of the specific types of actions that may be considered "bad faith" activities. Bad faith bargaining activities that an employer may engage in include; making a proposal to employees before or without making the proposal to the union that represents those employees, encouraging employees to decertify the union or take any other action that would adversely affect the union's ability to negotiate and making any changes in the favor of the employer to the terms and/or conditions under which the employees of the organization work while the collective bargaining process is taking place. Bad faith bargaining activities that a union or an employer may engage in include hiding information related to the bargaining process, refusing to set and adhere to a reasonable time and place for the negotiations, taking any action that can be considered an unfair labor practice and other similar activities.

Categories
The three categories that the National Labor Relations Board (NLRB) uses to describe the subjects that can and cannot be discussed during the collective bargaining process are illegal, mandatory, and voluntary. Illegal subjects are topics that cannot be discussed during the collective bargaining process. These subjects are usually related to activities that are specifically forbidden by law such as hot cargo agreements, clauses that prevent individuals from being employed by the organization if they do not join the union before assuming their position and other similar activities. Mandatory subjects are topics that must be discussed during the collective bargaining process. These subjects are usually related to the basic terms and conditions of an individual's employment including the benefits, hours, regular pay, safety protections, special pay and other similar terms and conditions related to an individual's employment. Voluntary subjects, also known as permissible subjects, are topics that the parties involved in the collective bargaining process may choose to discuss, but cannot be required to discuss. Voluntary subjects therefore include any topic that is not illegal or mandatory.

Agreements
The information that should be included in a collective bargaining agreement can vary from organization to organization, but all collective bargaining agreements should include

information related to the basic terms and conditions of employment that the parties have agreed upon, the contract grievance process, the disciplinary process and a zipper clause. The basic terms and conditions of employment such as the benefits, regular pay, and special pay that employees will receive and the hours and conditions under which employees are expected to work is an essential component of any collective bargaining agreement. The contract grievance process that will be used if there is a dispute over the terms or conditions established by a certain section of the agreement and the specific process that the organization will use to take action against employees that violate the terms of their employment should also be clearly stated. Finally, a zipper clause that clearly establishes that the agreement is final and that anything outside of the agreement cannot be discussed until the contract runs out is also an essential part of the agreement.

Negotiating strategies

The four main negotiating strategies that a union can use to negotiate with an organization during the collective bargaining process are single-unit bargaining, coordinated bargaining, multi-employer bargaining, and parallel bargaining. Single unit bargaining is a commonly used union bargaining strategy in which the representatives from a single unit meet with one organization at a time and the union's representatives focus all of their attention on the agreement for that specific organization. Coordinated bargaining, also known as multi-unit bargaining, is a union bargaining strategy in which a group of separate unions that each represent different employees within the organization negotiate with an organization as a group to reach an agreement that is in the best interest of everyone. Multi-employer bargaining is a union bargaining strategy in which a union negotiates with several different organizations that employ members of the union. Parallel bargaining, also referred to as leapfrogging or whipsawing, is a union bargaining strategy in which a union negotiates with one organization at a time and uses the agreement achieved with that organization as a model for the next organization.

Approaches

The two main approaches that the representatives of an organization or the representatives of a union may choose to use to negotiate during the collective bargaining process are distributive bargaining and principled bargaining. Distributive bargaining, which is also known as positional bargaining, refers to an approach in which a party establishes a specific objective that they wish to achieve or a specific position for each issue before the negotiations begin. As the negotiations proceed, the party will then attempt to achieve that objective or defend that position whenever possible. Principled bargaining, on the other hand, refers to an approach in which a party identifies the issues that are most important to each side. As the negotiations proceed, the party will then attempt to discuss possible solutions and encourage the other party to suggest possible solutions for each issue so the union and the organization may reach an agreement that will benefit the employer and the employees.

Contract grievance process

The specific contract grievance process that a particular employee or union will need to go through in order to address a contract issue can vary greatly from agreement to agreement. However, the first step for a typical grievance process is for the employee or union representative to file a written or verbal complaint with a supervisor. If the supervisor offers a solution to the contract issue and the employee or union accepts that solution, then the grievance process ends. If the employee or the union considers the solution unacceptable or the supervisor does not offer a solution, then the employee or union may file a complaint with a manager. If the manager solves the issue, the grievance process ends. If the manager does not solve the issue, the employee or union may file a complaint with the organization's upper management. Finally, if the organization's upper management fails to solve the issue, the employee or union may seek arbitration. This arbitration is usually binding and the employer and the union will therefore have to accept the decision of the arbitrator.

Differing unions

There are a variety of different ways in which unions may differ from country to country. Some of the common differences between a union located in one country and a union located in another country include differences related to the structure and size of the typical union in the country, differences related to the influence of the typical union in the country and differences in the bargaining process. The structure and size of a typical union can vary greatly from country to country as certain countries may have enormous unions that represent large numbers of people in a variety of different industries while other countries have virtually no union activity at all. The influence of a typical union can also vary greatly from country to country as certain countries have strict regulations controlling unions while other countries may actually have political parties that are strongly motivated or even controlled by unions. The bargaining process can also vary drastically from country to country as certain countries give bargaining power to unions while other countries give the power directly to employees.

NAALC

The North American Agreement on Labor Cooperation (NAALC), affected in 1994, is designed to help protect employees working in Canada, Mexico and the United States from questionable employment practices. This agreement specifically establishes a series of labor guidelines for the United States, Canada and Mexico related to a number of different labor concerns including child labor guidelines, equal employment opportunity guidelines, occupational health and safety guidelines, minimum wage guidelines and union rights guidelines. In addition to establishing these guidelines, this agreement also created the National Administrative Office (NAO), which was created to enforce the agreement. However, it is important to note that this agreement did not actually establish any specific labor regulations, but instead created a number of guidelines that the NAO could enforce through existing national laws.

ILO

The International Labor Organization (ILO) is designed to help protect the labor rights of employees that work within countries belonging to the United Nations (UN). In fact, the ILO is actually a UN agency that encourages UN members to grant certain labor rights to employees through recommendations and conventions. These rights are encouraged through guidelines related to child labor standards, equal employment opportunity standards, occupational health and safety standards, minimum wage standards and union rights standards. It is important to note that the ILO does not actually have any official authority to enforce its recommendations or conventions as it can only encourage each UN member to adhere to its guidelines.

WTO

The World Trade Organization (WTO) is designed to set a series of rules and   regulations that each nation in the WTO is expected to follow when carrying out trade negotiations. The WTO also attempts to ensure that each party involved in a trade agreement upholds their end of the agreement by imposing sanctions and assessing damages on nations that violate trade agreements.

Important terms

Fair Employment Practices Agency: A fair employment practices agency (FEPA) is a state or local organization that enforces anti-discrimination laws and regulations within the state or local area that the organization is located.

Charge: A charge, in terms of equal employment opportunity, is a formal discrimination claim filed with a FEPA and/or with the Equal Employment Opportunity Commission (EEOC). It is important to note that a FEPA, in certain situations, may file a charge with the EEOC while continuing to investigate the charge if the alleged discrimination is a violation of both state and federal law. In certain situations, the EEOC may also file a charge with a FEPA while continuing to investigate the charge if the alleged discrimination is a violation of both state and federal law.

Complainant: A complainant or charging party is an individual that claims that he or she has been a victim of an act that is considered discrimination by law.

Respondent: A respondent is the individual or party that is accused of committing an act that is considered discrimination by law.

Remedy: A remedy, also referred to as a relief, is the specific way in which an individual or organization attempts to relieve or "remedy" the effects of unlawful discrimination. In other words, a remedy is the specific amount of money that an individual or organization has to pay; or the specific action that an individual or organization has to take in order to rectify the effects that the unlawful discrimination has had upon the complainant.

Back Pay: Back pay refers to a type of remedy in which an individual or organization must pay the complainant an amount equal to what the complainant would have earned if he or she continued working for the individual or organization.

Front Pay: Front pay refers to a type of remedy in which an individual or organization must pay the complainant an amount equal to the future pay that the complainant would earn if the complainant returned to the organization.

Employee Communication Strategy: An employee communication strategy is a method that an organization uses to encourage employees within an organization to communicate with each other and with members of management. Usually, an employee communication strategy refers to a specific communication medium that employees and managers can use to exchange important information. The specific employee communication strategy that an organization should use depends on a variety of different factors including the size of the organization, the importance of the information and other similar factors.

Employee Involvement Strategy: An employee involvement strategy is a method that an organization uses to encourage employees within an organization to become involved in the operations of the organization. Usually, an employee involvement strategy refers to a specific program an organization can use or a specific action that an organization can take to allow an individual more control over the organization's decision-making.

Delegating Authority: Delegating authority refers to an employee involvement strategy in which an organization grants an individual the power to make decisions related to his or her position. This strategy specifically allows an individual to become more involved in the organization by allowing the individual to make certain decisions without having to receive permission.

Employee Surveys: An employee survey, also known as a climate survey, is an employee involvement strategy in which an organization gathers information about the priorities and concerns of the organizations' employees by having each employee fill out and submit a form.

- 112 -

Suggestion Programs: A suggestion program is an employee involvement strategy in which an organization gathers ideas for how to handle the concerns of the organization's employees and/or ideas for how to control or eliminate problems within the organization by allowing employees to submit anonymous ideas. Suggestion programs usually use suggestion boxes, voice mail and other similar systems.

Committee: A committee, in this context, is a group of employees within an organization that work together in order to make decisions related to a particular concern of the organization or activity within the organization. Employees may be assigned to a committee temporarily or permanently depending on the specific concern or activity that the committee is designed to handle.

Employee-Management Committee: An Employee-Management committee, also referred to as an employee participation group, is a group of employees that work with the supervisors and managers of the organization to make decisions related to a particular concern of the organization or activity within the organization. Employees, supervisors and managers may be assigned to an employment-management committee temporarily or permanently depending on the specific concern or activity that the committee is designed to handle.

Task Force: A task force is a group of employees that work together in order to determine the cause of a particular problem and ultimately identify a solution to the problem. Employees are usually only assigned to a task force until the cause of a particular problem is identified and/or solved.

Brown-bag Lunch Program: A brown-bag lunch program is an employee involvement strategy in which an organization organizes an informal meeting to discuss various organizational concerns and issues. Brown-bag lunches are usually organized to take place while employees are having lunch and allow managers and employees to discuss various issues and concerns in a more relaxed setting.

Department Meetings: A department meeting is a formal gathering in which the employees, supervisors and managers of a particular department within the organization discuss the various concerns and issues affecting that particular department. Department meetings usually take place on a regular basis.

Town hall Meetings: Town hall meetings, also known as all-hands staff meetings, are formal meetings in which all of the employees, supervisors and managers within an organization attend a formal assembly to distribute important information about the organization. Town hall meetings are usually conducted in a similar fashion to a large lecture and may or may not allow for effective two-way communication.

Compressed Work Weeks: A compressed workweek is a flexible scheduling method in which employees are allowed to work several long shifts in a row so the employee will receive an additional day or an additional two days off each week or every other week. In other words, a compressed workweek for a full-time employee may consist of four 10-hour days, three 12-hour days or five 9-hour days during one week and only four 9-hour days during the following week.

Flextime: Flextime is a flexible scheduling method in which employees are allowed to set their own hours as long as they report for work for a certain number of hours a week and/or report during certain required time periods.

Part-time Scheduling: Part-time scheduling is a flexible scheduling method in which employees are allowed to work shorter hours and/or fewer hours a week.

Featherbedding: Featherbedding refers to an unfair labor practice identified by the Labor Management Relations Act in which a union requires an employer to keep paying employees that are in positions that are no longer necessary. Featherbedding usually occurs if a new technique or new technological advancement eliminates the need for a particular position within an organization.

Hot cargo agreement: A hot cargo agreement is a verbal or written contract that guarantees that an employer will not trade or engage in business activities with a particular individual or organization. Hot cargo agreements are identified as unfair by the Labor Management Relations Act and are usually the result of a union's desire to prevent an employer from purchasing goods or services from nonunion workers.

Secondary Boycott: A secondary boycott is a situation in which a union encourages individuals outside the union to stop trading or engaging in business activities with a particular organization. Secondary boycotts are identified as unfair by the Labor Management Relations Act.

Jurisdictional Strike: A jurisdictional strike refers to a situation in which employees refuse to work in order to convince an employer to distribute or redistribute work to union workers instead of nonunion workers. Jurisdictional strikes are considered to be an unfair labor practice and are therefore illegal.

Sit-down Strike: A sit-down strike refers to a situation in which employees refuse to work, but also refuse to leave the worksite owned and/or operated by the employer. Sit-down strikes are prohibited by the National Labor Relations Board.

Wildcat Strike: A wildcat strike refers to a situation in which employees refuse to work even though they are working under a contract with a no-strike clause. Wildcat strikes are considered to be an unfair labor practice and are therefore illegal.

Work Slowdown: A work slowdown refers to a situation in which employees do not actually stop working, but instead deliberately work more slowly so the organization continues functioning, but not effectively. Work slowdowns are also prohibited by the National Labor Relations Board.

Risk Management

Risk and return

In order for an organization to make an educated decision regarding a particular investment or business venture it is essential for that organization to consider the potential risk and the potential return associated with each specific investment or venture. The potential risk of an investment or venture is a measurement of the likelihood that the undertaking will offer some sort of return to the organization versus the likelihood that the investment or venture will fail and the organization will lose any resources that it has devoted to that particular undertaking. The potential return of an investment or venture is a measurement of how much monetary value can be achieved from a particular undertaking. It is extremely important for an organization to be able to assess both the risk and return of each specific investment or venture, as the higher the potential risk associated with a particular undertaking, the higher the potential return needs to be for that particular undertaking to be worthwhile.

ERM

Enterprise risk management (ERM) refers to a variety of different techniques that an organization can use to identify and minimize the effects of any risks that may prevent the organization from achieving its objectives. In other words, enterprise risk management is the process by which an organization identifies risks that may pose a threat to the organization and then handles those risks by attempting to eliminate them or reduce their ability to affect the organization. The process of enterprise risk management usually takes place after the organization has identified threats or opportunities related to a particular objective from a SWOT or PEST analysis. Once the threat or opportunity is identified, the organization then attempts to determine the level of risk associated with the threat or opportunity by assessing the likelihood that the risk will affect the organization and by attempting to determine the potential effect that the risk will have if it does affect the organization. The organization can then attempt to determine the appropriate response based on the level of risk associated with the threat or opportunity.

Managing risk effectively

It is important for an HR professional to be able to manage risk effectively because, in most cases, a great deal of the organization's financial risk will be related to the organization's human resources. There are a variety of different risks that an organization may have to deal with at some point, but some of the most costly risks that an organization will usually have to handle are related to liability and other similar legal concerns. These concerns include risks such as the organization being held liable for the unethical, illegal, or inappropriate actions of its employees, the organization being fined for not filling out and/or filing government forms correctly and other similar financial risks. Since many of these risks can be controlled or almost eliminated through careful monitoring and intelligent risk management, it is essential for an HR professional to be able to identify risks as they appear and to find ways to reduce the chance that those risks will affect the organization.

Identifying potential risks

There are a variety of methods that an HR professional can use to identify potential risks to the organization. The most common method is known as an HR audit. An HR audit usually consists of a checklist, survey or other similar type of communication that is designed to assess whether a particular employee or department actually understands and is adhering to the policies, procedures and regulations set by the organization. In addition to making sure that each employee is adhering to the policies and procedures of the organization, an HR audit is also usually designed to make sure that each employee is adhering to all of the laws and regulations set by the local, state and federal government. The exact format used for an HR audit will often vary from audit to audit, as each audit can be designed to identify a wide range of various risks to the organization or to make sure that a specific risk, such as fines associated with a newly passed law regarding requirements for the sale of certain products, can be avoided.

OSHA

There are a series of record keeping and reporting actions that an employer must take in order to comply with the regulations established by the Occupational Safety and Health Administration (OSHA). First, any employer covered by the record keeping regulations established by OSHA must record and keep information on file about any work-related injury or illness. Second, any employer covered by these regulations must keep an accident report log that includes information that may be provided to an employee or an employee representative upon request. Third, any employer covered by these regulations must file an OSHA report for any accident that results in the death of an employee or the hospitalization of at least three employees within eight hours of the accident. Finally, employers are required to allow employees to make reports to OSHA offices regarding OSHA violations without fear of retaliation. The record keeping regulations established by OSHA apply to any employer with more than 10 employees unless that employer is in an industry that is specifically identified as "low-risk."

Injury situations
An employer is not required to record any injury or illness that is not work-related, so it is important for an employer to be aware of the specific situations in which an injury or illness is non-work-related. An incident should be considered non-work-related if the illness or injury became apparent in the workplace, but the employee was not in the workplace to perform work, the employee's illness or injury is the result of conditions or activities outside of the workplace or the employee was performing personal activities at the workplace before or after his or her scheduled hours. An incident should also be considered non-work-related if the illness or injury occurred because the individual was in a motor vehicle accident on company property during a commute to or from work, if the illness or injury occurred as a result of eating food or drinking beverages prepared by the employee, if the illness or injury occurred as a result of medication that the individual was taking for a non-work-related illness or if the illness or injury was deliberately self-inflicted.

Regulations
There are a series of posting and training actions that an employer must take to comply with the regulations established by the Occupational Safety and Health (OSH) Act. First, any employer covered by the OSH Act must inform the employees of the organization of the rights and regulations established by Occupational Safety and Health Administration (OSHA) and the specific health and safety standards that apply to the employees of the organization. Second, any employer covered by the OSH Act must train employees to recognize and use the specific procedures that must be followed for a particular work environment to remain safe. Third, any employer covered by the OSH Act must post warning signs identifying potential hazards as required by OSHA and post an OSHA poster in a location that is visible to all employees.

Finally, any employer covered by the OSH Act must train employees to use safety equipment and train employees to use tools and equipment in the safest way possible.

Rights to employers

In addition to establishing a series of regulations that employers are required to follow, the Occupational Safety and Health (OSH) Act grants several specific rights to employers. First, the OSH Act specifically allows an employer the right to influence health and safety standards by writing to the Occupational Safety and Health Administration (OSHA) Standard Advisory Council or appearing at a hearing related to a specific standard or set of standards. Second, the OSH act specifically allows an employer to obtain information regarding whether a particular substance used in the workplace is toxic or not by contacting the National Institute of Occupational Safety and Health. The OSH act specifically establishes that an employer that is covered by the OSH Act may request a permanent or temporary waiver if it is impossible for the employer to meet OSHA standards in a specific situation. Third, the OSH Act grants employees the right to receive copies of records related to an individual's past injuries, illnesses, treatment and/or the individual's exposure to potentially harmful substances. Fourth, the OSH Act grants employees the right to view OSHA citations and other records related to the safety and health conditions within a particular workplace. Finally, the OSH Act grants employees the right to file a complaint against an employer with OSHA if the employer discriminates against an employee because he or she took advantage of a right granted by the OSH act.

OSHA investigations

In certain situations, the Occupational Safety and Health Administration (OSHA) may decide that it is necessary to conduct an on-site investigation into the working conditions of a particular worksite. These investigations are usually unannounced, but each investigation will follow a set of specific procedures established by OSHA, which an employer or HR professional should keep in mind. First, a trained investigator from OSHA known as a Compliance Safety and Health Officer (CSHO) will travel to the worksite and inform the employer or a member of the employer's staff that he or she has come to perform an investigation of the worksite. Once the employer has verified that the CSHO's credentials are in order, the CSHO will inform the organization's management of exactly what is being investigated at the worksite and why the investigation is taking place at an opening conference. The CSHO will then tour the facilities with a member of management and usually with an employee. Once the CSHO has completed his or her tour, the CSHO will inform the employer of any violations at a closing conference.

Investigation priority system

In certain situations, the Occupational Safety and Health Administration (OSHA) may decide that it is necessary to conduct an investigation into the working conditions of a particular worksite. However, the number of investigations that OSHA can conduct is relatively limited as OSHA only has a limited number of Compliance Safety and Health Officers (CSHO) available at any given time. As a result, OSHA uses a priority system to identify which worksites should be investigated first based on the level of danger associated with the worksite. This priority system includes five levels and each priority level represents a certain amount of danger associated with the worksite. The five levels of the priority system from lowest priority to highest priority are follow-up inspections, planned or programmed high-hazard inspections, inspections resulting from employee complaints, inspections resulting from catastrophes and fatal accidents and inspections resulting from imminent danger.

Lowest priority levels

The OSHA investigation priority system consists of five levels. The three lowest priority levels include follow-up inspections, planned or programmed high-hazard inspections and employee complaints. Follow-up investigations refer to any investigation conducted by a Compliance Safety and Health Officer (CSHO) to verify that an employer has taken action to eliminate any health or safety violations that the CSHO previously identified. Follow-up investigations are considered to be the fifth priority level, which is the lowest priority assigned by OSHA. A planned or programmed high-hazard inspection is an investigation that is scheduled for a particular worksite because the worksite is involved in an industry that has been identified as extremely dangerous. These investigations are considered to be the fourth priority level, which is the second lowest priority assigned by OSHA. Investigations that result from an employee complaint include any situation in which OSHA has received a specific complaint from an employee about unsafe or unhealthy working conditions and that employee has requested an investigation. These investigations are considered to be the third priority level, which is the mid-level priority.

Highest priority levels

The OSHA investigation priority system consists of five levels. The two highest priority levels are the catastrophes and fatal accidents level and the imminent danger level. Investigations that result from catastrophes and fatal accidents refer to any investigation that is required because at least 3 employees have been hospitalized due to an accident at a worksite or at least one employee has died from an accident at a worksite. These investigations are considered to be the second priority level and are therefore, given the second highest priority. Investigations that result from imminent danger refer to any investigation that is required because it is likely that an individual will die or be seriously injured in the near future due to the working conditions of a particular worksite. Investigations at the imminent danger level are assigned the highest priority by OSHA and are usually investigated first.

Off-site OSHA investigation

In certain situations, the Occupational Health and Safety Administration (OSHA) may decide that it is necessary to conduct an off-site investigation into the working conditions of a particular worksite. OSHA may conduct an off-site investigation if the employees at a worksite do not appear to be in imminent danger of harm due to the health and safety violations that may be occurring at a worksite, the worksite is not related to an industry that is identified as high risk or already scheduled for an investigation, the employer does not have a history of any serious violations and the employer has complied with any OSHA requests made prior to the complaint or report. If OSHA determines that an off-site investigation is necessary, but an on-site investigation is not, OSHA will contact the employer by phone and identify the specific violation(s) that have been reported. Once the employer has been contacted, the employer has five days to mail or fax a written description of any health and safety issues that have been identified and how the organization plans to address those issues.

Violations: There are six different types of violations that an OSHA investigation can identify. These are de-minimus, other-than-serious, serious, failure to abate, repeat, and willful. A de-minimus violation is a violation of a standard that is not currently affecting the health or safety of the employees. A violation identified as other-than-serious is a violation of a standard that is affecting the health and safety of the employees, but there is no imminent danger of harm. A violation identified as serious is a violation of a standard in which there is imminent danger that an employee may be seriously injured or even killed. A violation identified as a failure to abate will be issued if the employer continues to violate a specific standard past the abatement date established by a previous OSHA investigation. A violation will be identified as a repeat violation if the

- 118 -

employer continues to violate a standard that is the same or similar as a violation identified by a previous OSHA investigation. Finally, a willful violation will be issued if the employer has intentionally violated or ignored OSHA standards.

Penalties: There are six different types of violations that an OSHA investigation can identify. Each type of violation has a different penalty range associated with it. In the case of a de-minimus violation, the employer will be informed of the violation, but will not be cited for the violation. In the case of other-than serious or serious violations, the employer will receive a citation and may have to pay fines up to $7,000 per violation. In the case of a failure-to-abate violation, the employer will receive a citation and may have to pay fines up to $7,000 per day for each day that the violation continues after the abatement date. In the case of a repeat violation, the employer will receive a citation and may have to pay fines up to $70,000 per violation. Finally, in the case of a willful violation, the employer will receive a citation and may have to pay fines of $5,000 - $70,000 and may be subject to additional penalties and jail time if an employee death resulted from the violation.

OSHA standards

General Duty Standard: The general duty standard is designed to hold employers responsible for the health and safety of their employees. This standard establishes the foundation for all of the other health and safety standards established by OSHA, as it requires employers to take action to eliminate safety and health hazards from the workplace, requires employees to adhere to all of the rules and standards that apply to employees and requires employers to adhere to all of the rules, regulations and standards that apply to their particular organization.

Hazard Communication Standard: The hazard communication standard, also known as the employee right-to-know standard, is designed to make sure that employees are informed about dangerous chemicals in the workplace. This standard requires employers to create a written Hazard Communication Program that informs employees of the presence of dangerous substances, the properties of the substance, the dangers associated with the substance and how to avoid the dangers associated with the substance.

Emergency Action Plan Standard: The emergency action plan standard is designed to make sure that there is a set procedure in place that employees should follow in order to handle and/or escape a fire or other similar emergency at the worksite. This standard establishes that an employer should create an emergency action plan with information such as how employees will escape the building, how the employer will make sure that all employees have left the building, what shutdown or emergency procedures must be followed to ensure that additional problems will not be caused by the emergency, who is responsible for shutting down systems or carrying out emergency procedures and other similar information. All employers are encouraged to design emergency action plans, but only employers in certain industries are legally required by OSHA to adhere to this standard.

Exit Route Standard: The exit route standard is designed to make sure that there is actually a clear path that an employee can use to escape a building or worksite in an emergency and requires that employers make sure that each escape route meets certain OSHA requirements.

Specifications for Accident Prevention Signs and Tags : Specifications for Accident Prevention Signs and Tags are designed to make sure that hazards in the workplace are appropriately marked. This standard requires employers to use color-coded signs that indicate the level of danger associated with a hazard by associating different danger levels with the color and size of the sign and indicate the type of danger by the design on the sign.

Fire Prevention Plan Standard: The Fire Prevention Plan standard is designed to make sure that there is a set procedure in place that employees should follow in order to prevent fires at the worksite. This standard establishes that an employer should create a fire prevention plan that identifies fire hazards, procedures for avoiding fire hazards, fire prevention methods related to fire hazards present in the workplace and actions employees should take to minimize the risk to themselves and others in the case of a fire. All employers are strongly encouraged to design fire prevention plans, but only employers in certain industries are legally required to adhere to this standard.

Occupational Noise Exposure Standard: The Occupational Noise Exposure standard is designed to protect employees from the stress and hearing damage that may result from loud sounds in the workplace. This standard requires employers to measure the amount of noise in a workplace using specific procedures. If the noise level present in a particular workplace is higher than the maximum acceptable level established by OSHA, this standard requires an employer to take action to preserve and monitor the hearing of the organization's employees.

Personal Protective Equipment Standard: The Personal Protective Equipment standard is designed to make sure that employees have access to the equipment necessary to protect themselves from hazardous substances, materials and environments. This standard requires employers to supply and maintain safety equipment, referred to as personal protective equipment, which employees can use to protect themselves from radiation, chemical burns, electric shocks and any other similar hazards present in the workplace.

Selection and Use of Electrical Work Practices Standard: The Selection and Use of Electrical Work Practices standard requires employers to provide training and/or equipment that will help protect employees from electrical shock. This standard applies to employees that work with electrical systems.

Sanitation Standard: The Sanitation standard is designed to make sure that each employee is working in as healthy a work environment as possible. This standard specifically requires an employer to maintain a work environment that is as clean and sanitary as possible for the industry in which the employee is working.

Medical Services and First Aid Standard: The Medical Services and First Aid standard is designed to make sure that employees have access to immediate medical attention in case of an emergency. This standard requires an employer to provide first aid supplies, make sure that first aid supplies are readily accessible and have personnel trained in basic first aid present at the worksite. The specific supplies, personnel and other requirements that a specific employer must maintain at the worksite to adhere to this standard depends on the specific industry that the employer is a part of and the type of work being performed at the worksite.

Lockout/Tagout Standard: The Lockout/Tagout standard, also known as the control of hazardous energy standard, is designed to protect employees from machinery that may operate or release hazardous substances without warning. This standard requires any employer with machinery that starts and/or stops operating automatically and/or employers with machinery that may discharge electricity, hazardous fluids or cause other similar hazards without warning to use a safety device that will prohibit the machine from operating when an employee is working on or near the machine.

Machine Guarding Standard: The Machine Guarding standard, also known as the general requirements for all machines, is designed to protect employees from dangerous machinery. This standard requires any employer working with tools identified as potentially hazardous, such as saws or welding tools to use guards or electronic safety devices that will prevent or reduce the chance that the tool or equipment will injure an individual.

Blood-borne Pathogens Standard: The Blood-borne Pathogens standard is designed to help protect employees that handle bodily fluids in the workplace from infectious diseases. This standard requires employers to create a written exposure control plan that identifies illnesses that employees may be exposed to in the workplace, identifies procedures that employees should follow to limit or eliminate their exposure to any illnesses that may be present in the workplace, identifies procedures that should be followed if an employee is exposed to an infectious disease and other similar information. This standard also requires employers to keep a log of each incident in which an employee is exposed to an infectious disease.

Permit-required Confined Spaces Standard: The Permit-required Confined Spaces standard is designed to protect employees from entering dangerous environments in which an individual may find it difficult or impossible to escape. This standard requires employers to have a special permit if employees must enter spaces in which they may become trapped, injured and/or killed and requires employers to test the confined/dangerous space to make sure that it is safe prior to an employee entering the space.

Respirator Standard: The Respirator standard is designed to help protect employees that work in environments with extremely poor air quality or in environments with airborne contaminants. This standard requires employers to provide respirator equipment to any employee that can reasonably be assumed at risk of being injured, becoming ill or dying from the condition of the air in the area at which the individual works.

Walking/Working Surfaces Standard: The Walking/Working Surfaces standard is designed to help protect employees from physical hazards at a worksite that may lead to accidents and injuries in the workplace. This standard requires employers to make sure that any surface which employees need to walk on or work on such as floors, stairs, ladders, and other similar surfaces are designed in as safe a fashion as possible and that each surface is appropriately maintained to ensure that employees are unlikely to trip or fall.

Important legislation

OSH Act

The Occupational Safety and Health (OSH) Act, which was passed in 1970, is designed to protect employees from having to work in work environments that are unsafe and/or unhealthy. This act specifically establishes a government system for setting the health and safety standards that an employer is legally required to meet in order for a work environment to be considered safe and healthy. This act also establishes that it is the responsibility of the employer to ensure that each employee is working in an environment in which there are no apparent hazards that may lead to the employee's injury or death. In addition to these regulations that apply to employers, this act also establishes specific regulations regarding the appropriate practices, procedures and standards that employees must use or meet in order to safeguard their own health and safety.

MSH Act

The Mine Safety and Health (MSH) Act, which was passed in 1977, is designed to protect mine workers from unsafe and/or unhealthy working conditions. This act specifically requires employers in the mining industry to follow a set of specific health and safety standards to ensure that employees are working in the safest environment possible. This act also requires employers in the mining industry to submit to mandatory inspections as requested by the Mine Safety and Health Administration (MSHA) and requires that all surface mines receive at least two inspections from the MSHA each year and each underground mine receive at least four inspections from the MSHA each year. This act applies to all mines within the United States and miners and mine operators are required to adhere to the standards established by the MSHA and the MSH Act.

Drug-Free Workplace Act

The Drug-Free Workplace Act, which was passed in 1988, is designed to prevent drug use in the workplace and to prevent accidents that may occur from employees working under the influence of illegal substances in organizations that receive federal funding or federal contracts. This act specifically requires each employer to establish a drug-free policy that prohibits employees from using, distributing, manufacturing or being in possession of drugs in the workplace or working under the influence of controlled substances. Each employer must also notify employees in writing that these actions are prohibited and notify employees of the type of disciplinary and/or legal action that will be taken if an individual violates the employer's drug-free policy. This act also specifically requires employers to establish a drug-free awareness program that will inform employees of the problems that workplace drug use can cause and identify places that employees may seek help. This act applies to any individual or organization that receives federal funding and any federal contractor with at least $100,000 in contracts per year.

Needlestick Safety and Prevention Act

The Needlestick Safety and Prevention Act, which was passed in 2000, is designed to help protect the safety of healthcare workers. This act requires an employer in an industry that handles needles or other sharp equipment to identify and use safe alternatives to needles or other sharp devices or identify and use the safest possible needle devices available. This act also requires an employer to keep a detailed injury log of any employee injury and/or illness that is caused by a needle or sharp device. In addition to these regulations, this act also requires an employer to include employees that will actually be using the needles or sharp devices in the organization's safe needle or sharp identification and decision-making process.

Sarbanes-Oxley Act

The Sarbanes-Oxley Act, which was passed in 2002, is designed to hold the senior executives of an organization responsible for any inappropriate or questionable financial practices. This act specifically holds the senior executives of an organization responsible for any sort of corporate accounting fraud, record tampering or any other similar action taken by a member of the organization's management if that action conceals or alters the financial information that the organization is legally required to provide to the organization's shareholders and/or the Security Exchange Commission. In addition to these anti-fraud regulations, this act also establishes higher penalties associated with white-collar crimes and requires employers to provide detailed financial reports and disclosures to the SEC at regular intervals and whenever there is a significant change in the financial status of the organization.

Risk assessment

Risk assessment is a process in which an organization attempts to identify each factor that may have an adverse effect on the organization, how likely it is for each factor to have an adverse effect on the organization and the costs that the organization may be faced with if that factor actually effects the organization. In other words, a risk assessment is an evaluation that an organization can perform to identify factors that may pose a risk to the organization and identify exactly how much risk is associated with each factor. The amount of risk associated with a particular factor is usually measured in terms of the financial cost that the organization will have to pay if an adverse effect occurs and the probability that the adverse effect will actually occur in the future.

MSDS

A material safety data sheet (MSDS) is a written document that describes a particular chemical substance, the types of hazards associated with the substance and how an individual should protect themselves from the hazards associated with the substance. These data sheets specifically include information such as the ingredients that make up the substance, whether the substance is considered stable or unstable, the substance's chemical properties, such as how it reacts to temperature or pressure, other substances that the substance may react violently with and the ability of the chemical to enter the body through contact, ingestion or inhalation. Material safety data sheets are ultimately designed to inform employees of the dangers associated with a particular substance and how to avoid those dangers. This is important because employees that are unaware of the dangers associated with a particular substance are much more likely to be adversely affected by the substance. As a result, employers are legally required to provide a material safety data sheet for each chemical present in the workplace.

Stress

The three main types of stress that an individual may experience are emotional stress, mental stress, and physical stress. Emotional stress is a type of stress in which an individual's mood, emotions and ability to socially interact are affected by a perceived or real threat in the individual's environment. Mental stress is a type of stress in which an individual's ability to think clearly, an individual's memory and an individual's ability to focus are affected by a perceived or real threat in the individual's environment. Physical stress is a type of stress in which an individual's body begins to lose its ability to function normally and the individual becomes more likely to become physically ill due to a perceived or real threat in the individual's environment.

Signs of extreme stress
The specific signs that indicate a particular individual is suffering from extreme stress can vary from person to person, as stress affects each person differently. There are a variety of common signs and symptoms that may indicate that an individual is suffering from the effects of extreme stress. Signs and symptoms that may indicate that an individual is suffering from extreme emotional stress include anxiety, panic attacks, mood swings, depression, personality changes and other similar symptoms. Signs and symptoms that may indicate that an individual is suffering from extreme mental stress include an inability to focus, an inability to recall information, an inability to make decisions, an inability to think clearly, excessive procrastination and other similar symptoms. Signs and symptoms that may indicate that an individual is suffering from extreme

physical stress may include headaches, sweating, raised heart rate, teeth grinding, unexplained fatigue, frequent illness and a variety of other similar symptoms.

<u>NIOSH contributing factors</u>
The National Institute of Occupational Safety and Health (NIOSH) recognizes six factors that may contribute to stress in the workplace. These include career concerns, environmental conditions, interpersonal relationships, management style, task design and work roles. Career concerns include any threat to an individual's employment or an individual's ability to advance within an organization. Environmental conditions refer to any physical workplace condition that may make it difficult for an individual to function normally such as extreme heat, extreme cold, loud noises, bright light and other similar conditions. Interpersonal relationships include any threat to an individual's ability to socially interact or receive emotional support. Management style factors include any threat that causes an individual to feel uninvolved in the organization, uninformed regarding important information or that the individual's needs are unrecognized by the organization. Task design factors include any task, practice or procedure that regularly requires an individual to perform unusual, unpleasant, meaningless or labor-intensive work. Factors related to work roles include any threat that may cause an individual to question his or her place within the organization.

Employee assistance program

Employee assistance programs are programs that are designed to help employees cope with or address personal problems that may or may not be affecting their work. These assistance programs can be designed to handle a variety of different issues including family problems, financial issues, legal issues, substance abuse problems, stress and a variety of other similar problems. Many organizations use employee assistance programs because they allow an organization to help employees cope with issues that are not directly related to their work. This is important because external issues or internal issues that are not directly related to an employee's work may have a large effect on the individual's ability to perform as expected. As a result, it is important for an organization to make sure that each employee has access to the resources that are necessary for an individual to handle personal problems in order for the individual to continue to perform the tasks associated with his or her position in a safe and effective manner.

Substance abuse program

Substance abuse programs are programs that are designed to inform employees about the problems associated with substance abuse, encourage employees to avoid substance abuse and/or help employees that have a drug problem. Many organizations use substance abuse programs because they allow an organization to help make sure that employees are not working under the influence of illegal substances. This is important because employees that use illegal substances at the workplace or frequently come to work under the influence of illegal substances are not only less likely to perform as expected, but are also much more likely to cause accidents or safety issues. As a result, these programs are primarily designed to prevent employees from using illegal drugs so that the organization can ensure that employees are performing as effectively and as safely as possible.

U.S. Department of Labor's Working Partners for an Alcohol and Drug-free Workplace initiative

The U.S. Department of Labor's Working Partners for an Alcohol and Drug-free Workplace initiative identifies five main elements that are necessary for an effective substance abuse program. These elements include a workplace substance abuse policy, drug tests, management/supervisor training, employee substance abuse education, and employee assistance programs. The workplace substance abuse policy is a written document that informs employees that substance abuse is strictly prohibited in the workplace and that disciplinary action will be taken against employees that violate the substance abuse policy. The drug tests included in the program should include tests that the organization can regularly perform to verify that employees are not taking illegal substances. The management/supervisor training included in the program should include activities related to informing management of the substance abuse policy and how to enforce that policy. The employee substance abuse education included in the program should include activities related to informing employees of the substance abuse policy and activities that discuss why employees should avoid substance abuse. Finally, the employee assistance program should specifically offer aid to employees with substance abuse problems.

Drug test programs

There are a variety of different drug test programs that an organization can establish. Some of the most commonly used drug test programs include pre-employment drug screening, pre-promotion drug screening, random drug testing and reasonable cause testing. In a pre-employment drug-screening program, each new employee hired by an organization receives a drug test prior to assuming his or her new position. In a pre-promotion screening program any employee accepting a higher position in the organization must receive a drug test prior to assuming his or her new position. In a random drug testing program the organization will test everyone in a specific team, department, or every employee within the entire organization without any advanced warning. In a reasonable cause testing program any employee suspected of using illegal substances in the workplace or suspected of working under the influence of illegal substances will receive a drug test to verify or refute the suspicions of the employee's supervisors and or managers.

Business continuity planning

Business continuity planning is a process in which an organization attempts to make sure that the organization will be able to continue functioning, even after an emergency. This type of planning is important because there are a large number of different types of emergencies that an organization can face and each one may impact the ability of the organization to continue functioning normally. As a result, business continuity planning is a process that organizations use to create a plan or group of plans that will help the organization return to normal after a natural disaster or other similar emergency occurs. The process of business continuity planning usually begins with an organization conducting a threat assessment such as a SWOT analysis. Once the organization has identified the threats that exist, the organization can rank those threats based on the risk associated with each threat. Finally, the organization can create a plan or group of plans that establish a system that the organization can use to recover from emergencies, which the organization can continually update as threats to the organization change.

Emergency response plans

There is a variety of different information that should be included in an emergency response plan. The specific information included in an emergency response plan can vary greatly from organization to organization. There is certain information that should be included in every organization's emergency response plan. All emergency response plans should identify the records and resources that are essential to the organization, identify the individuals responsible for protecting those records and resources and describe the procedures that individuals should follow in order to safeguard the records and resources that are essential for the organization to continue functioning. Emergency response plans must also establish a system that the organization can use to continue communicating with vendors and the public during and after an emergency.

Security threats

There are a variety of different security issues that an organization may have to address at some point. Some of the more common security threats that an organization may have to handle include natural disasters, technological issues, theft and violent acts. Natural disasters include any naturally occurring event that may pose a threat to an organization, such as earthquakes, fires, floods, hurricanes, lightning strikes, tornadoes and any other similar natural disaster that may pose a threat to an organization's resources. Technological issues include any problems related to modern equipment or technological systems that may pose a threat to an organization such as computer viruses, identify theft and catastrophic system failure. Theft includes any action in which the resources of the organization are illegally seized by an individual within the organization or by an individual outside the organization. Violent acts include any situation in which an individual is harmed by another individual in the workplace or an individual inside the workplace is harmed by an individual or group outside the workplace, such as in the case of a terrorist attack.

Emergency action plan

There is a variety of different information that should be included in an emergency action plan. The specific information included in an emergency action plan will vary from organization to organization. However, there is certain information that should be included in every organization's emergency action plan. All emergency action plans should explain the alarm system that will be used to inform the employees and other individuals at the worksite that they need to evacuate, should include in-depth exit route plans that describe which routes employees should take to escape the building and should include in-depth plans that describe what actions employees should take before evacuating such as shutting down equipment, closing doors, etc. All emergency action plans should also include detailed systems for handling different types of emergencies and a system that can be used to verify that all employees have escaped the worksite.

Fire prevention plan

There is a variety of different information that should be included in a fire prevention plan. The specific information included in a fire prevention plan will vary from organization to organization. However, there is certain information that should be included in every organization's fire prevention plan. All fire prevention plans should provide detailed descriptions of the specific areas in which employees can find fire extinguishers and other similar fire prevention equipment, detailed descriptions of the types of fire hazards present in the workplace and detailed descriptions of the appropriate procedures that should be followed to avoid these fire hazards. Fire prevention plans should also provide detailed descriptions of any hazardous waste that may be a fire hazard and the appropriate way to dispose or store hazardous waste in order to avoid a fire.

Disaster recovery plan

There is a variety of different information that should be included in a disaster recovery plan. The specific information included in a disaster recovery plan can vary greatly from organization to organization, but there is certain information that should be included in every organization's disaster recovery plan. All disaster recovery plans should identify specific locations or equipment that the organization may be able to use temporarily to continue functioning immediately after an emergency, identify agencies and personnel that may be able to help the organization continue functioning immediately after an emergency and establish a set of procedures that the organization can use to bring the personnel and equipment together after an emergency. Disaster recovery plans should also identify alternative sources that the organization can use to receive supplies or products if the emergency disabled the organization's normal supply chain.

Employee privacy policy

There is a wide range of different information that should be included in an employee privacy policy. The specific information included in a particular policy will vary from organization to organization. However, there is certain information that should be included in every organization's employee privacy policy. All employee privacy policies should inform employees that the organization may conduct monitoring activities and/or employee searches, identify the specific methods that the organization will use to monitor employees, identify the specific types of employee actions that will be monitored and identify the specific situations in which the organization may conduct a search of the employee's workspace and/or personal items. In addition, employee privacy policies should also establish the specific search procedures that the organization will use if it becomes necessary to conduct a search, establish the specific process that the organization will follow to investigate misconduct detected through employee monitoring and explain how information taken from employee monitoring will be used.

Investigating employee misconduct

The specific process that an organization should use to investigate employee misconduct can vary from organization to organization and may vary to from situation to situation. However, for most organizations the investigation process begins if the organization receives a complaint or if the organization determines that there is reasonable cause to investigate an employee's conduct. Once the organization has determined an investigation is necessary, the organization should identify exactly what is being investigated, what sort of evidence is needed to prove or disprove the misconduct, who should be interviewed during the investigation and identify which questions need to be asked in order to gather the necessary evidence. Next, the organization can interview the individual that made the complaint, interview the individual that the complaint has been made against and interview any other employees that may have information relevant to the investigation. Finally, once the organization has interviewed all of the individuals involved in a particular situation, the organization can come to a decision based on the information gathered during the investigation and take the appropriate action.

ELPI

Employment Practices Liability insurance (ELPI) is a risk management tool that an organization can use to share some of the financial risk associated with employee lawsuits. In other words, ELPI is a type of insurance that an organization can pay for to help protect itself against some of the legal costs that an organization may face if an employee brings a civil suit against the organization. ELPI can be an extremely useful tool for any organization, as there are a large number of costs that an organization will have to pay for if the organization is sued. In fact, there are many situations in which an employee may bring a lawsuit against an organization because the employee feels that his or her rights have been violated and the organization may end up paying a large amount in legal costs such as lawyer's fees and court fees even if the organization wins the suit. As a result, ELPI can be extremely useful as it helps cover some of the unexpected costs that may result from an employee's civil suit.

Important terms

Environmental Health Hazard: An environmental health hazard is a specific dangerous element in an employee's work environment that may have an adverse effect on an employee's health. In other words, an environmental health hazard usually refers to a specific condition, substance or other similar factor present at a worksite that may cause an employee to become injured or ill. Environmental health hazards are usually divided into three categories, which are biological health hazards, chemical health hazards and physical health hazards.

Biological Health Hazard: A biological health hazard is a specific activity, condition or contaminated object that exposes an employee to an infection or a disease. Biological health hazards include needle sticks, unsanitary procedures or conditions, contaminated food and other similar hazards that may expose an employee to an infectious disease

Physical health hazard: A physical health hazard is a condition, design flaw or unsafe object in an employee's work environment that may adversely affect an individual's health. Physical health hazards include extreme temperatures, poor ventilation, extreme physical stress, objects at the workplace that are not appropriately marked as dangerous and other similar physical hazards that may injure an individual or cause an individual to become ill.

Chemical health hazard: A chemical health hazard is a substance that an employee handles or that is present in the employee's work environment that may adversely affect an individual's health. Chemical health hazards include toxic chemicals, radioactive substances, substances that violently react under certain conditions, chemicals that studies have shown may cause cancer and other similar substances that may inure an individual or cause an individual to become ill.

Test

Practice Questions

1. Which of the following questions is not one of the questions that a human resources professional needs to address in a Human Management Capital Plan (HCMP) during strategic planning?
   a. Where have we come from?
   b. Where are we now?
   c. Where do we want to be?
   d. How will we get there?
   e. How will we know when we have arrived?

2. Which of the following best describes an environmental scan that might occur during strategic planning?
   a. Reviewing policy and procedures for any non-compliance with environmental regulations
   b. Analyzing indoor conditions to ensure overall employee health
   c. Collecting details that will help the company project a goal for growth and development
   d. Using research and development techniques to create an effective business plan
   e. Collaborating with the Environmental Protection Agency (EPA) for improving the company's green standards

3. Why is an understanding of the legal process so valuable for the human resources professional?
   a. Human resources professionals are the ones responsible for contacting members of Congress in the event that legislation should be proposed
   b. The business world is increasingly involved with the legislative process, and the human resources professional is a company's outside contact for legislation
   c. Understanding the legislative process is essential for small businesses to become corporations
   d. Legislation influences the relationship between employers and employees, and the human resources professional is responsible for understanding this relationship
   e. Human resources professionals are expected to function as lobbyists to Congress should legislation need to be enacted

4. After several months of meetings, the owners of Pearson Fishing Service, an oilfield service company, have agreed on an idea affecting employee health benefits. They believe their concept should be submitted to become a congressional bill. Janice, who is their human resources professional, has participated extensively in the meetings, so the company owners ask her to advise them on the necessary steps to submit the idea. Which is the first step that must be taken for an idea to be presented as a bill to Congress?
   a. Submit the idea to the House of Representatives for review
   b. Submit the idea to a senator or representative from the congressional district
   c. Present the idea to a congressional committee for discussion
   d. Acquire signatures from a statewide petition in order to demonstrate the importance of the idea
   e. Present the idea to a congressional hearing to see if it passes review

5. Which of the following legislative acts do not provide protection for whistleblowers (employees who choose to speak out against corrupt business practice)?
   a. The Occupational Safety and Health Act
   b. The Foreign Corrupt Practices Act of 1977
   c. The Toxic Substances Control Act
   d. The Sarbanes-Oxley Act
   e. The Railroad Safety Act

6. Which of the following is not a step in the strategic planning process?
   a. Environmental scanning
   b. Formulating strategy
   c. Creating business plan
   d. Implementing strategy
   e. Making adjustments to strategy

7. Richard, who heads up a team within a large corporation's human resources department, is known for his laid-back style of management. For the most part, the team works well together and there are few problems with member interaction on the team. When a problem does arise, Richard's first impulse is to encourage the team members to work out the issue amongst themselves before he intervenes. As a result, Richard's leadership style could be described as which of the following?
   a. Democratic
   b. Coaching
   c. Transactional
   d. Transformation
   e. Laissez-faire

8. Standard human resource budget responsibilities for a company might include all of the following except:
   a. Performance increases
   b. Payroll taxes
   c. Travel expenses
   d. Repairs and maintenance
   e. Employee benefits

9. The Fair Labor Standards Act (FLSA) retains a certification of age for all employees for how long?
   a. 1 year
   b. 2 years
   c. 3 years
   d. 5 years
   e. Until employee termination

10. As of July 24, 2009, the federal minimum wage was established at $7.25 per hour. Grace Clothing, a successful line of retail clothing stores located in California, will be hiring 10 new workers at minimum wage with the option for commission. California has a statewide minimum wage of $8.00 per hour, so the company owners have contacted human resources manager Edwina regarding the disparity in minimum wage pay at the state and federal level. Which statement below best quotes the policy Edwina would cite to help Grace Clothing resolve the difference?

    a. Grace Clothing is required to pay employees the lowest minimum wage of any state in the country, which is $5.15

    b. When a federal minimum wage is lower than a state minimum wage, companies may use the federal minimum wage as their standard

    c. When a state minimum wage is higher than the federal minimum wage, the company is required to pay the state minimum over the federal minimum

    d. The size of Grace Clothing makes it exempt from minimum wage requirements, so the company has no obligation to follow either federal or state minimum wage

    e. The presence of commission means that Grace Clothing can lower the minimum wage that it pays workers because the commission payments compensate for the lower minimum pay

11. Which of the following best describes adverse impact in the selection of employees for a company?

    a. A selection rate among a protected class of more than 95% the selection rate of the highest group

    b. The negative impact of failing to diversify the selection rate among employees

    c. Any non-compliance with the rules pertaining to the Uniform Guidelines on Employee Selection Process

    d. A selection rate among a protected class of less than 80% the selection rate of the highest group

    e. Willful discrimination against a specific group when selecting new employees

12. Which of the following is not involved in the human resources professional's analysis of staffing needs?

    a. Create a list of necessary KSAs that will encourage company growth

    b. Develop a list of employees who might be ready for promotion

    c. Review the economic situation to consider any changes to the company's hiring policy

    d. Consider various hiring options for any open positions, as well as positions that will be open in the near future

    e. Review the results of past hiring decisions to increase the potential success of future decisions

13. Philippa the head of the marketing department of Caledonia Coffee Company is planning to post a position that will allow current employees of the company to apply before that position opens to the public. Because the posting will be internal (arranged in-house), the process will differ from that of a public posting. Philippa contacts the human resources department to find out which type of application would be best for an internal position. The best type of application for this situation would be which of the following?

    a. Short-form application

    b. Weighted employment application

    c. Long-form application

    d. Job-specific application

    e. No application is needed – interested employees should submit resumes instead

14. What are the human resources professional's primary role in assisting a department with conducting an effective interview?
    a. To offer any requested advice on preparing for and setting up interviews
    b. To choose the members of the prospective interview board
    c. To create the official list of questions that will be asked during the interview
    d. To conduct all interviews for prospective employees of the company
    e. To work with the interview board to select the right candidate for the position

15. During the course of an interview, Adrian notices that the candidate he is interviewing is wearing a religious symbol on a chain around his neck. Adrian wants to ask a question about the employee's religious affiliation. Which of the following questions would be appropriate, according to the equal opportunity laws?
    a. What church do you attend?
    b. Do you belong to any organizations that might be relevant to the position?
    c. I noticed the symbol around your neck – do you attend services regularly?
    d. Have you ever attended a religious service?
    e. What does the symbol that you're wearing around your neck represent?

16. Caspar is responsible for interviewing the candidates who have passed the first round of the application process for a new position at a large technology firm in Nevada. The first candidate that Caspar speaks to is a young woman with a strong resume and an accessible personality. Caspar is highly impressed and continues to remember the first candidate when he is interviewing the others. As a result, he rates the other candidates lower than the first, even though two of the other candidates have more experience than the first candidate and have even received several awards that she has not received. In conducting the interviews, Caspar has displayed which of the following types of interview bias?
    a. Cultural noise
    b. Halo effect
    c. Contrast
    d. Leniency
    e. Negative emphasis

17. Louisa is in the process of interviewing the prospective employees for an open position in the accounting department of a small publishing company. She has already interviewed several strong candidates, but she is looking forward to interviewing one of the candidates whose resume has struck her as showing significant potential. When this employee enters the room, however, it is obvious that he has not fully conquered his pre-interview nerves, and he stumbles through the first few questions. By the end of the interview, however, the candidate is doing well, responding articulately and living up to the potential indicated in his resume. Louisa, though, is unable to overcome her disappointment with the candidate's earlier nervousness and fails to see his improvement during the interview. Louisa is thus displayed by which of the following types of interview bias?
    a. Knowledge-of-predictor
    b. Stereotyping
    c. Recency
    d. Nonverbal bias
    e. First impression

18. The Uniform Guidelines on Employee Selection Process (UGESP) requires which two qualities in testing?
    a. Fairness and reliability
    b. Validity and disinterestedness
    c. Equality and fairness
    d. Reliability and validity
    e. Consideration and reliability

19. Why does the Uniform Guidelines on Employee Selection Process (UGESP) require these qualities in testing?
    a. To ensure the same results from all tests
    b. To avoid discrimination against protected classes
    c. To quantify the success rate for the company doing the testing
    d. To create a better standard for testing
    e. To prevent qualified candidates from being overlooked

20. The WARN Act was designed to do which of the following?
    a. Prevent massive lay-offs that disrupt the economy
    b. Provide new positions for employees that have been laid off
    c. Create government funding to support a struggling company
    d. Establish full severance pay for those who have been laid off
    e. Ensure rights for employees who have been laid off

21. Which of the following provides the best definition of organization development?
    a. Creating a mutual understanding of the values within an organization
    b. Discovering methods of strategic intervention to address problems within the organization
    c. Establishing means of employee participation in decisions that are made within organizations
    d. Creating a sense of balance between employers and their employees in a company
    e. Analyzing the various elements of an organization's makeup and reviewing opportunities for improvement

22. Which of the following is not a part of the four categories of intervention, as defined by Thomas Cummings and Christopher Worley in their book Organization Development and Change?
    a. Techno-structural
    b. Human resource management
    c. Change management
    d. Strategic
    e. Human process

23. The head of the administrative department for a major university has asked Raisa, a human resources professional at the school, for a team-building exercise that will benefit the administrative department. The administrative department is composed of employees who work closely together daily but often run into conflicts that indicate a clash of personalities. The department head hopes to find a team-building exercise that will improve the relationships among staff members in the department. Which of the following should Raisa recommend to the department head?
    a. A team obstacle course
    b. Role-playing situations
    c. Team scavenger hunts
    d. The Meyers-Briggs Type Indicator
    e. Real-life scenario re-creation

24. Which of the following elements is not a part of the ADDIE model of instructional design?
    a. Administration
    b. Design
    c. Development
    d. Implementation
    e. Evaluation

25. Eamon is a human resources professional for a large firm of attorneys, and he has been assigned the responsibility of developing an instructional method that is most suitable for the support staff at the firm. The support staff has been struggling with problem-solving issues, and Eamon has been instructed to utilize a training method that will allow the staff members to discuss problems and potential resolutions under the supervision of a third party expert. Which of the following instructional methods will be most effective for this situation?
    a. Vestibule
    b. Facilitation
    c. Demonstration
    d. Conference
    e. One-on-one

26. What is the purpose of a total rewards strategy?
    a. To plan for establishing salaries among employees
    b. To represent the employee brand as effectively as possible
    c. To assist in creating teamwork among employees
    d. To use budget for rewards in order to retain employees
    e. To recognize organizational changes as they occur

27. Which of the following is not a major factor in establishing compensation within an organization?
    a. IRS rules
    b. Employee salary history
    c. Conditions in the labor market
    d. Current economic situation
    e. Competition from other companies

28. All of the following are part of the Fair Labor Standards Act except:
   a. Minimum wage
   b. Exemption conditions for employees
   c. Work conditions for children under 18
   d. Overtime
   e. Federal service contracts

29. Which of the following best expresses the definition of benchmark positions?
   a. Common jobs within all organizations
   b. Evaluation of current jobs
   c. Review of market conditions for salaries
   d. Change in significant jobs in a company
   e. Review of value in positions within an organization

30. Arthur is an employee of a distribution company and is looking to request FMLA-approved leave for personal reasons. Arthur contacts Brad, a human resources professional at the company, to find out if he is eligible for this type of leave. Arthur has worked for the company for 9 months. What is the minimum period of time that an employee needs to work for an employer to request leave according to FMLA guidelines?
   a. 8 months
   b. 10 months
   c. 12 months
   d. 15 months
   e. 18 months

31. The Consolidated Omnibus Reconciliation Act (COBRA) requires that companies employing a certain number of people – or more – must offer a specified amount of health benefits. What is the minimum number of employees that a company must have for COBRA guidelines to be in effect?
   a. 10
   b. 20
   c. 30
   d. 40
   e. 50

32. Which of the following is not a piece of legislation that covers employee deferred compensation programs?
   a. Family Medical and Leave Act
   b. Retirement Equity Act
   c. Small Business Job Protection Act
   d. Older Worker Benefit Protection Act
   e. Pension Protection Act

33. The Health Insurance Portability and Accountability Act (HIPAA) was added to ERISA to do which of the following?
   a. Establish new guidelines for employee health insurance programs within organizations
   b. Ensure that all employers are responsible for covering minimum health conditions among employees
   c. Link ERISA to COBRA to protect any employees that are covered under COBRA guidelines
   d. Forbid any discrimination based on pre-existing health problems or conditions
   e. Ensure that retired employees maintain healthcare coverage

- 135 -

34. Which type of voluntary benefit program utilizes a typical pension plan in which the employer adds an established benefit to the plan when the employee retires?
    a. Benefit accrual plan
    b. Defined contribution
    c. Nonqualified plan
    d. Defined benefit
    e. Qualified plan

35. Which type of voluntary benefit plan goes beyond IRS guidelines and tends to be offered to shareholders and executives?
    a. Qualified plan
    b. Nonqualified plan
    c. Defined contribution
    d. Defined benefit
    e. Participation benefit

36. The so-called Glass Ceiling Act, which was an amendment to Title II of the Civil Rights Act of 1991, identified which three barriers to women advancing in the workplace?
    a. Internal, societal, governmental
    b. Federal, internal, societal
    c. Societal, personal, economic
    d. Personal, federal, internal
    e. Economic, governmental, societal

37. The Latin phrase quid pro quo, used to describe a type of sexual harassment that is forbidden under Title VII of the Civil Rights Act of 1964, means which of the following?
    a. Actions not words
    b. From the stronger
    c. Action follows belief
    d. This for that
    e. Limit before which

38. The National Labor Relations Act (NLRA) provides the right for employees to engage in "concerted activities for the purpose of collective bargaining or other mutual aid or protection" to which types of employees?
    a. Full-time employees only
    b. Part-time employees only
    c. Union employees only
    d. Non-union employees only
    e. All employees

39. Which of the following best defines featherbedding?
    a. When an employer ceases to do business with another employer
    b. When an obsolete job is retained to ensure an employee is not terminated
    c. When a union coerces an employee to participate in union activities
    d. When a union overcharges employees the union fees
    e. When an employer treats an employee badly for acting as a whistleblower

40. Which of the following best represents what an employer can do when employees begin to unionize?
    a. Employers may contact union leaders and forbid unionization.
    b. Employers may block employees who begin the process of unionization
    c. Employers may threaten to replace workers who choose to unionize
    d. Employers may explain problems with unionization to employees
    e. Employers are not allowed to discuss unionization with employees

41. The risk areas that the human resources professional is responsible for considering include all of the following except:
    a. Workplace privacy
    b. Legal compliance
    c. Safety and health
    d. Business continuity
    e. Labor relations

42. Which of the following best defines the purpose of a human resources audit?
    a. Reviewing the organization of the human resources department and making any necessary changes
    b. Taking stock of current compliance with labor relations laws and updating company policies accordingly
    c. Considering overall improvements that human resources can make within the company
    d. Reviewing current training programs to consider internal improvement
    e. Analyzing the organization's recruiting methods and policies

43. The Drug-Free Workplace Act of 1988 applies to which of the following types of organizations?
    a. Large corporations
    b. Federal contractors
    c. Government agencies
    d. Local businesses governed under municipal laws
    e. Academic organizations

44. Which of the following acts requires workplaces to maintain an environment that is "free from recognized hazards that are causing or are likely to cause death or serious physical harm"?
    a. Occupational Safety and Health Act
    b. Americans with Disabilities Act
    c. Drug-Free Workplace Act
    d. Sarbanes-Oxley Act
    e. Fair Labor Standards Act

45. Which of the following is not a stated category of OSHA violation?
    a. Serious
    b. Repeat
    c. Accidental
    d. Failure to abate
    e. Other-than-serious

46. The minimum number of employees that are required for an organization to complete OSHA forms is which of the following?
    a. 10
    b. 11
    c. 12
    d. 15
    e. 17

47. The Needlestick Safety and Prevention Act of 2000 requires organizations to do which of the following?
    a. Quarterly audits to check for sharp objects that could cause workplace injuries
    b. Removal of specified sharp objects from workplace due to potential for injury
    c. Listing of sharp objects recognized for having caused workplace injuries in the past
    d. Report workplace injuries from sharp objects, pay a fine, and provide worker's compensation
    e. Report workplace injuries from sharp objects and consider replacement object to prevent future injuries

48. Which of the following steps is not a part of the human resources professional's role in observing the guidelines of the Americans with Disabilities Act when an employee requests ADA accommodation?
    a. Request that the employee acquire medical certification of condition
    b. Meet with department supervisor to discuss employee accommodation
    c. Set up and mediate meeting between supervisor and employee
    d. Provide for all employee accommodation requests to ensure continued employment
    e. Send full review of accommodation process to upper-level management

49. OSHA requires that organizations develop three types of plans that will ensure employee protection. Two of these types of plans include an injury and illness prevention plan and an emergency response plan. Which of the following represents the third type of plan?
    a. Drug prevention
    b. Fire prevention
    c. Environmental protection
    d. Clean air
    e. Terrorism response

50. Which of the following is a necessary part of the three plans that all organizations must develop?
    a. Company policy about employee protection
    b. Disaster recovery
    c. Hazard assessment
    d. Union policy for employee protection
    e. Fellow servant rule

51. Which of the following is not a part of the due diligence process that a human resources professional must review during a merger?
    a. Affirmative Action plans
    b. Employment contracts
    c. Whistleblower prevention
    d. OSHA compliance
    e. Union activity

52. What is the human resource professional's strategic role in organizations within a company or corporation?
　　a. Produce definitive change
　　b. Encourage employees in their personal strengths
　　c. Manage relationships between employees and the company
　　d. Handle any issues arising from compliance problems
　　e. Manage all employee problems

53. Which of the following does not represent steps in Enterprise Risk Management (ERM)?
　　a. Identify risks
　　b. Identify those responsible for risks
　　c. Identify mitigation options for risks
　　d. Make decisions about dealing with risks
　　e. Reduce risks

54. Harold, the head of the human resources department for a large industrial machine manufacturing company, has discovered an issue that requires ERM, or Enterprise Risk Management. Upon review of important employee documentation, he has found out that that required forms are not being completed, placing the human resources department at the risk for non-compliance with federal guidelines. Using the guidelines of ERM, what should Harold consider doing to prevent further non-compliance?
　　a. Terminate the employee responsible for failing to ensure correct documentation
　　b. Create a new department within the human resources department that keeps an eye on completing the documentation
　　c. Contact the federal agency responsible for documentation and request a reprieve
　　d. Establish quarterly reviews of the documentation to ensure that it is completed as required
　　e. Create a series of checklists that will make certain all company documentation is complete and up to date

55. Which of the following end results represents a way that a human resources professional can measure how the HR department is bringing value to a company?
　　a. A reduced number of lawsuits against a company
　　b. Increased expense within the human resources department
　　c. An increased number of employee complaints indicating corporate problems
　　d. The addition of new employees to the human resources department
　　e. A reduced level of outsourcing from a company

56. Which motivational theory resulted in the idea that job enrichment can improve the overall quality of work and the workplace for employees?
　　a. Herzberg Motivation/Hygiene Theory
　　b. Alderfer ERG Theory
　　c. Adams Equity Theory
　　d. Skinner Operant Conditioning Theory
　　e. Vroom Expectancy Theory

57. Which of the following motivational theories explores two different managerial approaches: providing rigorous structure and supervision because employees are only working for financial reward versus providing an atmosphere conducive to dialogue, growth, and modification of structure because employees work not just for financial reward, but the betterment of themselves and others?
a. Maslow Hierarchy Theory
b. Skinner Behavioral Theory
c. McGregor X and Y Theory
d. McClelland Acquired Needs Theory
e. Adams Equity Theory

58. Which motivational theory focuses on the ability to alter behavior through intervention options, such as positive or negative reinforcement?
a. Alderfer ERG Theory
b. Skinner Operant Conditioning Theory
c. Maslow Hierarchy Theory
d. Vroom Expectancy Theory
e. Herzberg Motivation/Hygiene Theory

59. Abbey, the head of the human resources department for a book distribution service, accidentally discovers information about one of the company employees. She learns that the employee has a genetic disease that could potentially affect the employee's ability to continue in the job. According to the Genetic Information Nondiscrimination Act of 2008, all employee genetic information is private, and companies are not allowed to locate or make decisions based on employee conditions. Now that Abbey has discovered this information, what is her responsibility?
a. Abbey is required to report the information to her superiors, but they will not be allowed to alter the employee's work situation
b. Abbey must inform the Department of Labor about her inadvertent acquisition of the knowledge
c. Abbey must let the employee know what she has discovered and counsel the employee to consider requesting a change in the employee's job situation
d. Abbey must place the information in the employee's company file, but it cannot be accessed unless absolutely necessary
e. Because the information was gained accidentally, Abbey is not legally responsible for it, but she is not allowed to divulge any of the information or change the employee's working situation

60. According to Marcus Buckingham and Curt Coffman in First, Break All the Rules, which of the following is not one of the four factors that help to create eager and content employees?
a. Terminate employees who fail to connect with other members of the team
b. Create clear goals for all employees and provide rewards for completed goals
c. Focus on the strengths of each employee and encourage individual growth
d. Identify potential employees who demonstrate versatility and a combination of KSAs (knowledge, skills, and abilities)
e. Locate the most advantageous work situation for each employee

61. What is the purpose of the Training Adjustment Assistance (TAA) program?
    a. To create funding for employees who have been terminated for any reason
    b. To help employees who lose their jobs due to a rise in the number of imports
    c. To establish health benefits for employees after they have been laid off
    d. To improve the quality of employee working conditions
    e. To work in coordination with the welfare system to support employees

62. Gabriela is a human resources professional who has been given the responsibility of filling a position within the HR department. She is ready to begin making the details of the position available to interested candidates and pursuing potential employees who will fill the requirements of the job as best as possible. This process is known as which of the following?
    a. Hiring
    b. Sourcing
    c. Tracking
    d. Selection
    e. Recruiting

63. During succession planning, a human resources professional may categorize employees as all of the following except:
    a. Employees who are ready for a new position on the company
    b. No employee is necessary because the position is now obsolete
    c. Employees who show indications that he or she is ready for a promotion
    d. Employees who fulfill all of the requirements of the position
    e. Employees who are expected to or will be required to leave the position soon

64. Eric is in charge of interviewing candidates for an open position in a hotel chain. As he considers each candidate, he finds himself quick to write off one young man in particular. This candidate has a strong resume and excellent credentials, but Eric decides that he just does not like this person and is disinclined to consider him a contender for the position. In doing so, Eric is demonstrating which of the following interview biases?
    a. First impression
    b. Cultural noise
    c. Gut feeling
    d. Leniency
    e. Nonverbal bias

65. Jocelyn has the responsibility of interviewing the candidates who have applied for an open position as a mechanic in an auto repair shop. As she meets and interviews the various candidates, she is not pleased with the potential employees that she encounters during this interview. One of the candidates, however, is a strongly built young woman with a tough demeanor. Despite this woman's limited resume and experience, Jocelyn decides that this particular candidate is the best employee choice because her appearance fits the image that the auto repair shop will need. In this, Jocelyn is demonstrating which of the following interview biases?
    a. Stereotyping
    b. Similar-to-me
    c. Recency
    d. First impression
    e. Gut feeling

66. Which of the following is the best definition of an employee brand?
    a. The public relations strategy for a company's success
    b. The human resources policy of marketing the company to prospective employees
    c. A clear portrayal of the company's identity
    d. The total rewards philosophy for a company
    e. The logo that represents a company

67. A data management company is looking to hire several new candidates who will be responsible for researching current data and cleaning up outdated files within the database. The database clean-up will cover four separate departments within the company, so the new employees will be required to work with the heads of each of the department. Lydia, who is the human resources professional for the company, has been asked about which type of interview would be most effective for this position. Considering the job situation, what type of interview should Lydia recommend?
    a. Panel
    b. Behavioral
    c. Patterned
    d. Stress
    e. Nondirective

68. How do conditions in the labor market affect a company?
    a. Ability for a company to consider and hire the right candidates
    b. Potential for negative effect on the company's bottom line
    c. Analysis of competition with other companies
    d. Geographic changes to the economic situation as a whole
    e. Changing educational expectations for potential employees

69. The Foreign Corrupt Practices Act (FCPA) was designed to do which of the following?
    a. Prevent illegal trafficking of merchandise
    b. Curtail extensive imports to bolster domestic manufacturing
    c. Maintain fair standards in American businesses that have locations abroad
    d. Prevent American businesses from bribing foreign governments
    e. Protect American workers who go to work overseas

70. A private company works as a contractor for federal defense agency. As a result of this agreement, many of the contractor employees will be engaging in positions of extreme sensitivity, and the contractor would like to give polygraph tests to employees. What is the federal policy regarding polygraph tests in this situation?
    a. All contractor employees may be given polygraph tests
    b. Federal law makes polygraphs illegal for anyone or any institution but the government to administer
    c. The employer may utilize anyone in the company to administer the polygraph
    d. Because the contractor does other work outside of his or her work with the defense agency, polygraphs are not allowed
    e. The polygraph test may be administered only to those who will be working in defense-related jobs

71. Which of the following best defines the purpose of talent management for the human resources professional?
   a. Creating interest for potential employees and developing current employees with the potential for management and executive positions
   b. Locating new talent that will enable the organization to grow and improve
   c. Training all employees for expected promotions within the organization
   d. Setting apart employees who are currently ready or will be ready for higher positions
   e. Identifying employees who have the most potential and training them for management positions within the organization

72. Which of the following are not steps in an analysis of training?
   a. Establish a clear objective for training
   b. Collect data about potential problems and review it
   c. Analyze where the organization is lacking in its objective and its outcome
   d. Develop new and more effective training material
   e. Consider options with respect to the organization's available budget and time

73. Susannah, who is the head of the human resources department, will be responsible for a training session and must decide on the seating style in the space that she will be using. The training will include a large group and will involve a range of activities, including several lectures, film presentations, and a small amount of group work. Which of the following seating styles will be most appropriate for the training that Susannah will be conducting?
   a. Theater-style
   b. Chevron-style
   c. Banquet-style
   d. Conference-style
   e. U-shaped-style

74. Human resources professional Jacob conducts an evaluation that considers required changes and the outcome of those changes over the course of six months. Jacob begins with a written objective stated on the evaluation form and then returns to this objective at the end of the six months. Jacob is utilizing which of the following types of evaluations?
   a. Reaction
   b. Learning
   c. Pretest/Posttest
   d. Behavior
   e. Results

75. What is required in the role of the human resources professional when considering unique employee needs?
   a. Assessing the boundaries of the current policies of the organization
   b. Creating diversity initiatives by enabling employees to find a comfortable place within the company
   c. Recognizing that the most effective employees are those who are able to balance their work with situations outside of work
   d. Locating repatriation situations for employees who have the potential to benefit the organization outside the United States
   e. Establishing flexibility within the working arrangements of employees by providing daycare programs, nutrition and health training, and fitness centers

76. Which of the following best explains the primary role of fiduciary responsibility for the human resources professional?
   a. Creating unimpeachable trust
   b. Avoiding any indication of favoritism
   c. Handling the total rewards program at the organization
   d. Recognizing the need to handle sensitive material carefully
   e. Assuring a sense of trust in the organization's total rewards program

77. How are vacation pay policies established for organizations?
   a. Vacation pay policies are created under the guidelines of the FMLA
   b. Vacation pay policies are established by each company
   c. Vacation pay policies fall under the rules of ERISA
   d. Vacation pay policies fall under the jurisdiction of state-established guidelines
   e. Vacation pay policies are created by union policies within companies

78. Which of the following best explains workers compensation laws regarding an employer's responsibility?
   a. Employers are responsible for any work-related injuries or health problems
   b. Employers are responsible for any health problems that an employee develops while working for the employer
   c. Employers do not have to assume responsibility for employee problems unless the employee proves definitively that the problem is job related
   d. Employers may utilize federal aid for most work-related injuries and problems that employers develop on the job
   e. Employers are only responsible for a federally designated list of injuries and problems that employees develop on the job

79. Defined contribution plans for organizations include all of the following options except:
   a. 401(k)
   b. Money purchase plans
   c. Profit-sharing plans
   d. Cash-balance plans
   e. Target benefit plans

80. The "golden" benefits for executive compensation packages include all of the following except:
   a. Golden lifeboat
   b. Golden parachute
   c. Golden handshake
   d. Golden handcuffs
   e. Golden life jacket

81. What is the fiduciary role of the human resources professional regarding ERISA?
   a. Setting up pension accounts for employees
   b. Handling and managing pension funds
   c. Ensuring that the HIPAA guidelines of ERISA are observed
   d. Creating the rules that govern individual retirement account for employees
   e. Working with organization to locate the funds for pension accounts

82. How long after filing with the Department of Labor are ERISA records required to be maintained?
    a. 4 years
    b. 5 years
    c. 6 years
    d. 7 years
    e. 8 years

83. Which of the following pieces of legislation establishes guidelines for retaining and reporting employee identification records?
    a. Fair Labor Standards Act
    b. Fair Credit Reporting Act
    c. Consumer Credit Protection Act
    d. Small Business Job Protection Act
    e. Personal Responsibility and Work Opportunity Reconciliation Act

84. Which type of voluntary benefits plan offers specified tax benefits for employers as well as employees and does not provide extra benefits for shareholders or executives?
    a. Nonqualified plan
    b. Defined contribution
    c. Qualified plan
    d. Cash balance
    e. Defined benefit

85. Which type of voluntary benefits plan relies on unknown benefits that result from investments that are gained on the retirement account?
    a. Participation benefit
    b. Nonqualified plan
    c. Cash balance
    d. Qualified plan
    e. Defined contribution

86. Which of the following represents an occasion when picketing would be illegal?
    a. When an election for union representation has occurred within a 12-month period
    b. When employees try to provide potential customers with information about business practices
    c. When a union tries to encourage non-union employees to join the union
    d. When a union attempts to encourage the employer to recognize union representation
    e. When employees make efforts to inform the public about the employer's position regarding unions

87. All of the following represent collective bargaining strategies except:
    a. Single-unit bargaining
    b. Principled bargaining
    c. Parallel bargaining
    d. Multi-employer bargaining
    e. Multi-unit bargaining

88. Which of the following types of bargaining strategies between an employer and union employees is considered to be illegal?
    a. Double breasting
    b. Lockout
    c. Secondary boycott
    d. Common situs picketing
    e. Sit-down strike

89. An unfair labor practice (ULP) is defined as
    a. Any type of coercion on the part of employers against unions
    b. Discrimination against employees and union representatives during a strike
    c. Activity from employer or union that hinders employees from exercising rights
    d. Participating in strikes or boycotts that are prohibited by law
    e. Restraint that employers use to prevent employees from unionizing

90. During a lawful economic strike, employers have the right to do which of the following?
    a. Confront employees and require that they return to work at the risk of being fired
    b. Hire new employees to replace striking employees
    c. Encourage the union to disband or a suggest the formation of a new union
    d. Disband union bargaining and require new representation
    e. Restrict union bargaining if they negatively impact company's finances

91. Which of the following is not considered by OSHA to be a standard environmental health hazard?
    a. Ergonomic design
    b. Stress
    c. Plants
    d. Computer use
    e. Vibrations

92. Employers are legally allowed to check and review employee emails subject to which of the following requirements?
    a. Immediate notification from the legal department of impending review
    b. Evidence to suggest wrongdoing on the employee's part
    c. Written policy informing employees of potential for email searches
    d. No notification is required, therefore employers may check and review employee emails at any time
    e. Employers are not allowed to check or review employee emails without employee permission

93. The National Institute of Occupational Safety and Health (NIOSH) describes a certain workplace condition as "harmful physical and emotional responses that occur when the requirements of the job do not match the capabilities, resources, or needs of the worker." Which of the following workplace conditions does this quote define?
    a. Panic
    b. Depression
    c. Disorganization
    d. Insecurity
    e. Stress

94. Which of the following represents a legitimate reason for company management to conduct a workplace investigation?
    a. An employee is accused of inappropriate behavior toward other employees
    b. The company experiences a rapid reduction in the price of their stock
    c. Management becomes aware of a breach in legal compliance
    d. A supervisor reports a disagreement among co-workers in his or her department
    e. The human resources supervisor recognizes clear organizational problems within the human resources department

95. Risk management activities for Civil Rights are covered under which of the following pieces of legislation?
    a. EEOC
    b. SOX
    c. OSHA
    d. SEC
    e. MSHA

96. The phrase unholy trinity refers to which of the following organizational controls?
    a. OSHA logs for record of workplace injuries
    b. Top-tier leaders of the organization
    c. Steps of a human resource audit
    d. Common law doctrines for worker's compensation
    e. OSHA requirements for IIPP

97. OSHA 300 represents which of the following:
    a. Summary of Workplace Problems
    b. Injury and Illness Incident Report
    c. Log of Work-Related Injuries and Illnesses
    d. Employee Privacy Case List
    e. Record of Employee Complaints and Referrals

98. Employers will typically use which of the following in order to protect confidential company information?
    a. Lie detector test
    b. Nondisclosure agreement
    c. Employee contract
    d. Video surveillance
    e. Random searches

99. The components of an effective substance abuse program include all of the following except:
    a. A written statement regarding the company's no-tolerance policy about substance abuse
    b. Upper-level management support for all substance abuse programs and policies
    c. Educational awareness for incoming employees regarding the company's substance abuse policy
    d. Management training programs for implementing substance abuse policy
    e. Targeted drug testing for employees who have substance abuse problems

100. A large university is concerned about the possibility of an act of terrorism on campus, and the supervisor for the school's student affairs program has consulted Angelova, the head of the human resources department, about developing a program for responding to a terrorist attack and assisting students in the aftermath of an attack. Which of the following represents what Angelova could recommend to the student affairs supervisor?

    a. A counseling program that assists students in recovering from the trauma of a terrorist attack

    b. A relocation program that enables students to transfer to other schools in the aftermath of a terrorist attack

    c. A monthly email newsletter that provides recommendations for students should the school experience an act of terrorism

    d. Creation of new department specifically focused on responding to a terrorist attack on campus

    e. A school-wide emergency response program that gives students information on how to protect themselves during a terrorist attack

Answers and Explanations

1. A: A Human Management Capital Plan is forward thinking; the questions asked look at the present and into the future. As a result, a human resources professional who is setting up a HCMP should ask the following questions as demonstrated in answer choices B, C, D, and E: Where are we now? Where do we want to be? How will we get there? How will we know when we arrive? Answer choice A, which asks where have we come from, addresses an issue that does not apply to this portion of strategic planning, so it is correct.

2. C: An environmental scan has to do with the gathering of information that will help to project company growth and development. In other words, an environmental scan helps a company to review historical data to begin the process of preparing for expected or planned growth in the company. The environmental scan has nothing to do with environmental standards, federal or otherwise. This means that answer choices A, B, and E can be eliminated because all refer to outdoor or indoor environment, the EPA, and green standards. Answer choice D may be eliminated as well because the environmental scan does not relate to research and development techniques, nor is it specifically related to a business plan in the immediate sense.

3. D: Simply put, the legislation that will affect a business often will affect that business's relationship with its employees. Because the human resources professional is, in some ways, the intermediary between the employers and the employees, he or she should be at least somewhat familiar with legislation and the legislative process. Answer choice A is not correct because the human resources professional is not necessarily responsible for contacting a member of Congress about submitting legislation. Similarly, answer choice B is incorrect because the human resources professional is not required to act as the company's outside contact. Answer choice C is largely irrelevant to the larger question and, if true, would only refer to human resources professionals at small companies that are hoping to expand. Answer choice E is also incorrect because lobbying before Congress is a task that anyone can perform, but does not necessarily fall under the specific job description of the human resources professional.

4. B: Question 4 essentially asks the student to choose the first step in the legislative process for a bill to become a law. When an idea for a bill originates from an individual or business outside of Congress, the idea must first be submitted to a member of Congress (known as MOC). This MOC may be either a senator or a representative. The MOC will then sponsor the bill by submitting it to the part of Congress where he or she works, and the bill will begin its journey through legislation. Answer choice A is incorrect because no business or individual has the ability to submit a bill to either part of Congress. That obligation belongs to the MOC. Answer choices C and E are incorrect because they again overstep the boundaries of the MOC. First the MOC must sponsor the bill; then it goes into a congressional committee and/or hearing. Answer choice D is also incorrect because a statewide petition, while valuable for some processes, plays no real part in the legislative process.

5. B: The Foreign Corrupt Practices Act of 1977 establishes the rules for preventing bribery and penalizing occurrences of it within corporations that exist in several countries. Each of the other answer choices – A, C, D, and E – all provide some kind of protection for whistleblowers who reveal corrupt business practices.

6. C: Creating a business plan, while useful for businesses that are in their early stages, is not an identifiable step within the strategic planning process that a human resources professional may

complete. On the other hand, completing an environmental scan (answer choice A), formulating a strategy (answer choice B), implementing that strategy (answer choice D), and adjusting the strategy (answer choice E) are all significant steps in the strategic planning process. It is important to bear in mind that strategic planning is related largely to a company's future goals for growth and improvement.

7. E: Richard's laid-back mentality demonstrates a laissez-faire, or "let it be" attitude toward managing his team in the human resources department. A democratic leadership style (answer choice A) provides plenty of freedom among team members but still maintains a sense of order and control. A leader who demonstrates the coaching style (answer choice B) has a more hands-on approach to working individually with team members to help them with targeting their skills and giving them the means to function on their own. A transactional leader (answer choice C) sets goals and provides rewards to team members as they reach these goals, while a transformational leader (answer choice D) works on team dynamics for a united approach to reaching goals.

8. A: In terms of standard budget responsibilities, the human resources professional is expected to manage payroll taxes (answer choice B), travel expenses (answer choice C), repairs and maintenance (answer choice D), and employee benefits (answer choice E). The performance increases tend to fall under human resources in some cases but are not considered standard responsibilities, so answer choice A is correct.

9. E: The Fair Labor Standards Act requires that companies maintain a certification of age on file for all employees until their employment is terminated. The certification of age simply shows that the employee can legally work for the company in the capacity in which he or she was hired. Once the employment has been terminated, it is no longer necessary to maintain a certification of age. Answer choices A, B, C, and D all represents time periods that could be true depending on the time that an employee is with a company, but they are not technically correct based on the wording of the law.

10. C: Minimum wage law is as follows: the federal minimum wage is primary if the state minimum wage is lower than the federal minimum wage. If the state minimum wage is higher than the federal level, however, the company is required to pay the state minimum wage. In other words, companies are expected to pay whatever happens to be higher. There are, of course, a number of variables that can affect minimum wage and what a company is expected to pay, but in question 10 one should assume that Grace Clothing in California is required to pay whatever happens to be the higher minimum wage. This means that answer choices A and B are immediately incorrect. In the case of answer choice D, the question does not provide any information about the size of the company, so the answer choice becomes irrelevant to the discussion. (Again, it must be assumed based on the question that Grace Clothing is required to pay minimum wage; the real question is which minimum wage?) And answer choice E is incorrect because the presence of commission should not necessarily affect minimum wage. The minimum wage is the minimum a company is expected to pay employees. Any commissions represent an addition to payment, but because commissions cannot be guaranteed they cannot compensate for lower minimum wage.

11. D: The phrase adverse impact or unintentional discrimination refers to the selection rate of a protected class being less than 80% of the selection rate of the highest group. In other words, if the selection rate of females is less than 80% the selection rate of males, there is an adverse impact on females by the hiring process. Answer choice A is the opposite of the correct definition of adverse impact, so it is incorrect. Answer choice B is close to the meaning of adverse impact – in a broad sense – but it is not specific enough to be correct. Answer choice C is also too broad, particularly

because there is far more to the Uniform Guidelines on Employee Selection Process than just selection rate. And answer choice E is incorrect; while adverse impact might be interpreted as discrimination, it is not necessarily the direct result of discrimination.

12. C: While a consideration of the economic situation might be useful, it is not a part of the human resources professional's analysis of staffing needs. The other answer choices – creating a list of necessary KSAs that will encourage company growth, developing a list of employees who might be ready for promotion, considering hiring options for open positions, and reviewing the results of hiring decisions for future hiring – are all part of an analysis of staffing needs.

13. A: For applications that are completed in-house – that is, for internal applications that current employees complete – a short-form application is usually best. This is because the company will already have most of the employee's information on file and simply needs a formal application for the new job rather than an extensive application detailing information the company probably has. Answer choice B is incorrect because the weighted employment application, while specific to the job and excellent for considering the details of a candidate's qualifications, is far too costly to establish in this type of situation. Answer choice C is incorrect because the long-form application is simply unnecessary for internal hiring. Answer choice D is incorrect because the job-specific application (which is used largely for hiring a number of employees for similar positions) will not necessarily be useful for the company looking to hire internally. And answer choice E is incorrect because an application is almost always necessary, even for internal hiring.

14. A: When a department within a company is planning interviews to hire new employees, the human resources professional's role is primarily one of assisting. The human resources professional is not responsible for choosing the members of the prospective interview board (answer choice B), since this role will fall to the department and those who will be working with the new employee or employees. Additionally, the job of creating official list of questions for the interview (answer choice C), conducting the actual interviews for prospective employees (answer choice D), and working with the interview board to select the right candidate (answer choice E) belongs not to the human resources professional but to the manager or supervisor of department in which the employees will work.

15. B: Specific questions regarding a candidate's personal life and religious choices are entirely off limits for interviews. The only question that an interviewer may ask a candidate is whether or not the candidate belongs to an organization that may be relevant to the job. Unless the candidate volunteers information, all other questions about the religious symbol that the candidate is wearing are not appropriate during the interview. This is because a question could make a candidate uncomfortable. What is more, should the candidate be asked such a question and then receive the job – or not receive the job – the situation could be viewed as a form of discrimination.

16. C: Caspar's interview bias is one of contrast; he finds himself, however unconsciously, contrasting the other candidates with the first candidate that he interviews. A cultural noise bias (answer choice A) occurs when the candidate responds with pointed answers that are aimed at making the interviewer happy rather than responding in a more natural or general way. A halo bias (answer choice B) occurs when the interviewer considers only one quality of the candidate over his other qualities, such as shyness that might detract from the candidate's true record of achievement. A leniency bias (answer choice D) means the interviewer is lenient in regard to a candidate's potential weaknesses. A negative emphasis bias (answer choice E) means the interviewer places too much weight on the candidate's weaknesses.

17. E: Louisa's response to the candidate is influenced by her first impression of the candidate's behavior. A knowledge-of-predictor bias (answer choice A) means the interviewer responds to the candidate based on knowledge about the candidate's scores on evaluative tests that were given. A stereotyping bias (answer choice B) occurs when an interviewer bases a personal opinion about a candidate on a stereotype of the candidate rather than evaluating the candidate as objectively as possible. A recency bias (answer choice C) means the interviewer compares a candidate to the most recent candidate that was interviewed. A nonverbal bias occurs when the interviewer is over-influenced by body language instead of by the candidate's responses.

18. D: The Uniform Guidelines on Employee Selection Process (UGESP) requires that all testing be focused around reliability and validity. Answer choice A is incorrect, not because "fairness" is an undesirable quality but because it is intended to be a result of the requirements of validity and reliability. Answer choice B is also incorrect because "disinterestedness" is an intended result of the required qualities of reliability and validity. Answer choice C is incorrect, again because "equality" is an expected result, and answer choice D is incorrect because "consideration" is too vague of a requirement for establishing tests.

19. B: The required qualities of reliability and validity are established for the express purpose of avoiding discrimination against protected classes. Answer choice A is incorrect because it makes no sense to ensure the same results from all tests – the tests would have no value at that point. Answer choice C is incorrect because the testing of candidates for a new position is about assessing the qualifications of the candidates and not quantifying the success rate of the company. Answer choice D is incorrect because it is too vague. Such guidelines would always be intended to create better standards for testing, but this is not specific enough to be a correct answer. And answer choice E is correct in the larger sense but is also not specific enough, since the standards were created for very specific reasons.

20. E: The WARN Act is the Worker Adjustment and Retraining Notification Act, which was designed to offer rights for workers who have been laid off. Answer choice A is incorrect because the act was certainly not designed to prevent massive lay-offs but rather to give workers "adjustment and retraining" in the event of massive lay-offs. Answer choice B is incorrect because the act cannot necessarily provide new positions for workers who have been laid off. Answer choice C is incorrect; while the act creates government funding for workers who have lost their jobs, it does not create government funding for a struggling company. And answer choice D is incorrect because the act cannot provide severance pay for those who have been laid off.

21. E: Organization development is the process by which a human resources professional analyzes the elements of an organization's makeup and considers opportunities for improvement. Answer choice A is incorrect because the definition refers more to organization culture than it does to organization development. And answer choices B, C, and D are incorrect because they refer to elements of organization development but do not explain the larger definition of the process as a whole.

22. C: The four categories of intervention, as presented by Cummings and Worley in Organization Development and Change, are Techno-structural, Human Resource Management, Human Process, and Strategic. Change management is more of another way to describe intervention within an organization than it is a category of intervention.

23. D: In the workplace, the Meyers-Brigg Type Indicator is primarily used as a personality test to enable individuals to understand their personalities better and to assist staff members in

- 152 -

appreciating how to interact with their co-workers more effectively. Due to the nature of the administrative department and its situation – employees who work together quite frequently and run into personality conflicts – the Meyers-Brigg test will be Raisa's best recommendation. Answer choices A and C are incorrect because research has suggested a lack of long-term value in team-building activities such as obstacle courses and scavenger hunts. Answer choices B and E are also incorrect: while role-playing situations and real-life scenarios might be beneficial to those who work in highly active and often sensitive fields, they will not necessarily be as useful for employees whose jobs is more focused around completing and maintaining paperwork for a university.

24. A: The instructional design acronym known as the ADDIE model begins not with Administration but with Analysis. The other options – Design, Development, Implementation, and Evaluation – are all accurate elements of the ADDIE acronym.

25. B: Facilitation is an instructional method that enables employees to work together on problem-solving techniques while under the guidance of a facilitator, or third-party expert in helping different groups interact effectively. Answer choice A is incorrect because the vestibule instructional method is a type of simulation, in which the employees receive hands-on experience on the equipment they will be using. A demonstration is largely just a presentation of information in a lecture-style setting, so that would be inappropriate for this situation, making answer choice C incorrect. Similarly, a conference style of instructional method is primarily focused on presenting information without employee interaction, so answer choice D is also incorrect. And the one-on-one method would be instruction given from one person to another. This is hardly useful in the situation with which Eamon is presented, so answer choice E is incorrect.

26. D: The purpose of a total rewards strategy is one of reviewing the budget and finding out how much of the budget is available for establishing rewards that will retain employees. (Additionally, the total rewards strategy contributes to drawing potential employees and motivating them in their employment activities.) Answer choice A is incorrect. While a total rewards program might cover salaries, the total rewards strategy is larger than basic salary. Answer choice B is incorrect because the total rewards strategy is unrelated to employer brand. Answer choice C is incorrect because the total rewards strategy is unconnected to creating teamwork among employees. And answer choice E is incorrect because the total rewards strategy is unrelated to the recognition of organizational changes.

27. B: When establishing employee compensation within an organization, considering employee salary history might be a part of the larger process, but it is not a major factor in the process. Answer choices A, C, D, and E – IRS rules, conditions in the labor market, current economic situations, and competition from other companies – all play a major role in establishing employee compensation.

28. E: The McNamara-O'Hara Service Contract Act (1965) covers federal service contracts, but the Fair Labor Standards Act does not. The Fair Labor Standards Act does, however, cover minimum wage requirements, exemption conditions for employees, work conditions for children under 18, and overtime. As a result, answer choices A, B, C, and D are all incorrect.

29. A: Benchmark positions are simply the types of positions that are common within all organizations, such as administrative assistants. Benchmark positions do not, however, relate to an evaluation of current jobs (answer choice B), a review of market conditions for salaries (answer choice C), a change in significant jobs in a company (answer choice D), and a review of the value of various positions within an organization (answer choice E).

30. C: According to FMLA guidelines, an employee must work for an employer for a minimum of 12 months (not necessarily consecutively) in order to apply for FMLA-approved leave. Because Arthur has only worked for the company for 9 months, he will not be eligible to apply for type of leave, which is what Brad – as the human resources professional – will be required to explain to Arthur. Answer choices A, B, D, and E are incorrect because each represents the wrong period of time for FMLA leave.

31. B: COBRA regulations state that a company with at least 20 employees must provide a defined amount of health benefits for employees. Answer choices A, C, D, and E are all correct because they fail to recognize the requirements of COBRA regarding minimum number of employees.

32. A: Among the answer choices provided, only the Family Medical and Leave Act does not reference or cover employee deferred compensation programs. The Retirement Equity Act (answer choice B), the Small Business Job Protection Act (answer choice C), the Older Worker Benefit Protection Act (answer choice D), and the Pension Protection Act (answer choice E) all provide for deferred employee compensation programs in some way.

33. D: The Health Insurance Portability and Accountability Act was added to ERISA for the express purpose of forbidding any type of health benefit discrimination toward employees based on pre-existing health problems or health conditions. Answer choice A is incorrect for several reasons. On the one hand, it is simply too vague to explain the purpose of HIPAA. What is more, answer choice A does not simply establish new guidelines for employee health insurance programs, so it is incorrect. Answer choices B and C are incorrect because both refer to COBRA (answer choice B references COBRA inferentially), and HIPAA is not immediately connected to COBRA or to providing minimum health benefits for employees. Answer choice E is incorrect because it fails to specify the exact purpose of HIPAA and because HIPAA was not added to ERISA simply for the purpose of retired employees maintaining healthcare coverage.

34. D: Question 34 describes the defined benefit program, which starts with a basic pension plan. To this pension plan are added established benefits, thus explaining the name of the plan. Answer choice A is incorrect because the benefit accrual plan is not a type of voluntary benefits plan. Answer choice B is incorrect. Like the defined benefit plan, the defined contribution plan utilizes a standard pension plan but without the added benefits defined in advance. Answer choice C is incorrect because the nonqualified plan provides benefits to specified employees (for example, executives) and shareholders. And answer choice E is incorrect because a qualified plan is a 401(k) plan that receives special tax credits from the IRS.

35. B: Question 35 describes the nonqualified plan, which provides benefits to employees such as executives and shareholders. Answer choice A is incorrect because the qualified plan provides IRS-approved tax advantages but without any extra benefits for shareholders and executives. Answer choice C is incorrect because the defined contribution plan utilizes a standard pension plan without any added benefits defined in advance. Answer choice D is incorrect because the defined benefit program starts with a pension plan and adds specified benefits to it. Answer choice E is incorrect because participation benefit is not a type of voluntary benefits plan.

36. A: The Glass Ceiling Act noted that the three barriers to women advancing in the workplace are internal, societal, and governmental. Answer choices B and D are incorrect because the term "federal" encompasses government at the federal level but does not include any local or state governmental barriers that might exist for women in the workplace. Answer choices C and E are

incorrect because an economic barrier would be a result of other barriers or would fall under "societal" barriers.

37. D: The Latin phrase quid pro quo translates simply as this for that and under sexual harassment laws it suggests that an employee is expected to provide sexual favors for improved (or continued) employment situation. Answer choices A, B, C, and E are incorrect because they do not reflect a correct translation of this Latin phrase.

38. E: The rights that are provided by the NLRA apply to all employees of an organization and are not limited to specific employees within that organization. As a result, the other answer choices that limit the employee coverage to full-time employees only (answer choice A), part-time employees only (answer choice B), union employees only (answer choice C), and non-union employees only (answer choice D) are all incorrect.

39. B: Featherbedding occurs when a union requires that an otherwise obsolete job remains intact at an organization in order to avoid terminating an employee. Answer choice A is incorrect because it describes a hot cargo agreement. Answer choice C is incorrect because it simply describes a type of union coercion. Answer choice D is incorrect because it describes another type of union coercion or restraint of employees. And answer choice E is incorrect because it describes a type of employer coercion or restraint, but it does not describe featherbedding.

40. D: When an employer discovers that employees are beginning to unionize, the employer is not allowed to prevent unionization. The employer can, however, provide information to employees about the problems involved with unionization. Answer choice A is incorrect because the employer may not contact union leaders and forbid unionization. Answer choice B is incorrect because employers are not allowed to block employees who begin to unionize. Answer choice C is incorrect because employers may not threaten to replace workers who choose to unionize (although employers may replace workers during a lawful economic strike). Answer choice E is incorrect because employers are allowed to discuss unionization with employees; however, the substance of that discussion can be restricted by law.

41. E: The category of labor relations is not considered to be one of the larger risks that a human resources professional must consider. Compliance with labor relations laws would fall under the category of legal compliance as a whole, but it is not a separate area of risk management. Answer choices A, B, C, and E are all incorrect because they represent distinct areas of risk that a human resources professional must consider.

42. C: The purpose of a human resources audit can be fairly extensive in scope--to consider overall improvements that can be made within the company. Answer choice A is incorrect because a human resources audit is certainly not limited to the human resources department, nor would a review of the organization within the human resources department represent an audit. Answer choice B is incorrect because it is too limited in focus. A human resources audit might include a review of compliance with labor relations laws, but it is not the only focus of a human resources audit. Answer choices D and E are also incorrect because they are do not include the larger purpose of the human resources audit and focus only on elements of the audit.

43. B: The Drug-Free Workplace Act of 1988 applies specifically to federal contractors (specifically, the contractors that make at least $100,000). Answer choices A, C, D, and E are incorrect because they inaccurately reflect the types of organizations to which the Drug-Free Workplace Act of 1988 refers. Specifically, answer choice A is incorrect because it is far too vague. A federal contractor

might be a large corporation, but not all large corporations are going to be federal contractors. Answer choice C is incorrect because federal contractors might be funded through government agencies but are entirely different organizations. Answer choice D is incorrect because it simply makes no sense: all local businesses will, in some way, be governed under municipal laws. Answer choice E is also incorrect because academic organizations – like most business that are not federal contractors – are responsible for developing their own substance abuse policies for the workplace.

44. A: The piece of legislation to which the quote refers is the Occupational Safety and Health Act of 1970 (OSHA). The Americans with Disabilities Act (ADA) is focused specifically on providing rights for employees with disabilities in the workplace. The Drug-Free Workplace Act is focused on the substance abuse policy for federal contractors. The Sarbanes-Oxley Act is focused on the legal obligation that organizations have to record and report financial information. And the Fair Labor Standards Act refers to the legal requirements that companies have to provide a workplace environment that is fair to all employees.

45. C: The stated categories of OSHA violations include willful, serious, other-than-serious, repeat, failure to abate, and de minimus (or minimal violations). Accidental is not one of the categories officially noted by OSHA, so answer choice C is correct. Answer choices A, B, D, and E all reflect actual categories, so they are incorrect.

46. B: Organizations with up to 10 employees are not required to file OSHA forms. As a result, organizations with a minimum of 11 employees must file OSHA forms. Answer choices A, C, D, and E are incorrect because they reflect the incorrect number of employees for filing OSHA documentation.

47. E: The purpose of the Needlestick Safety and Prevention Act is to require the employers report workplace injuries as a result of sharp objects and consider replacement objects to prevent further injuries. Answer choice A is incorrect because the purpose of the act is not to require that companies perform quarterly audits. Answer choice B is incorrect because the Needlestick Safety and Prevention Act does not require that organizations remove specified sharp objects but instead recommend the replacement of dangerous sharp objects. Answer choice C is incorrect because the act does not create a list of sharp objects that are recognized for having caused workplace injuries but instead leaves the decision about these objects up to the organization. Answer choice D is incorrect because the act does not require that companies pay a fine for workplace injuries from sharp objects.

48. D: The human resources professional is not required to provide for all employee accommodation requests to ensure continued employment. Human resources professionals are expected to discuss possible employee accommodations with management and to recommend the implementation of certain requests, but there is no requirement to implement all requests. Answer choices A, B, C, and E are all steps in the human resources professional's role in observing the guidelines of ADA, so they are incorrect.

49. B: The three primary types of plans that OSHA requires organizations to develop include an injury and illness prevention plan, an emergency response plan, and a fire prevention plan. Answer choice A is incorrect because OSHA does not require a drug prevention plan. Such a plan might fall under illness prevention, but ultimately a drug prevention plan is voluntary on the part of the organization. Answer choice C is incorrect because OSHA does not require an environmental protection plan. This too might fall under illness prevention, but it is not specified under OSHA's rules. Answer choice D is incorrect because OSHA does not require a clean air plan. Additionally,

answer choice E is incorrect because OSHA does not require that organizations create a terrorism response plan.

50. A: However organizations choose to create their plans, a company policy about employee protection is required for all of them. This policy lets employees know what the organization's approach to employee protection is. Answer choice B is incorrect because a disaster recovery plan is not a necessary part of the three plans. Answer choice C is incorrect because organizations are not obligated to include hazard assessment in all three plans. Answer choice D is incorrect because organizations are not required to include a union policy about employee protection. And answer choice E is incorrect because organizations are not required to create a fellow servant rule. In fact, the fellow servant rule is a part of common law doctrine that is now considered obsolete.

51. C: A due diligence process during a merger should focus primarily on recording the following basics of company employee details: documentation regarding employee names, employment contracts, I-9 forms, benefit contracts, compensation information, company policy and procedures (such as handbooks for employees), compliance documentation for equal opportunity, information about company labor relations (including labor activity), all information about potential legal situations (such as legal violations, sexual harassment claims, and disputes about employee terminations), and legal compliance documentation for COBRA, FMLA, WARN, and OSHA. This means that answer choices A, B, D, and E all fall within the boundaries of due diligence for a merger, leaving only answer choice C. What is more, whistleblower prevention is not necessarily legal – as there are a number of laws designed to protect whistleblowers – so a company could not legally retain or utilize whistleblower techniques.

52. B: In many cases, the human resources professional is responsible for acting as a kind of median between the company and its employees. In organizations, the role of the human resources professional is somewhat more specific; the HR professional is expected to encourage employees in their strengths and when necessary, help employees in building their strengths. Answer choice A is incorrect. While the HR professional's responsibility is related to change in organizations, it cannot produce definitive change if the need is too great. Answer choice C can be correct in the greater sense of the HR professional's job, but is not specific enough for the HR professional's responsibility within organizations. Similarly, answer choices D and E relate to the HR professional's job description but not within organizations.

53. B: The steps for Enterprise Risk Management are focused primarily on identifying risk and pursuing means of managing and reducing risk. As a result, this includes answer choices A, C, D, and E. The steps of Enterprise Risk Management do not, however, include identifying the employees who are responsible for the risk. This might be part of the larger process of understanding risk, but it does not fall under the primary steps of Enterprise Risk Management. Answer choice B is, therefore, correct.

54. D: According to the expectations of ERM, a human resources professional should apply reasonable techniques to correcting a problem. In Harold's case, the best option for addressing the problem of the incomplete documentation would simply be to establish a quarterly review of the paperwork to ensure that it is completed. As for the other answer choices, they each contain extreme responses that do not fit with the requirements of ERM. Terminating the responsible employee does not guarantee that the problem will be fully addressed. Creating a new department simply adds more paper work that can further complicate the process of completing the documentation. There is nothing within the process of ERM that suggests a human resources professional can request a reprieve from a federal agency; the rules are in place already and need to

be observed. And while creating a series of checklists sounds good, it also sounds vague and has the potential to be as ineffective as the current system.

55. A: A reduced number of lawsuits against a company definitely indicates that the human resources department is bringing value to a company. Lawsuits often occur when serious policy mistakes are made. If policy mistakes are being reduced or eliminated, the company is moving in a positive direction. Answer choice B is incorrect because an increase in expenses within the human resources department indicates nothing more in the immediate sense than that the human resource department is spending more money. Whether or not that money is being put to good use is not explained sufficiently. Answer choice C makes no sense because an increase in employee complaints cannot indicate if any department – and definitely not the human resources department – is bringing value to the company. Similar to answer choice A, answer choice D does not show anything tangible in terms of value; an increase in employees within human resources only shows that more people are needed and not that better work is being done. And answer choice E has no real relevance to human resources. Outsourcing occurs for a variety of reasons that may or may not relate to the value that the human resources department brings to a company.

56. A: The Herzberg Motivation/Hygiene Theory, developed by Frederick Herzberg in 1959, was the result of Herzberg's study on what motivated employees and the way that positive motivation could bring quantifiable results to a company. Herzberg concluded that giving employees the opportunity to excel in something will bring overall success to the entire company.

57. C: The McGregor X and Y Theory broke management up into two different styles, called X and Y for the study. McGregor concluded that the X-style manager is focused more on close supervision and control of employees, while the Y-style manager seeks to create a rewarding work environment for all employees. McGregor's theory is based on Maslow Hierarchy Theory, but it achieves separate conclusions, so answer choice A is not correct.

58. B: B.F. Skinner is famous as a behaviorist, concluding that all human actions can be conditioned through behavior modification, or different types of behavioral reinforcement.

59. E: The Genetic Information Nondiscrimination Act of 2008 does not make employers responsible for information acquired by accident. With that information, however, employers have no legal right to make decisions or change an employee's work situation, so Abbey's only option is to keep the information to herself and take no action. Answer choice A is incorrect because the law does not require Abbey to report the employee's personal information to her superiors, nor should she take such a step. Answer choice B is incorrect because the Department of Labor does not need to be updated on this type of individual employee information (and reporting it could make Abbey legally responsible for divulging an employee's personal details). Answer choice C is incorrect because Abbey has no legal responsibility to discuss the situation with the employee, nor should she counsel the employee about changing the work situation. Answer choice D is also incorrect because employee genetic information – if obtained by accident – should not be documented. In fact, documenting it could create legal problems for the company, so Abbey's only choice is to proceed as though she does not know the information.

60. A: Marcus Buckingham and Curt Coffman's First, Break All the Rules takes a positive approach to improving the situation for employees; terminating an employee would not necessarily create a positive situation. Instead, Buckingham and Coffman suggest that a human resources professional work on the steps provided in answer choices B, C, D, and E, which are creating goals, focusing on

individual employee strengths, identifying employee KSAs, and locating the most advantageous work situation for employees.

61. B: The Training Adjustment Assistance (TAA) program was designed specifically to provide assistance to employees who have lost their jobs due to a rise in the number of imports. In other words, when import levels shift and companies in the US begin importing items that were previously manufactured here, the manufacturing companies might close as a result leaving employees without jobs. Answer choice A is incorrect because the TAA was designed for a far more particular reason than just employees losing their jobs for any reason. Answer choice C is incorrect because the TAA is related to providing training for laid-off workers to receive new jobs instead of providing them with health benefits. Answer choice D is incorrect because the TAA program is designed for workers who have already lost their jobs rather than for those who currently have jobs. Answer choice E is incorrect because the TAA does not specifically work with welfare, while the Workforce Investment Act (WIA) does.

62. E: The process described in question 12 is that of recruiting, or making the details of making the position available to interested candidates and pursuing potential employees who will fill the requirements of the job as best as possible. Answer choice A is incorrect because the process of hiring follows the process of recruiting. Answer choice B is incorrect because the process of sourcing is related more to acquiring the names and other information of potential candidates but is considered separate from recruiting. Answer choice C is incorrect because tracking is also a separate process from recruiting. Answer choice D is incorrect because selection is the next step beyond recruiting but does not belong within the recruitment process.

63. B: The process of succession planning requires that a human resources professional consider employees within their current positions. As a result, answer choice B falls outside the focus on employees within the positions and instead focuses on the position itself. This is not a part of succession planning. Answer choices A, C, D, and E all belong to the process of categorizing employees who are currently in positions within an organization.

64. C: By allowing his intuition to guide his preference, Eric is relying on the bias of his gut feeling. Answer choice A is incorrect because a first impression bias means the interviewer allows an immediate impression of a candidate to determine a decision. Answer choice B is incorrect because a cultural noise bias means the candidate responds with pointed answers that are aimed at making the interviewer happy rather than responding in a more natural or general way. Answer choice D is incorrect because a leniency bias is occurs when the interviewer is lenient in regard to a candidate and fails to take potential weaknesses into account. Answer choice E is incorrect because a nonverbal bias occurs when the interviewer is over-influenced by body language instead of by the candidate's responses.

65. A: In this case, Jocelyn is allowing a stereotyping bias (how she perceives a female mechanic) to guide her decision about which candidate will be best for the position in the auto repair shop. Answer choice B is incorrect because a similar-to-me bias occurs when the interviewer is influenced by similar interests or a similar background in the candidate. Answer choice C is incorrect because a recency bias occurs when the interviewer compares a candidate to the previously interviewed candidate. Answer choice D is incorrect because a first impression bias happens when an immediate impression of a candidate determines a decision. And answer choice E is incorrect because a gut feeling bias relies on a preference or intuition to make a decision about a candidate.

66. C: An employer brand is simply a clear indication of a company's identity; it is essentially the unique characteristic(s) that define a company. An employer brand might be related to a public relations strategy (answer choice A), but it is not contained entirely within the public relations strategy. Similarly, the human resources policy of marketing (answer choice B) might reflect the employer brand, but this is not a clear definition of it. The total rewards philosophy is a separate part of a company's identity, so answer choice D is incorrect. And while the company might design a logo that reflects its employer brand, the logo is not equivalent to the brand.

67. A: Because the new employees will be working with the heads of several departments, the panel interview style is best. It enables each of the department heads to be there during the interview process. A behavioral interview might be useful in some cases, but there is nothing specific about this case that would require candidates to indicate how their prior behavior would affect the current position. A patterned interview might be useful, but it will not necessarily be the most useful type of interview for this situation. A stress interview is unnecessary for this type of position (database management). Finally, a nondirective interview has no clear value for the type of position being filled.

68. A: Simply put, the conditions in the labor market can influence the available candidates for open positions in a company. Answer choice B might be correct in the larger, but conditions in the labor market do not have to have a negative effect on the bottom line. An analysis of competition with other companies might result from overall economic changes, but changes in the labor market do not necessarily cause this, so answer choice C is incorrect. Answer choice D might also be accurate in a broad way, but this is not clear enough for an immediate connection to the changes in the labor market and the way that they affect a company. Answer choice E contains interesting information, but it is not relevant to the way that changes in the labor market affect a company.

69. D: The Foreign Corrupt Practices Act (FCPA) was created specifically to prevent American businesses from bribing foreign governments. This act has nothing to do with the illegal trafficking of merchandise (answer choice A) or changing the level of imports (answer choice B). And while the larger role of the act is to maintain fair standards, answer choice C is incorrect because it is not clear about the nature of these fair standards. And answer choice E is incorrect because the FCPA is not relevant to protecting American workers overseas but rather focuses on the relationship between American businesses and foreign governments.

70. E: Polygraph tests are allowed among federal defense contractors but may only be administered to those who will be working in the defense-related jobs. Most large contractors will not limit their contract work to the government, so it is entirely possible that the company will have employees doing work that is unrelated to the defense jobs. What is more, the employees who do work in connection with the defense agency but do not necessarily do sensitive work will not require polygraph testing. As a result, answer choice A is incorrect because there is no justification for testing all employees of the contractor. Answer choice B is incorrect because federal law does allow for polygraph testing in certain situations. Answer choice C is incorrect because it does not really address the question and because the information is not accurate--polygraph tests must be administered by certified professionals. Answer choice D is also incorrect because the nature of the contractor's work for the defense agency will likely justify polygraph testing for many of the employees.

71. A: The purpose of talent management is twofold: to create a reputation and working situation that draws in new talent and to hold on to the talent by constantly maintaining the most effective work situation for employees. Answer choice A best summarizes this description, so it is correct.

Answer choices B, D, and E all contain descriptions that are part of talent management, but each fails to encompass the entire purpose of talent management. As a result, answer choices B, D, and E are all incorrect. Answer choice C is also incorrect because it steps beyond any purpose of talent management. The goal of this process is not to train all employees for promotion but rather to attract employees with significant talent and to maintain them within the organization.

72. D: The development of new and more effective training material might be an end result of training analysis, but it is not necessarily one of the primary steps within the process. Answer choices A, B, C, and E, however, all reflect specific steps within the process of analyzing training and are thus incorrect.

73. B: As the question states, the training will encompass several features – lectures, film presentations, and group work. Among the available styles of seating, the chevron-style – with the chairs angled in a V-shape toward the stage or front of the meeting space – will offer the most versatility for trainees. Answer choice A is incorrect because the theater-style seating would be useful for lectures and film presentations but would offer no good way for trainees to break into groups. Answer choice C is incorrect because the banquet-style seating would be excellent for group work but would be impractical for lectures and film presentations. Similarly, answer choice D is incorrect because the conference-style seating would place participants around one large table, which would not necessarily be useful for any of the three activities that will occur in the training. And answer choice E is incorrect because the U-shaped seating would be useful only for lectures but would not benefit the trainees in a film presentation or in group work.

74. E: Question 24 describes a results-based evaluation--an evaluation in which a goal or objective is noted in advance and then reviewed after a stated period of time. Answer choice A is incorrect because a reaction-style evaluation usually consists of a survey of some kind, which does not apply to the situation described in the question. Answer choice B is also incorrect because the learning-style evaluation focuses on whether or not employees actually learned required information correctly instead of whether or not a stated objective was reached. Answer choice C is a subset of answer choice B (the pre-test / posttest of the learning-style evaluation), so it is incorrect. Answer choice D is incorrect because the behavior-style evaluation takes a broader look at an employee's work and accomplishments instead of focusing on a stated goal and evaluating whether or not it was reached.

75. C: The responsibility of the human resources professional in is to recognize that employees need a balance of work and situation outside of work in order to be the most effective in the workplace. Answer choices A, B, D, and E all contain aspects of considering unique employee needs – in particular, with the focus on diversity initiatives, flexibility in work situation, and repatriation – but only answer choice C encompasses all of the HR responsibility.

76. C: The primary role of fiduciary responsibility for the human resources professional is to handle the total rewards program for an organization. Answer choices A, B, D, and E are incorrect, not because they are unrelated to fiduciary responsibility, but because they do not represent the primary role of fiduciary responsibility for a human resources professional. While handling a total rewards program, the human resources professional is expected to create unimpeachable trust, avoid any indication of favoritism, recognize the need for handle sensitive material carefully, and assure a sense of trust in the organization's total rewards program.

77. B: Each company is responsible for establishing the vacation pay policies that will apply to the employees of that company. The FMLA does not specify vacation pay policies, so answer choice A is

incorrect. ERISA is the Employee Retirement Income Security Act of 1974, so it does not relate to vacation pay policies; therefore, answer choice C is incorrect. States do not establish vacation pay guidelines (apart from basic compensation requirements established at the federal level), so answer choice D is incorrect. And unions might vote for changes within vacation pay policies, but they are not responsible for creating these policies, so answer choice E is incorrect.

78. A: Workers compensation laws state that employers are responsible for any work-related injuries or problems that employees sustain on the job. Answer choice B is incorrect because employers are not responsible for all or any of an individual's health problems unless of course they were sustained at work. Answer choice C is incorrect because the workers compensation laws do not necessarily place the full burden of proof on employees to prove the nature of the injury or problem. Answer choice D is incorrect because the workers compensation laws do not provide for federal aid. Answer choice E is incorrect because there is no federally designated list of injuries for which employers are responsible.

79. D: Cash-balance plans fall under the category of deferred contribution but not under the category of defined contribution. Answer choices A, B, C, and E – 401(k), money purchase plans, profit-sharing plans, and target benefit plans – do, however, fall under defined contribution from employers toward employee retirement accounts.

80. A: The "golden" benefits for executive compensation packages include the golden parachute (answer choice B), the golden handshake (answer choice C), the golden handcuffs (answer choice D), and the golden life jacket (answer choice E). There is no golden lifeboat, however, so answer choice A is correct because it does not fall within this category of benefits for executive compensation packages.

81. B: The fiduciary role of the human resources professional regarding ERISA is primarily one of handling and managing the pension funds that the organization provides for retirement accounts. Answer choice A is incorrect because the fiduciary role does not include setting up pension accounts for employees. (This might be another part of the human resources professional's job, but this is not the immediate fiduciary role with respect to ERISA.) Answer choice C is incorrect because the fiduciary role has nothing to do with ensuring that HIPAA guidelines are observed. Answer choice D is incorrect because human resources professional is not responsible for creating retirement account rules. And answer choice E is incorrect because the fiduciary role of the human resources professional is not necessarily one of locating the funding but rather of managing it.

82. C: Once a company has filed ERISA records with the Department of Labor, that company is required to maintain those records for a minimum of six years. Answer choices A, B, D, and E are incorrect because they do not reflect accurate federal guidelines for ERISA record keeping.

83. E: The Personal Responsibility and Work Opportunity Reconciliation Act, which went into law in 1996, establishes and updates rules for retaining and reporting employee identification records. Answer choice A is incorrect because the Fair Labor Standards Act has no immediate requirement about record keeping and instead focuses on establishing fair compensation for employees. Answer choice B is incorrect because the Fair Credit Reporting Act governs employee credit reporting but not the retention of employee identification records. Answer choice C is incorrect because the workplace application of the Consumer Credit Protection Act relates to wage garnishing. And answer choice D is incorrect because the Small Business Job Protection Act relates to employee deferred compensation plans.

84. C: Question 34 describes the qualified plan, which provides IRS-approved tax advantages but without any extra benefits for shareholders and executives. Answer choice A is incorrect because the nonqualified plan provides benefits to specified employees (i.e., executives) and shareholder. Answer choice B is incorrect because the defined contribution plan utilizes a standard pension plan but without the added benefits defined in advance. Answer choice D is incorrect because the cash balance plan is a combination of the defined benefit and defined contribution plan but does not fall under the immediate grouping of voluntary benefits programs. Answer choice E is incorrect because the defined benefit program starts with a pension plan and adds specified benefits to it.

85. E: Question 35 describes the defined contribution plan, which utilizes a standard pension plan but without the added benefits defined in advance. Answer choice A is incorrect because participation benefits do not refer to a voluntary benefits program. Answer choice B is incorrect because the nonqualified plan provides benefits to specified employees (i.e., executives) and shareholder. Answer choice C is incorrect because the cash balance plan is a combination of the defined benefit and defined contribution plan but does not fall under the immediate grouping of voluntary benefits programs. And answer choice D is incorrect because it provides IRS-approved tax advantages but without any extra benefits for shareholders and executives.

86. A: Though picketing is legal under certain circumstances, one instance when picketing is illegal occurs when an election for union representation has occurred within a 12-month period. Answer choices B, C, D, and E are all incorrect because they represent occasions when picketing would be considered legal.

87. B: Principled bargaining is considered a collective bargaining position, but it is not considered a collective bargaining strategy. Answer choices, A, C, D, and E are all incorrect because they represent four types of collective bargaining strategies.

88. E: While some types of strikes are fully legal, a sit-down strike is considered illegal. Double breasting is a reference to different types of businesses-- one being union and the other being non-union--and it has no immediate connection to bargaining strategies, so answer choice A is incorrect. A lockout is the result of an employer stopping work indefinitely, but it is not a bargaining strategy, so answer choice B is incorrect. A secondary boycott is the result of a union attempting to require the participation of a secondary employer who is not directly involved in a union issue with the primary employer, so answer choice C is incorrect. Common situs picketing is the result of two employers sharing a business location when one of the employers is engaged in a labor dispute with employees, so answer choice D is incorrect.

89. C: An unfair labor practice is defined as any activity from an employer or a union that hinders employees from exercising their rights. Answer choices A, B, D, and E are incorrect. While they describe types of unfair labor practices, they fail to provide a complete definition of ULP. Each offers a type of unfair labor practice, but does not encompass the total definition.

90. B: During a lawful economic strike, employers do have the right to hire employees to replace the striking employees. Answer choices A, C, D, and E are incorrect because they each represent types of unfair labor practices. Employers may not fire employees who refuse to cease striking instead of returning to work. They also may not encourage the union to disband and/or suggest the formation of a new union. Nor may the employer disband union bargaining and require new representation, or restrict union bargaining if this negatively impacts company's finances.

91. D: OSHA does not list computer use as one of its standard environmental health hazards. Computer use might contribute to other hazards (such as ergonomic design or stress), but it is not in itself a health hazard. Answer choices A, B, C, and E are incorrect because each represents one of OSHA's environmental health hazards.

92. C: Employers are legally allowed to check and review employee email as long as they provide a written policy informing employees of the potential for email searches. Without this written policy, employers could legally file concerns about invasion of employee privacy. Answer choice A is incorrect because immediate notification from the legal department of impending review would not be sufficient. Answer choice B is incorrect because evidence of employee wrongdoing is too late for an employer to implement a search policy. Answer choice D is incorrect because notification is required. Although employers technically own the emails that employees send and receive, they are not advised to search emails without a written search policy. Answer choice E is incorrect because employers are allowed to check and review employee emails.

93. E: According to NIOSH, this is the definition of stress that affects employees in the workplace. Answer choice A is incorrect because it should be considered an effect of stress but does not fulfill the requirements of the definition. Answer choice B, C, and D are incorrect because they too could be considered by-products of stress but do not reflect the definition provided by NIOSH.

94. A: If an employee is accused of inappropriate behavior toward other employees, the company management has an obligation to conduct a workplace investigation. Answer choice B is incorrect because a workplace investigation is related to activities and behavior in the workplace; a rapid reduction in the price of the stock would not require a workplace investigation. Answer choice C is incorrect because company management would not require a workplace investigation due to a breach in legal compliance. Answer choice D is incorrect because disagreements among co-workers are par for the course in the workplace. It is the substance of the disagreement that might cause a workplace investigation. Answer choice E is incorrect because management would not require a workplace investigation due to organizational problems within the human resources department.

95. A: The EEOC, or the Equal Employment Opportunity Commission, is responsible for risk management activities that cover Civil Rights. The SOX (The Sarbanes-Oxley Act) covers a company's obligation to report financial matters. OSHA (the Occupational Safety and Health Act) covers safety and health in the workplace. The SEC (Securities and Exchange Commission) covers workplace security – and primarily financial security. And the MSHA (Mine Safety and Health Administration) covers mine safety for workers in different types of mines.

96. D: The unholy trinity refers to the common law doctrines of the fellow servant rule, the doctrine of contributory negligence, and the voluntary assumption of risk that traditionally reflected worker's compensation guidelines in the U.S. Answer choices A, B, C, and E are incorrect because they fail to provide the accurate items contained within the phrase unholy trinity.

97. C: OSHA 300 is officially the Log of Work-Related Injuries and Illnesses. Answer choice A is incorrect because it more closely reflects OSHA 300A, which is a separate log. Answer choice B is incorrect because the Injury and Illness Incident Report is officially OSHA 301. Answer choices D is incorrect because it reflects an element of OSHA 300 but does not encompass the correct title of the log. Answer choice E is incorrect because it refers to one of OSHA's inspection priorities but not to the Log of Work-Related Injuries and Illnesses.

98. B: Organizations typically use the nondisclosure agreement to protect their confidential company information. The lie detector test is only legal within certain boundaries, so answer choice A is incorrect. An employee contract generally binds an employee to the company for a specified length of time, but it does not necessarily protect confidential company information, so answer choice C is incorrect. Organizations utilize video surveillance and random searches to ensure that employees are performing their tasks appropriately, but these activities alone do not protect confidential company information, so answer choices D and E are incorrect.

99. E: Effective substance abuse programs require that drug testing be completely fair, and targeted drug testing for employees who betray substance abuse problems would not necessarily fall under the description of "fair." Answer choices A, B, C, and D are incorrect because all represent components of an effective substance abuse program within an organization.

100. A: As a human resources professional, Angelova's best recommendation would be a counseling program that assists students in recovering from the trauma of a terrorist attack. Answer choice B is incorrect because the human resources professional would not do well to recommend a relocation program for students away from the university. Answer choice C is incorrect because a monthly email newsletter providing recommendations for students would hardly suffice to help students in the aftermath of a terrorist attack. Answer choice D is incorrect because the human resources professional is not generally authorized to advise the creation of a new department. Answer choice E is incorrect because a school-wide emergency response program might be useful in preparing students for a terrorist attack, but it would not necessarily assist them in the aftermath of the attack, and certainly not as well as a counseling program.

Special Report: Additional Bonus Material

Due to our efforts to try to keep this book to a manageable length, we've created a link that will give you access to all of your additional bonus material.

Please visit http://www.mometrix.com/bonus948/sphr to access the information.